The Emotional Brain

Physiology, Neuroanatomy, Psychology, and Emotion

EMOTIONS, PERSONALITY, AND PSYCHOTHERAPY

Series Editors
Carroll E. Izard, *University of Delaware, Newark, Delaware*
and
Jerome L. Singer, *Yale University, New Haven, Connecticut*

THE EMOTIONAL BRAIN: Physiology, Neuroanatomy, Psychology, and Emotion
P. V. Simonov

EMOTIONS IN PERSONALITY AND PSYCHOPATHOLOGY
Carroll E. Izard, ed.

FREUD AND MODERN PSYCHOLOGY, Volume 1: The Emotional Basis of Mental Illness
Helen Block Lewis

FREUD AND MODERN PSYCHOLOGY, Volume 2: The Emotional Basis of Human Behavior
Helen Block Lewis

GUIDED AFFECTIVE IMAGERY WITH CHILDREN AND ADOLESCENTS
Hanscarl Leuner, Gunther Horn, and Edda Klessmann

HUMAN EMOTIONS
Carroll E. Izard

THE PERSONAL EXPERIENCE OF TIME
Bernard S. Gorman and Alden E. Wessman, eds.

THE POWER OF HUMAN IMAGINATION: New Methods in Psychotherapy
Jerome L. Singer and Kenneth S. Pope, eds.

SHYNESS: Perspectives on Research and Treatment
Warren H. Jones, Jonathan M. Cheek, and Stephen R. Briggs, eds.

THE STREAM OF CONSCIOUSNESS: Scientific Investigations into the Flow of Human Experience
Kenneth S. Pope and Jerome L. Singer, eds.

A Continuation Order Plan is available for this series. A continuation order will bring delivery of each new volume immediately upon publication. Volumes are billed only upon actual shipment. For further information please contact the publisher.

The Emotional Brain

Physiology, Neuroanatomy, Psychology, and Emotion

P. V. Simonov

Director, Institute of Higher Nervous Activity and Physiology
Academy of Sciences of the USSR
Moscow, USSR

Translated from Russian by
Marie J. Hall

PLENUM PRESS • NEW YORK AND LONDON

Library of Congress Cataloging in Publication Data

Simonov, P. V. (Pavel Vasil'evich)
The emotional brain.

(Emotions, personality, and psychotherapy)
Translation of: Emotsional'nyi mozg.
Bibliography: p.
Includes index.
1. Emotions—Physiological aspects. 2. Brain—Localization of functions. I. Title. II. Series. [DNLM: 1. Emotions. 2. Psychophysiology. WL 103 S599e]
QP401.S57813 1986 152.4 86-15098
ISBN 0-306-42363-4

Printed in the United States of America

Contents

Introduction

This book deals with the results of theoretical and experimental studies of the emotions which my colleagues and I carried out over the last two decades.

An interest in the psychology of emotions prompted us to undertake an analysis of the creative legacy of K. S. Stanislavsky. A result of this analysis was the book, *The Method of K. S. Stanislavsky and the Physiology of Emotions*, written in 1955-1956 and published by the Academy of Sciences of the USSR in 1962. I am grateful to the first reader and critic of the manuscript, Leon Abgarovich Orbeli. In 1960, having transferred to the Institute of Higher Nervous Activity and Neurophysiology of the Academy of Sciences of the USSR, I had the opportunity to conduct experiments on problems that had interested me for a long time. In close scientific association with Peter Mikhailovich Ershov, director and teacher of theater, I began a systematic study of the involuntary and electrophysiological shifts in actors during voluntary production of various emotional states.

Here comparatively quickly we became convinced that the fruitfulness of such studies rests on an absence of any kind of developed, systematic, and sound *general theory* of the emotions of man and the higher mammals. We will illustrate our difficulties if only with one example. We had frequently read of the so-called "emotional memory." According to this hypothesis, an emotionally colored event not only leaves an ineradicable trace on the human memory, but having become a memory, invariably evokes a strong emotional reaction every time any kind of association recalls the shock that was experienced earlier. Pursuing this axiom confidently, we asked our subjects to recall the events in their lives that were connected with the strongest emotional experiences. How surprised we were when these kinds of deliberate recollections were accompanied in only a very limited percentage of cases by clear shifts in skin potentials, heart rate, respiration, and frequency-amplitude of the electroencephalogram characteristics. At the same time, recollections of persons, encounters, or life episodes by no means connected in anamnesis with any kind of feelings resulting from them evoked exceptionally strong, stable, objectively recorded shifts that were not extinguished with repetition. A more careful analysis of the cases in the second category showed that emotional coloring of recollections does not depend on the strength of the emotions experienced at the moment of the event itself, but on the *actuality* of these recollections for the subject at a given moment. We could not help but remember Chekov's Ionich who smiles ironically as he rides past the home of a girl he once loved, past the balcony where he spent a night in a state of shock and rapture. It becomes clear that what we are concerned with is not the "emotional memory" nor the emotions in themselves, but something else hidden behind the facade of emotional feelings. It becomes all the more clear that the simple accumulation of facts of relatively objective "correlates" of human emotional reactions will add little to the physiology of emotions without a proper attempt to answer the question that has arisen many times in the history of science, the sacramental question: "What is emotion?"

We looked for an answer to this question in experiments, in literature, and in seminars of young colleagues at the institute for the study of the methodological principles of the science of brain activity. Very important for us was a conference with the physicist, Anatolii Nikitich Malyshko, who invariably required the most precise (either professional, or "personal!") determination of concepts used in argument. The "formula of the emotions" appeared in February, 1964, and we devoted all the subsequent years to a theoretical and experimental working out of this formula from all its aspects.

Our approach to the problem of emotions tends entirely toward the Pavlovian in the study of higher nervous (psychic) activity of the brain. And here we are not concerned only with the fact that Pavlov's idea that the formation and disruption of the dynamic stereotype as a critical link involving the brain apparatus of emotions was the beginning point of the "information theory of emotions." Perhaps even more important was the general methodological approach of Pavlov to the problem of the physiological and the psychological in the study of higher forms of brain activity.

Pavlov wrote: "Whatever the basis, how could we differentiate, separate one from the other, what the physiologist calls the temporal connection and the psychologist, association? In this case, the one is completely merged, completely absorbed by and identified with the other" (Pavlov, 1973a, p. 489). This consequent monism of the great physiologist gave rise to myths that persist even now about Pavlov's rejection of the psychological aspect of the study of brain activity. I have come across one of the later papers of Luria which criticizes the "many investigators of higher nervous activity, taking the position of reductionism and considering it possible to understand psychological processes in man as physiological processes constructed on the principle of conditioned reflexes" (Luria, 1977, pp. 68 and 72). Shvyrkov believes that "the physiological reflex theory gave a 'purely physiological' explanation of the causes and mechanisms of behavior in which the reflection by the brain of objective reality is limited by the physiological processes and the psyche is simply not necessary" (Shvyrkov, 1978, p. 14). However, Pavlov himself, formulating his investigative strategy, maintained that "first of all, it is important to understand psychologically, and then to translate to physiological language" (Pavlov, 1954, p. 275). If the psychological and the physiological are one and the same thing, if "the psyche is not necessary," then where did Pavlov get this "first of all" and "then"? How is it possible to "translate to the physiological language" what simply does not exist? In a speech at a general meeting of the XII Congress of Naturalists and Doctors on December 28, 1909, Pavlov said: "I do not reject psychology as knowledge of the internal world of man. Even less am I inclined to reject anything from the deeper tendencies of the human spirit. Here and now I only assert and confirm the absolute, indisputable rights of scientific thought wherever and whenever it may show its power. And who knows where this possibility will end?" (Pavlov, 1973, p. 88). It is not difficult to see that Pavlov's real views differ greatly from the treatment accorded these views by his commentators.

A unique correlation between the neurophysiological and psychological was proposed by Dubrovsky (1976, 1978), who developed the information approach to the problem of "consciousness and the brain." In his opinion, "the brain neurodynamic system responsible for the existence of an image is the material carrier of information. The relation between the subjective image and the brain neurodynamic system that corresponds to it is the relation of information to its carrier" (Dubrovsky, 1978), and the information is invariant in relation to its carrier. Two positions formulated by Dubrovsky arouse protest.

It is difficult to accept invariance with respect to the carrier because it is difficult to assume that any change in content of the mental image would not have as its basis a corresponding change in neurodynamics. What is this mysterious mental indifference to its physiological "code?" Modern genetics, from which concepts on information and its carriers have been borrowed, indicates that any change in the code leads to a more serious change in the content of hereditary information when it is "taken into account" in the process of ontogenetic development. But the idea of a "brain code" is even less acceptable, since there is the question of the "recipient" of the information. Dubrovsky would have to answer this kind of question. "Every manifestation of consciousness entails in principle a reflective character and, consequently, represents certain information *for the personality*" (Dubrovsky, 1978a, p. 94; author's emphasis). But who is the receiver, reader, of information coded in the neurophysiological systems? It is the personality! And what is a "personality" in the context of the "information approach" of Dubrovsky? Something that is "above" the neurodynamic systems and the information encoded in them? And does not the capacity of "directing certain classes of brain neurodynamic systems of one's own brain" (Dubrovsky, 1978a, p. 96) engender amazement? Who is it that directs these systems? Again the omnipotent "personality?"

Pavlov's monism, the nucleus of his methodology, does not consist in that he "denied" the psychic or "reduced" it to the neurophysiological. The strength and depth of Pavlov's *dialectical* thinking lies in recognizing the *various aspects* of the study of the *unity* of the neuropsychological (higher nervous) process according to its objective nature. The psychological problem arose at a time when the activity of the brain was being studied by two sciences, physiology and psychology. The creation of a science of higher nervous (psychic) activity through the fact of its being produced marked the first step toward a dialectical "release" of *the problem itself*. In the history of science, it has happened more than once that its development led not to the solution of a problem that had agitated the minds of investigators for a long time, but to the elimination of the problem itself as being improper and fruitless in the light of new achievements of the human mind.

The science of higher nervous activity is neither physiology nor psychology in the traditional sense; it cannot be unequivocally referred to the biological or social sciences because it includes elements of both these branches of science. It is another matter that the single process of reflecting objects and phenomena of the external world can be considered from its various aspects:

- from the aspect of the mechanisms of this process, that is, as being neurophysiological, material;

- from the aspect of its content, meaning, its relation to the objects of the external world that it reflects and the needs of the subject, that is, as psychological, subjective, ideal.

The qualitative property of the science of higher nervous activity consists in considering both aspects of the reflective activity of the brain in their interconnection and interdependence. It is in this truly *systemic* approach of Pavlov to the study of the activity of the brain that the dialectical substance and revolutionary spirit of his discoveries were embodied most completely and clearly.

But we must mention still another aspect, one hypostasis above the nervous (psychic) activity of the brain which clearly evades the "awesome power of physiological investigation" and forms a basis for speaking of the sovereignty of purely psychological analysis. The essence of this aspect was formulated very well in a paper by Dubrovsky. "I cannot study pain as such if I do not take into account that fundamental circumstance that it is a phenomenon of the subjective reality of another person. Otherwise the object of my studies will not be pain, but something else, most of all, the objective changes in the organism of a man who tells me that he is experiencing pain" (Dubrovsky, 1978a, p. 54).

Let us make this example even more clear with the help of a mental experiment. Let us imagine that there appeared on Earth an investigator from another planet completely without the sensation of pain. As a result of his experiments, he found that, by amplifying various mechanical, thermal, sonic, and other such stimuli, at a given moment he could elicit a number of characteristic, objectively recorded shifts in the human organism: typical mimicry, vocal reactions (complaints), elevation of blood pressure, etc., even to changing the activity of nerve cells in certain sections of the brain. We can say that such a highly intelligent extraterrestrial might leave the Earth thinking, what is pain, but a subjective reality of experience? Of course, this is impossible. We comprehend the pain of another exclusively because of our own capacity to experience the sensation of pain. We have no other way of penetrating into the internal world of another person. The aspect of the psyche of which we are speaking lies beyond the limits of *scientific* knowledge in the generally accepted meaning of the word "science."

Other people are an irreplaceable mirror in which the subject not only recognizes himself as man, but also confirms his humanity, the universality of his perception of the reality that surrounds him. "Only by regarding the man, Paul, as a person similar to himself, does man begin to regard himself as a human being. Moreover, Paul as such, in all his embodiment as Paul, becomes for the man a manifestation of the genus man" (Karl Marx and Friedrich Engels, *Works*, 2nd edn., Vol. 23, p. 62). Comprehending the nature of man and, therefore, one's own nature, can have the character of scientific knowledge in all its variety (philosophy, psychology, anthropology, sociology, physiology, etc.). But the reflective activity of the brain is not exhausted by the knowledge attained through science. There is another way whose significance in the development of civilization remains, at times, as if in the shadow of the triumphal achievements of scientific thought. "Co-experience" functions together with "co-knowledge."

In studying the human brain, science deals with the correlates (vocal, electrophysiological, biochemical) of the psychological processes, but their subjective side remains inaccessible to science. Scientific methods are not in a position to acquaint us with the *experience* of pain, satisfaction, joy, despair, or other emotions of another person.

Such a possibility is presented only by co-experience, the role of which has not been evaluated thus far by either theory or by practice in education.

It would be a mistake to assume that the functions of the mechanism of co-experiencing are limited just to uniting ourselves with the internal world of other people. The concept of co-experience as something archaic, crude, roughly comparable to thinking, and having in mind its refined logic, is indeed unfair: to empathize is no less profound than to ponder. The world of experiences that accompany the process of associating with people may be exceptionally rich, complex, and subtle, and remain nonverbalized. It is enough to mention the emotions that arise with the contemplation of works of art. Although one and the same work elicits its own series of emotions in each viewer, these emotions have something in common, which is the instance of co-experiencing. If this were not the case, every work would have only a very small circle of admirers and would not serve millions of people over the ages.

The dual nature of the psyche, the dependence of the process of reflection on the object of reflection and the subject with his many needs, gave rise to two basic versions, two branches of human culture complementary to each other: science and art. The subjective aspect of a person's internal world is not the subject of neurophysiology since it is not the subject of science in general. Avoiding related disciplines that follow on his heels, such as neurophysiology, ethology, anthropology, sociology, etc., the psychologist at a given moment finds himself in a territory where he feels himself to be beyond the reach of representatives of these branches of science. Relieved, he looks around and finds that he is in the land of ... art.

It was important to us to consider common methodological problems in order to determine immediately and unequivocally our approach to the problem of emotions. The information theory of emotions, the subject of the rest of this work, is not only "physiological" nor only "psychological," and certainly not only "cybernetic." It is inextricably involved with the Pavlovian system by the nature of its approach to the study of higher nervous (psychic) activity. This means that the theory, if it is valid, must be equally productive for both the analysis of phenomena that relate to the psychology of emotions and the study of the brain mechanisms of emotional reactions of man and animals. We must be able to demonstrate its truth or falsity in both psychological and neurophysiological experiments. Finally, we must be confirmed in pedagogical and clinical practice and in works of art that describe the inner world of man.

In conclusion, I would like to express appreciation to my colleagues whose work supplied the concrete, factual content of one part or another of the experimental work on the problems that were of interest to us: I. I. Vainshtein, M. N. Valueva (Rusalova), I. N. Gryzlova, A. P. Ershova, A. A. Zanicheva, I. S. Ivanov, C. E. Izard, A. N. Luk'yanov, V. A. Markevich, A. Ya. Mekhedova, N. G. Mikhailova, R. A. Pavlygina, D. I. Paikin, M. L. Pigareva, T. G. Pimenova, L. A. Preobrazhenskaya, V. A. Puchkov, K. Yu. Sarkisova, O. A. Sidorova, S. E. Skorikova, S. I. Tabachnikova, V. L. Taubkin, V. D. Trush, M. V. Frolov, and S. N. Chugunov. Many of our experiments were set up with their participation, and their enthusiasm and time, in keeping with the tradition, are represented by initials in the logs of our experiments. I am grateful to all of them — experienced actors and those studying in theater schools, sportsmen—parachutists and flight controllers, students and laboratory technicians. Their emotions, recorded by the pens of recording apparatus, remain on the pages of our books, dissertations, and papers.

It is with special feeling that I express unlimited gratitude to my teachers, Vasilii L'vovich Simonov and Ezras Asratovich Asratyan.

What Is Emotion?

"The path of definition and classification followed by psychology over the course of several centuries led to the fact that of all the chapters of this science, the psychology of feelings appeared to be fruitless and tedious" (Vygotsky, 1970, p. 127). Definitions of the term "emotion," which, in their most focused form, would of necessity have to reflect the degree of our penetration into the nature and internal structure of the given phenomenon, are, as a rule, of the abstract—descriptive type or require additional explanation. Let us cite some examples of such definitions in order to demonstrate the reason for the dissatisfaction that led us to seek a fundamental answer to the question: "What is emotion?"

"Emotion is one of the most important aspects of psychological processes and characterizes man's experiencing of reality. Emotions represent the internal expression of a changed tonus of neuropsychological activity which is reflected in all aspects of the human psyche and organism" (Lebedinsky and Myasishchev, 1966, p. 222). Definitions of emotion as experiences (and experiences as emotion) can be found not only among psychologists but also in physiological works: "Emotions are the physiological state of an organism that has clearly expressed subjective coloring and encompasses all types of feelings and experiences of man, from deep, traumatizing suffering to exalted forms of joy and social sensations of life" (Anokhin, 1964, p. 339). It is true that the physiological approach to defining emotions displays, as a rule, but not in the case of all investigators by any means, a close connection between emotions and the needs of an organism. "From the point of view of physiology, we have before us the task of identifying the mechanism of those concrete processes that are, in the last analysis, responsible for both a negative (need) and a positive (satisfaction) emotional state" (Anokhin, 1964, p. 355).

The connection between emotion and need is indisputable, but it would be totally incorrect to consider emotion as the function of need alone. An *unsatisfied* need is no less indispensable for positive emotions than for negative emotions. To be convinced of this, it is enough to imagine the state of a person who is invited to sit at the table again after a lavish meal. Nevertheless, homeostatic identification of emotions with the bare fact of an arousal or satisfaction of needs (with reduction of drive) continues to wander through the pages of scientific works. Makarenko (1972, p. 224) writes: "A decrease or elimination of motivation is evaluated as something pleasant, and increase in motivation as something unpleasant. Thus, motivations are always specific, almost always negative (since they reflect the presence of need), and always cyclical."

In the definitions of emotions, together with need, there is the factor of self-regulation. According to Shingarov (1970, p. 7), emotion is a form of "reflecting reality, the essence (!) of which consists in the self-regulation of the functions of the organism in keeping with the requirements of the conditions of the external world." But the so-called "self-regulation of functions" is an immeasurable concept much broader than emotions. The great mass of processes of self-regulation that take place in the living organism is not accompanied by any kind of emotional experience. And Shingarov himself takes the next step toward dissolving the emotions into multifaceted manifestations of life activity: "... any psychological process takes place according to the principle: cause—reaction—reinforcement (as "removal" of the cause). What is the place of emotions in this basic scheme of the activity of the nervous system? They exist at all stages of this activity" (Shingarov, 1971, p. 137).

Together with the categories of need and regulation that we already know, the factors of relation, significance, and sense appear in the definitions of emotions. "Emotions are a special class of psychological processes and states connected with instincts, needs, and motives. Emotions fulfill the function of regulating the activity of the subject by reflecting the significance of external and internal situations for carrying out his life activity" (Leont'ev, 1970, p. 553). With the appearance of the category of significance (relation, evaluation, sense, "significant experience," "personal sense," and other variants on this theme), the definitions of emotions become remarkably similar to each other regardless of whether they belong to a philosopher, psychologist, physiologist, pharmacologist, etc. Emotions are "the activity of evaluating information that comes into the brain concerning the external and internal world, the sensations and perceptions of which are coded in the form of subjective images" (Dodonov, 1978, p. 29). "Emotional processes are a specific class of processes of psychological regulation, triggered by factors significant for the individual" (Reikovsky, 1979, p. 354). "Emotion is a form of reflective psychological activity in which a relation to the surrounding information appears first, in which information signals are transformed in personal terms" (Waldman, 1978, p. 132). This is perhaps a word or a question that requires further explanation: what is meant by "relation," or "personal terms," and how are information signals "transformed in personal terms?"

"Emotions as a form of reflecting the biological quality of the stimulus, its usefulness or harmfulness for the organism, which enter into the functional system of behavioral growth, can modulate its direction and final result to a significant degree" (Waldman et al., 1976, pp. 161-162). It is of no consequence that what is useful for the organism is evaluated by it as "pleasant, or emotionally positive," and what is harmful, as "unpleasant, or emotionally negative." Let us imagine for a minute what would have become of evolution if living entities would strive for everything harmful and disruptive and avoid everything that was positive and necessary for life. To say that what is useful is pleasant and what is harmful is unpleasant adds nothing to the self-evident situation.

We will conclude our linguistic excursion with a definition of the term "emotion," in the third (last) edition of the *Great Soviet Encyclopedia*: "Emotions...are the subjective reactions of man and animals to the effect of external and internal stimuli that appear in the form of satisfaction or dissatisfaction, joy, fear, etc. Accompanying almost any manifestations of the life activity of an organism, emotions reflect, in the form of direct experience, the significance (sense) of phenomena and situations and serve as one of the principal mechanisms of internal regulation of psychological activity and behavior directed toward satisfying actual needs (motivations)" (Leont'ev and Sudakov, 1978, p. 169). Such a definition can be accepted as true in its broadest form, but it requires further refinement without which we risk being left with somewhat vague phraseology. What determines significance (sense) for the subject? Why can this significance be exceptionally great in one case and practically nonexistent in another? How are significance and sense connected with needs and behavior? Answers to these questions are the essence of resolving the problem of emotions as a specific form of reflection of the real environment.

However, by no means is the function of reflection acknowledged for emotions by all authors. "In studying cognitive processes, it is usually possible to base the work on two kinds of phenomena: objective and subjective, reflected and reflecting. With respect to subjective reflection, the first kind, the objective, may serve as a unique example or "standard" of what, for example, must or might be perceived, imprinted, memorized, attained by thinking, etc. But in the study of emotions, there is no such possibility. Emotions fulfill a function not of reflecting objective phenomena, but of the expression of subjective relations to those phenomena. For this reason, data on one emotional experience or another can be compared only with data on other emotional experiences of one and the same person or of other people, and not with any objective "standard." Thus, emotions are "an expression without reflection"; they can be compared not with objective factors that give rise to and determine these emotions, but only with other emotions. The psychology of feelings has gone far since the time when Vygotsky pronounced his melancholy sentence!

Not finding an answer to the question formulated above, we turned to the scientific legacy of Pavlov. His works point to two factors that inextricably involve the brain mechanisms of emotions. First, Pavlov identified the needs and inclinations of the organism as innate (unconditioned) reflexes. "Among the unconditioned, more complex reflexes (instincts), who would segregate the physiological or somatic from the psychological, that is, from the experiencing of the powerful emotions of hunger, sexual drive, anger, and so forth?" (Pavlov, 1951, p. 335). Pavlov, however, understood that the infinite variety of the world of human emotions cannot be reduced to a complement of innate (even "complex," or vitally important) unconditioned reflexes. Second, it was Pavlov who discovered the key mechanism through which the brain apparatus responsible for the formation and realization of emotions is involved in conditioned-reflex activity (behavior) of higher animals and man. Pavlov made his discovery known for the first time on August 24, 1932, at the 10th International Psychological Congress in Copenhagen. The direct cause for Pavlov's turning to the problem of emotions was the experiments of Asratyan and other colleagues in Pavlov's laboratory; the subject of these experiments was the phenomenon of "systemicity" (Asratyan's term) or dynamic "stereotypy" (Pavlov's term) in the working of the cerebral hemispheres.

On the basis of these experiments, Pavlov came to the conclusion that under the influence of an external stereotype of repetitive actions, a stable system of internal neural processes is formed in the cortex of the cerebral hemispheres, and the "formation and installation of a dynamic stereotype is neural work of exceptionally varied intensity, considering, of course, the complexity of the system of stimuli on the one hand, and the individuality and state of the animal on the other" (Pavlov, 1973, p. 429). No less, and sometimes even more, intense "mental" (Pavlov's term) work is the reorganizing of the stereotype that emerges and exchanging it for a new stereotype. According to Pavlov, "these physiological processes in the cerebral hemispheres correspond to what we subjectively ordinarily call feelings in the general sense of positive and negative feelings and these have a vast array of shades and variations, or differing intensities, inherent in them or in their combination. There may be a feeling of difficulty or ease, cheerfulness or weariness, satisfaction or grief, joy, exultation and despair, and so forth" (Pavlov, 1973, p. 431).

A week later, on September 2, 1932, Pavlov returned to the same topic in his paper at the 14th International Physiological Congress in Rome. At the podium of the Congress, Pavlov said, "We must recognize that in installing and maintaining the dynamic stereotype, the neural processes of the hemisphere are what is usually called feelings in their two basic categories: positive and negative, in their broad gradation of intensities. The processes of installing a stereotype, completing the installation, and maintaining the stereotype or disrupting it are also subjectively varied positive and negative feelings, as has always been apparent in the motor reactions of an animal" (Pavlov, 1973, p. 423).

We have frequently found this Pavlovian idea of noncoincidence (today we would say, error) of the internal stereotype prepared by the brain and the altered external stereotype in one form or another in the works of authors who have undertaken the study of emotions. According to Hodge (1935), emotions arise when the higher brain centers cannot provide an adequate response to a perceived situation or when there is doubt or indecision with respect to the possibility of a successful response. Hodge believed that the strength of the emotional reaction is inversely proportional to the possibility of the higher brain centers to respond adequately to a given situation. Emotions represent a lack of successful integration at the cerebral cortex level.

Similar theoretical concepts were developed later by Hebb (1946) using the example of activation of the innate mechanism of fear. According to Hebb, this mechanism is involved in the process of behavior when the situation appears to be "strange," partly familiar and partly not, and not fully understood. The reaction of fear is based more on experiencing error than on an actual sensory perception of the developing circumstances. The results of systematic experiments with the disruption of different structures of the so-called limbic system led Arnold (1960) to state that emotions are the result of activating commands of the neocortex where there is a "merging of expectations with the sensory representation of the evaluation of a situation."

The biological theory of emotions of P. K. Anokhin (1964) is directly linked to his more general theory of the functional system of the behavioral act. Anokhin believes that the neural apparatus of negative and positive emotions is triggered when there is a perception of noncoincidence or coincidence of the acceptor of the action (an afferent model of the expected results) with impulsation signalling the actually achieved effect. We will conclude the review of this line of investigations, intrinsically close to the idea Pavlov formulated in 1932, with a reference to Pribram's paper, "New Biology and the Neurology of Emotions. A Structural Approach," published in 1967 after Simonov's paper, "The Information Theory of Emotions," was published (1964), and delivered at the 17th International Psychological Congress (1966). Noting the significance of Hebb's experiments and those of Lindsley (1951) showing that the degree of emotional stress can be quantitatively determined by its impact on effector organs, Pribram concludes: "Changes in vegetative function may be measured as information.... Thus, we must acknowledge that the model of the activation theory of emotions of 1967 is constructed on the basis of measuring indeterminacy.... Such a theory would best be called a 'theory of indeterminacy' or a theory of dependence of emotions on the degree of indeterminacy" (Pribram, 1967, p. 833). "Emotions express the relation between perception and action.... Emotions are connected with the information process and mechanisms of control.... On the basis of experience, emotions arise every time that probability of reinforcement of an action appears to be low" (Pribram, 1967, p. 836).

We note that the stage of pragmatic indeterminacy occurs not only with the formation of a complex system of conditioned reactions, the dynamic stereotype, but also with the formation of a single conditioned reflex, which also represents a *system* consisting of two or several unconditioned reflexes (Asratyan, 1953, p. 208). As early as 1924 the Soviet psychiatrist Osipov insightfully termed the first stage of the formation of any conditioned reflex (the stage of generalization) the "emotional," as distinct from the later "intellectual, cognitive" stage of a well consolidated reflex (Osipov, 1924). These two stages (the dynamics of weakening and then gradual dissipation of emotional stress) can be easily demonstrated using the example of development of a defensive conditioned reflex in man. Subjects were asked to press a key 20 sec after a short sound signal (Fig. 1). If the subject pressed the key sooner than 19 sec after the signal or later than 21 sec, he received a painful electric shock with a current on the order of 60-90 V. The subject was informed about his reaction time after each trial. The degree of emotional stress was measured by the change in frequency of heartbeat. The galvanic skin response (GSR) was measured at the same time. An increase in frequency of heart beat was judged according to the total duration of the first three heartbeats after the sound signal and the last three heartbeats before the motor reaction (rate of paper movement, 1.5 cm/sec). During the first ten presentations of the conditioned signal, the subject knew that there would be no electric shock. Then an isolated electric shock was administered several times to determine the intensity of the current that would exceed the pain threshold by no less than a factor of three. This intensity was maintained over the course of the whole experiment.

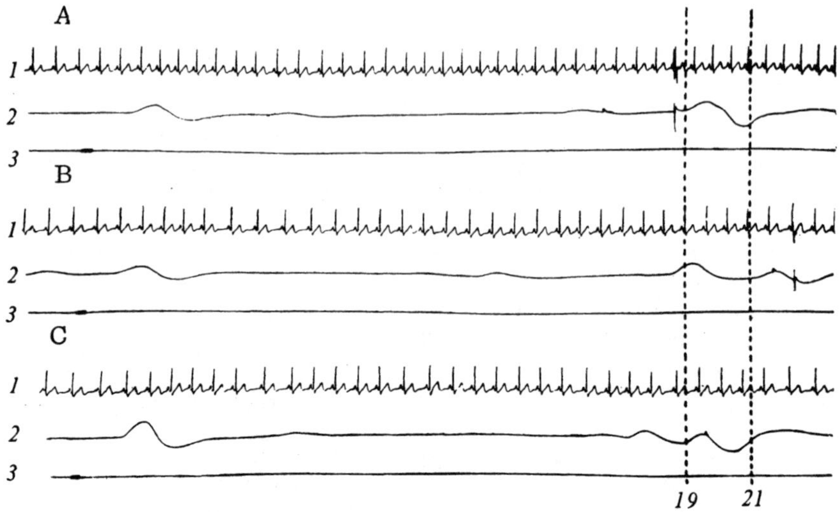

Fig. 1. Conditioned defensive reflex in man. A, B) Error reactions accompanied by painful electric shock; C) correct reaction; 1) EKG; 2) GSR, notation of reaction and current; 3) sound signal. Dotted lines mark the "safe zone."

In Fig. 2, the solid curve indicates the time of motor reactions in subsequent trials. Electric shocks were administered when the errors exceeded the allowed deviation (indicated by two horizontal lines). The dotted line indicates the changes in duration of six heart contractions computed according to number of beats per minute. The upper horizontal line represents the average normal pulse frequency before development of the conditioned reflex.

If we compare the two stages of the experiment containing the same number of trials and the same amount of painful electric shocks, we are convinced that the total deviations of the frequency of heartbeats from the original in the two parts of the experiment are different. Consequently, it does not depend solely on the number of punishments. Experiments with nine subjects demonstrated that the total change in frequency of heartbeat is proportional to the total deviation of time of the motor reactions from the designated value, that is, proportional to the degree of efficiency, precision, and reliability of the conditioned defensive re-

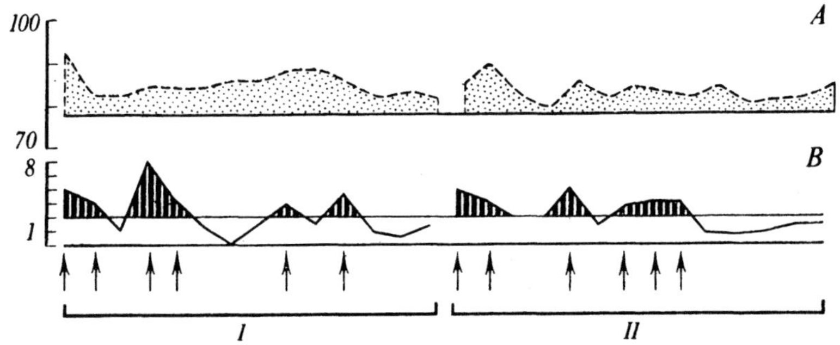

Fig. 2. Development of a conditioned defensive reflex. A) Increase in frequency of heartbeat in comparison with the basal rate (beats/min); B) deviation in time of motor reactions from the designated value (sec). Abscissa: sequential trials during two stages of the experiment, I and II. Arrow: electric shock.

TABLE 1. Relation of Total Change in Frequency of Heart Beat to Total Value of Errors in Experiments with Nine Subjects

Index	Subjects								
	I	II	III	IV	V	VI	VII	VIII	IX
Number of reactions in each of two parts of the experiment	8	14	9	9	15	8	17	9	10
Number of electric shocks	2	6	3	3	8	5	7	7	3
Ratio of pulse and size of errors in the first part	7.5	1.56	3.28	5.4	3.08	0.48	0.66	0.42	0.73
Ratio of pulse and size of errors in the second part	6.1	1.55	3.11	5.8	3.19	0.46	0.83	0.40	0.61

flex (Table 1). This rule holds also for those cases where the value of errors (but not their number nor the number of painful electric shocks) increased as the frequency of heart beat increased and where, consequently, the dynamics of the involuntary shifts could not have been explained by adaptation to the painful stimuli due to repetition.

Experiments with animals also show that the brain predicts the probability of punishment on the basis of the degree of efficiency of an instrumental motor reflex. Preobrazhenskaya developed a conditioned defense reflex in dogs in a situation where lifting a front paw to a specific level and keeping it at that level for 10 sec prevented a painful electric shock of the opposite hind paw (methodology of G. P. Zeleny, G. V. Skipin, R. L. Vinnik, and others). The conditioned sound signal was presented 10 sec before the painful shock. Combining the sound with the painful shock before developing the conditioned motor reflex led to an increase in the amplitude and percentage content of the theta rhythm in the frequency spectrum of the electrical activity of the dorsal hippocampus (Fig. 3). Quantitative analysis disclosed a positive correlation between the changes in total stress of the hippocampal theta rhythm (measured by integrator records) and the frequency of heartbeat. Both signs were noticeably diminished with the stabilization of the motor adaptation that reliably saved the animal from pain. Any difficulties in making movements made the theta rhythm increase again. Thus, the experiments of Preobrazhenskaya (1969; see also Konorski et al., 1968) demonstrated that the intensity of the hippocampal theta rhythm depends not on the motor activity in itself, but on the efficiency of the motor acts and on their effect on the probability of preventing painful shocks. Also, the degree of emotional stress is affected by the need-motivation factor: in experiments with conditioned defense reflexes, the total stress of the theta rhythm and increase in heart rate were expressed significantly more strongly than in experiments with food reflexes.

Concluding a review of the data that are evidence for the elimination of emotional stress to the degree that adequate conditioned reactions are developed, P. Fress writes: "Most of all it must be stressed that there is no situation that generates emotions of itself. It depends on the relation between motivation and the potentials of the subject" (Fress, 1975, p. 133). The idea that even a firmly established instrumental conditioned defensive reflex continues to be motivated by fear as if replacing the need to avoid pain has been subjected to criticism supported by argument by Newton: "...the need to avoid a painful stimulus continues to be effective (until the animal learns that the sig-

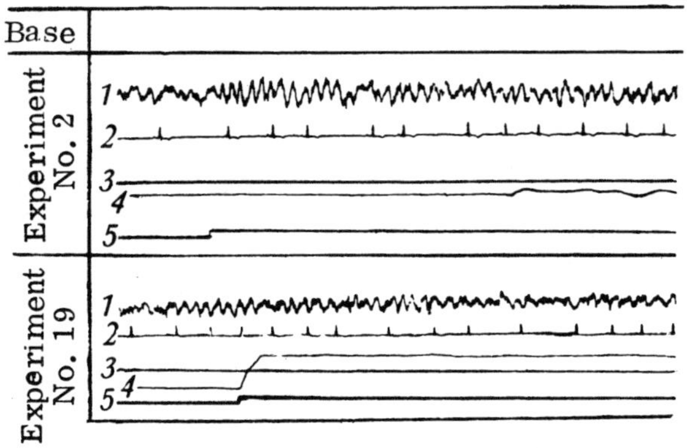

Fig. 3. Change in hippocampal theta rhythm and frequency of heart rate during development of an instrumental conditioned defensive reflex in the dog. 1) EG of the dorsal hippocampus; 2) EKG; 3) level at which current was switched off; 4) raising of the front paw, which switched off the current; 5) conditioned sound signal (after Preobrazhenskaya).

nal does not predict danger), but since the animal expects neither pain from the stimulus nor the threat of a dangerous situation, it no longer exhibits the emotional reaction of fear" (Newton, 1975, p. 70).

The literature is full of experimental data indicating the dependence of emotional stress on the magnitude of need (motivation) and predicting the probability of its satisfaction. For example, it has been established that pulse frequency in bank employees depends on the degree of their responsibility (counting of bank notes of various denominations) and the amount of information contained in one operation (Gantchev et al., 1967). The emotional reactions of monkeys regularly depend on changes in probability of food reinforcement (Melges and Popper, 1976). According to the data of Menitsky and Khananashvili (1969), the greatest emotional stress in dogs (squealing, howling, scratching, scratching the feed trough) was observed when probability of reinforcement was 1:4, and as the experiment continued, it became 1:2. The significance of the information factor appears with particular clarity in experiments with paired animals when both partners receive the same number of electric shocks, but only one of them can avoid punishment by an appropriate instrumental reaction. It was demonstrated that it was precisely in such an animal that the characteristics of fear gradually disappeared and ulceration of the mucous membrane of the stomach and intestine was averted (Desiderato and Newman, 1971; Jonas and Jonas, 1975; Starr and Mineka, 1977). Motivation and information factors in the genesis of emotional stress have different weights in different animals of the same species. According to data of Preobrazhenskaya (1974), the maximum increase in heart rhythm was observed in some dogs with a 30% food reinforcement and, in others, at 5%. Consequently, for dogs of the second group, total "failure" to satisfy the need for food had a greater significance than the indeterminacy of the experimental situation.

We also have information to indicate that two components of emotional stress have different effects on the magnitude of various involuntary shifts. In experiments with people, the amount of incentive (amount paid for a correct solution) had the greatest effect on pulse and respiration frequency and the level of electrical resistance of the skin, and the difficulty of the task (number of selections) had the greatest effect on pulse magnitude and the galvanic skin response (Wilkinson et al., 1972). The principal connection between the galvanic skin response and the information factor was found also in experiments where the galvanic skin response was weaker when a painful electric shock was highly probable than when the shock was less frequent, but more difficult to predict (Epstein and Bahm, 1971).

THE REFLECTIVE-EVALUATIVE FUNCTION OF EMOTIONS

Lobachevsky wrote: "The first concepts with which any science begins must be clear and reduced to the least possible number. Only then will they serve as a firm and adequate basis for science" (Lobachevsky, 1976, p. 39). Summarizing the final results of our own experiments and data in the literature, in 1964 we came to the conclusion that *emotion is a reflection by the brains of man and animals of any real need (its qualities and magnitude) and probability (possibility) of its satisfaction, which the brain evaluates on the basis of genetic and earlier acquired personal experience.*

In its most general form, the rule for the development of emotions can be represented in the form of a structural equation:

$$E = f[N, I_n - I_a), \ldots],$$

where E is emotion, its degree, quality, and sign; N is the magnitude and quality of actual need; $(I_n - I_a)$ is the evaluation of probability (possibility) of satisfying the need on the basis of innate and ontogenetic experience; I_n is information on means predictably necessary for satisfying the need; I_a is information on means that the subject has available to him at the given moment.

Of course, emotion also depends on a number of other factors, one of which we know very well, and others which perhaps we only suspect. Among those we know are:

- individual (typological) traits of the subject, primarily individual traits of his emotionality, motivational environment, qualities of will, etc.;

- the factor of time, depending on which emotional reaction acquires a quality of rapidly developing *affect* or *mood* that sometimes persists for hours, days, or weeks;

- qualitative features of the need. Thus emotions that are based on social and spiritual needs have been called *feelings*. The low probability of avoiding an undesirable effect arouses *anxiety* in the subject, and a low probability of achieving a desirable goal, *frustration*; and there can be many more such examples.

But all of the factors enumerated and other similar factors promote only variations of infinitely variable emotions while there are two, and only two, and always only two factors which are *necessary* and *adequate*: need and the probability (possibility) of its satisfaction.

To avoid misunderstandings (we will deal with these in a later chapter), we will specify more precisely the concepts we are using. We use the term "information," having in mind its pragmatic meaning, that is, the change in probability of achieving a goal (satisfying a need) by reason of obtaining a specific communication (Kharkevich, 1960). Thus, we are speaking not about information that actualizes the need (for example, of a developing danger), but about information necessary for satisfying a need (for example, of how to avoid a danger). As information, we understand the reflection of the whole aggregate of means for achieving a goal: knowledge which the subject has, developed habits, energy resources of the organism, adequate or inadequate time for organizing appropriate action, etc. Should we, in this case, use the term "information?" We believe we should, and this is why. First, the brain that generates emotions deals not with habits alone (and this includes training of the peripheral performing apparatus), not with the organism's energy resources alone, etc., but with afferent factors of the external and internal environment of the organism, that is, with information about available means. Second, all the various knowledge about what is necessary to satisfy the need that has developed and is actually available to the subject at a given moment is transformed by the brain into a single, integral index, into an evaluation of the probability of achieving the goal (satisfying the need). The evaluation of probability by its very nature is the *informational* category.

We use the term "need," in its broad, Marxist sense; it cannot be reduced to only the preservation (survival) of an individual or a species. In *King Lear*, Shakespeare wrote:

> "Allow not nature more than nature needs,
> Man's life is cheap as beast's."

But even the needs of animals are not limited to self-preservation. We will consider the problem of needs in greater detail later; here we will limit ourselves to the most precise definition of the term. Frequently need is qualified as the need of something, but such a definition is nothing more than a play on synonyms. It is our opinion that *need is a selective dependence of living organisms on factors of the external environment essential for self-preservation and development, the origin of activity of living systems, the motivation and goal of their behavior in the surrounding world.* Correspondingly, we define *behavior* as *such form of life activity as can change the probability and duration of contact with an external object capable of satisfying the need of the organism.*

Serzhantov and Serzhantova (1976, p. 14) have correctly noted that it is precisely the category of need that can play the role of a "conceptual bridge" that links the knowledge of natural science, summarized in the concept "organism," with the psychological and social knowledge of the nature of man, conveyed by the concept "personality." We are in agreement with Diligensky in thinking that "the function of fixation of a specific tendency of various needs and the methods of proceeding to satisfy them are fulfilled by the tendencies, values, interests, and goals of the subject. In Marxist psychological literature, all of these levels of motivation are usually described as derivatives of needs" (Diligensky, 1977, p. 115).

Identifying a need that initiated one act or another is a most difficult task for both theoretical analysis and for practical training. Sukhomlinsky wrote: "In 30 years of work in school, I had the opportunity to analyze a hundred seemingly completely identical acts: a youngster concealed his teacher's unsatisfactory report from his parents. But in each case there were unique reasons, unique moral and emotional motives..." (Sukhomlinsky, 1979, p. 49). The heuristic value of emotions lies precisely in that, as distinct from an act, they can serve as one of the most subtle and objective indicators of the need we are interested in.

Most closely associated with the concept "need" is the phenomenon of motivation. A good historical presentation of the study of motivation is contained in a series of papers collected by Russell (1970). In comparison with the actualization of need, motivation is the second stage of organization of goal-directed behavior (Fig. 4); it may be considered as a "predetermined need." Motivation does not exist without a need, but it is entirely possible to encounter a need that is not prompted by motivation. Thus, man can experience the most urgent need for vitamins and not be motivated since he does not know the reason for his state. When a dog that has had the cerebral cortex of the brain removed is hungry (need of food), it develops a state of extreme motor excitation. Nevertheless, we cannot speak of food motivation here since the dog does not approach food lying at its feet. Therefore, *motivation is the physiological mechanism for activating traces (engrams), preserved in the memory, of those external objects that are capable of satisfying a need that the organism has and of those actions that are capable of leading to its satisfaction.* With this concept of the neurophysiology of motivation, we naturally find it difficult to agree with the notion of original motivational arousal of structures of the hypothalamus. Only by involving the hypothalamus in conditioned reflex activity (which we will discuss subsequently) can we ascribe a motivational character to the activity of the hypothalamic structures. Recently, Asratyan presented an elegant system of theoretical and experimental arguments in favor of the concept that the physiological mechanisms of motivation are the result of the interaction of the more complex, vitally important unconditioned reflexes with direct and reverse conditioned connections. Of special significance for understanding the mechanisms of motivation are the reverse conditioned connections, including their tonic variant which is responsible for the selective increase in the excitability of structures that receive the conditioned signal of possible reinforcement. Considering the problems of motivation of behavior in light of the reflex theory, Asratyan emphasized that: "...activation of reverse conditioned connections may result not only in a conditioned-reflex reproduction of the reflex to the first stimulus in a linked pair, but may be limited to only an increase in excitability of the central structures of that reflex" (Asratyan, 1974, p. 14).

Let us return to an analysis of the consequences of the "formula of emotions." The low probability of satisfying a need (I_n greater than I_a) generates negative emotions. Increase in the probability of satisfaction in comparison with the earlier prognosis (I_a greater than I_n) generates positive emotions. An example of the latter case may be the emotional reaction arising in a person in the process of solving a problem of differentiating visual signals.

In our experiments, sets of five figures, ones and zeros, were projected on a screen before the subject. The subject was warned that some of the sets with a common trait (for

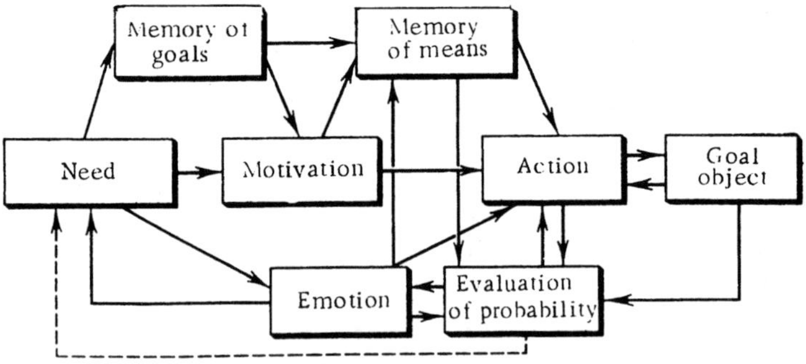

Fig. 4. Need, motivation, and emotion in the structure of a goal-directed behavioral act. Dotted line: inhibiting influence.

example, two zeros in succession), would be accompanied by a whistle. The task was to detect this common trait. In the course of the experiment, the subject had to use a microphone to tell the experimenter about the hypotheses that he was developing. Each set was exposed for 10 sec. Two electroencephalograms, an electrocardiogram, and the galvanic skin response (GSR) were being recorded. Before the subject was given the instructions, the GSR to the change in sets and whistles was extinguished.

Such a task is a typical example of creative intellectual activity in which the "requirements of the task" are formulated, but where the "unknown" still remains to be found (Brushlinsky, 1966). Before the first (usually erroneous) hypothesis is developed, relative to the reinforcing trait, neither new sets nor the whistle elicited a GSR (Fig. 5A). This fact once again indicates that there is no naturally occurring orienting reaction to a "new stimulus." The orienting reaction is a reaction to the result of comparing the external stimulus with the "neural model" (Sokolov, 1960) in its broadest scope, from the engram of the concrete stimulus to the generalized model of the whole situation, including its possible changes anticipated by the subject. The development of a hypothesis was accompanied by a GSR (Fig. 5B). Since the GSR has a comparatively long latent period, the figure clearly shows that fluctuations in skin potentials are linked with the moment of becoming aware of the hypothesis and not with the vocal message of the subject. Following the formation of the hypothesis, two situations are possible that we consider as experimental models of negative and positive emotional reactions.

The first case is presented in Fig. 5C. The hypothesis is incorrect, and set 25, containing the reinforced trait, does not elicit a GSR. But when the whistle indicates to the subject that he has made a mistake, there is a GSR as a result of disagreement of the hypothesis with the actual stimulus, a case predicted by the concepts of Anokhin's "acceptor of the results of an action," Sokolov's "neural model of the stimulus," and similar concepts. The subject changes his hypothesis a number of times, and at some point it begins to correspond to reality (Fig. 5D). Now the very appearance of the reinforced set 30 elicits a GSR, and its reinforcement with the whistle results in a still stronger shift in the GSR.

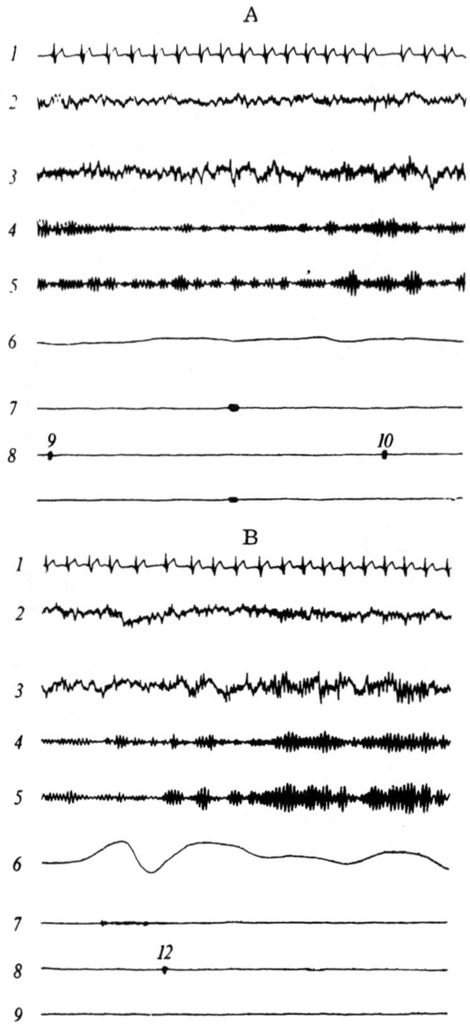

Fig. 5. GSR before the development of a hypothesis about the reinforced trait (A), at the moment of development of the hypothesis (B), in the case of error (C), and confirmation of the hypothesis (D). 1) EKG; 2, 3) EEG; 4, 5) analysis of the alpha rhythm of the EEG; 6) GSR; 7) oral response by subject; 8) change of sets; 9) horn. The numbers on the eighth line are set numbers.

C

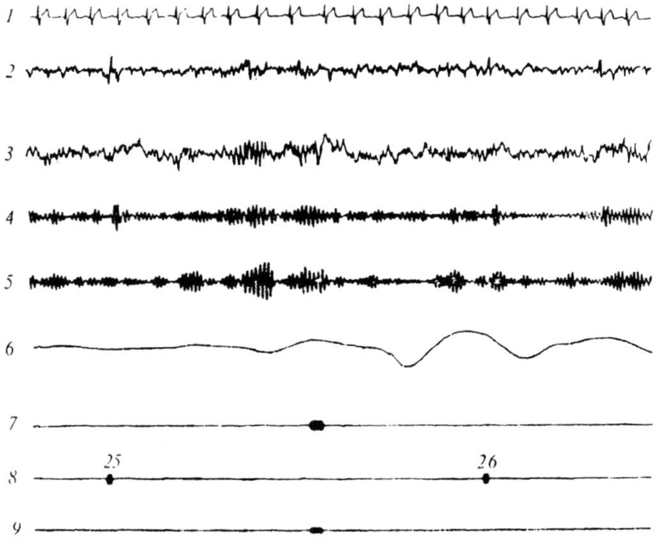

D

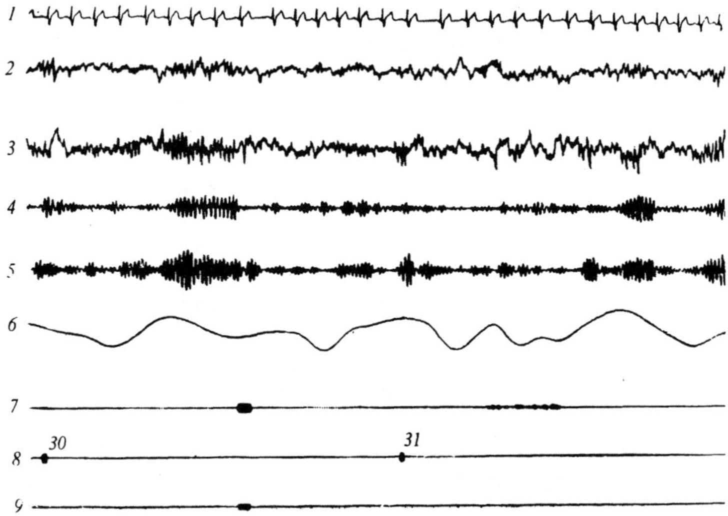

How can we understand this kind of effect? In this case, after all, there was complete agreement between the hypothesis ("acceptor of the result of the action," "neural model," etc.) and the stimulus present. Absence of error should have entailed absence of GSR and other involuntary shifts. Actually, in the latter case, we also find error, but it is error of a different kind than that of confirming a false hypothesis. The prognosis formed in the process of repeated combinations contains not only the afferent model of the goal, not only its semantics, but also the *probability* of attaining this goal. At the moment of reinforcing set 30 with a whistle, the predicted probability of solving the problem (correctness of the hypothesis) rose sharply, and this disagreement of the prognosis and the information coming in led to a strong GSR as an involuntary component of the positive emotional reaction. The significance of probability prediction for the genesis of positive emotions was described by Feigenberg (1965) in the study of disturbances in the affective sphere in schizophrenics.

The factor of positive disagreement was discovered in the field of esthetics. Wolkenstein (1931) defined the beautiful as a "desirable and complex (difficult) ability to surmount something." "There is beauty in chess when there is expediency of movement coupled with peripeteia, that is, an unexpected, paradoxical (at first glance) ability to overcome in a difficult situation. Such are the moments when sacrifices are made. If, however, victory is achieved by a gradual accumulation of small advantages that exhibit no fascinating combinations, but lead to gains by capturing pawns or by exchanges that lead to a true win, such a game may be termed solid, mature, or even instructive or subtle, but it cannot be called beautiful" (Wolkenstein, 1931, pp. 45-46). "Good days are the lot of the wise," writes Sigrid Undset, "but best days are given to him who dares to be mad."

The information theory of emotions is correct not only for comparatively complex behavioral and mental acts, but also for the genesis of *any* emotional state. For example, positive emotion during eating is due to the integration of the stimulation of hunger (need) and the afferentation from the oral cavity that is evidence of the growing probability of satisfying the given need. In a different state of need, that same afferentation would be emotionally indifferent or would generate a feeling of aversion.

Thus far we have spoken of the *reflective* function of emotions that corresponds with their *evaluative* function. Now we will turn our attention to the fact that the price in the most general sense of this concept is always the function of *two* factors: demand (need) and supply (possibility of satisfying the need). But the category of value and the function of evaluation become unnecessary if there is no need to compare or to exchange, that is, no need to compare values. For this reason, the function of emotions cannot be reduced to a simple signalling of the actions that are useful or harmful to the organisms, as proponents of the "biological theory of emotions" believe. Let us give an example that Anokhin uses (1964, p. 342). When a joint is damaged, the sensation of pain limits movement of the extremity, promoting healing processes. In this integral signalling of "harm," Anokhin saw the adaptive significance of pain. But an automatic mechanism may play an analogous role without the participation of emotions that inhibit movement that would be harmful to the damaged organ. The feeling of pain is a more flexible mechanism: when the need to move becomes very great (for example, when the very existence of the subject is threatened), movement is accomplished regardless of the pain. In other words, emotions play the role of a unique "currency of the brain," a universal *measure* of values, and not simply an equivalent functioning according to the principle harmful—unpleasant, useful—pleasant, as has been presented in scores of redundant papers.

From the essence of the reflective-evaluative function of emotions arise their *regulatory functions*. We will begin their analysis with the functions regulating individual behavior.

THE SWITCHING FUNCTION OF EMOTION

From the physiological point of view, emotion is the active state of the system of specialized brain structures that stimulates a change in behavior in the direction of minimizing or maximizing that state. Since positive emotion indicates the approach of satisfaction of need, and negative emotion a postponement of it, the subject tries to maximize (reinforce, continue, repeat) the first state and minimize (weaken, interrupt, reverse) the second. This hedonistic principle of maximizing and minimizing, equally applicable to man and to animals, makes it possible to overcome the seeming inaccessibility of the emotions of animals to direct experimental study.

As distinct from clinical-physiological studies in the process of which a doctor maintains verbal contact with the patient, an experimental physiologist must judge the emotions of an animal only on the basis of external behavioral manifestations of these emotions. And here an obstacle arises that has been analyzed again and again in the works of Waldman: "In the evaluation of response reactions of animals to electrical stimulation of the brain, many experimenters make overly simple evaluations and treat the essence of the behavioral reaction of the animal subjectively. Most of them proceed on the premise that emotion is a form of behavior. If an animal hides or runs away, it means that it is a reaction of fear; if it attacks, this is a reaction of rage" (Waldman, 1972, p. 13). However, it has been demonstrated many times that both under natural conditions and when the brain is stimulated electrically, it is possible to observe a completely goal-directed "cold" attack without outward traits of rage, completely precise reactions of avoiding danger without the symptoms of fright and ritual "warning" of an adversary (raising of the hair, baring of teeth, exposure of claws) without underlying anger.

On the basis of the results of his systematic studies, Waldman proposes to differentiate: 1) emotional reactions, complexes of motor-autonomic manifestations, characteristic for one emotion or another, that are not goal-directed (in the terminology of old authors, "pseudoaffects"); 2) emotional behavior, goal-directed behavioral acts which express traits of emotion; 3) emotional states that are manifested only when the appropriate test-object is present in the environment (experimenter, other animal, a danger signal, etc.).

In an experiment with animals, a shift in emotional state can be obtained with a weak (subthreshold) stimulation of those brain structures which when stimulated more strongly produce emotionally tinged behavior. In the opinion of Waldman, "Exactly such states, and not various manifestations that develop with stronger stimulation of these substrates of the brain, may and must be tested as analogs of emotions in animals" (Waldman, 1972, pp. 22-23).

In his experiments to identify the hidden "emotional state," Waldman evidently activated that system (and not a singular "point") of brain structures that realizes the given emotion. In the neurophysiological scheme, more than anything we have to deal with an "emotional dominant" (in Ukhtomsky's sense) that is elicited with supplementary activation with an external stimulus, the test-object. These structures continue to participate in the regulation of the animal's goal-directed activity and in the realization of "emotional behavior," and this is why it seems to us that it would be difficult to test as emotions only subthreshold "emotional states."

If Waldman thinks it is possible to consider the "emotional state" of animals as analogs of human emotions, including those that arise in patients during stimulation of deep structures of the brain, then the psychologist Vilyunas has a more pessimistic view: "A serious and, at first glance, insurmountable obstacle that makes it difficult to realize the principle of evolutionary development in the study of emotional phenomena is that fact that, over the whole course of biological evolution, the emotional sphere of psychic reflection is absolutely inaccessible to direct study....Even our judgments about the emotional experiences of the higher animals are, strictly speaking, only hypotheses, anthropomorphic projections, based on comparing situations and behavior" (Vilyunas, 1976, p. 75).

We cannot agree with the statement of Vilyunas. We believe that an experimenter has a minimum of three possibilities of judging the emotional state of the experimental animal objectively.

The first of these indices, which we have already mentioned, is the presence or absence of involuntary shifts and characteristic changes in the bioelectric activity of the brain under conditions that the animal's physical stress coupled with accomplishing a motor act remains constant or decreases in the process of developing adaptive actions. If the animal (and to the same degree, man) performs the same motor skill and the involuntary and electrophysiological shifts observed at earlier stages of training become weaker, we have a strong basis for speaking of a gradual decrease in the degree of emotional stress for at present it is impossible to propose any other kind of explanation for this phenomenon.

A second objective indicator of the emotional state of an animal may be the reaction of another individual of the same species to signals of emotional expression of the partner, the phenomenon of unique "emotional resonance"; we will return again to the significance of this. This device is one of the brilliant experimental finds of Waldman and his laboratory that has an important significance for the general methodology of studying emotions in animals. As distinct from a human observer, an animal is capable of distinguishing nuances of emotional expression of its partner so fine that they escape the experimenter.

But it is our deep conviction that the decisive criterion for the presence of *emotion* in an animal, and not some kind of other phenomenon of higher nervous activity, is the *attitude of the animal itself to the state of its brain.* It is specifically the direct stimulation of the brain with an electric current, as with no other methodological device, that makes it possible to identify a positive emotional state that the animal tries to maximize, that is, strengthen, continue, or repeat, or a negative emotional state that the animal tries to minimize, that is, weaken, interrupt, or reverse. We must emphasize that emotion in animals must be identified not according to the character of an external factor (food may elicit aversion in a sated subject, and a destructive narcotic, satisfaction), but according to an active attitude toward his condition, exhibited in behavior. It is precisely this behavioral criterion, and not expression in the form of baring of teeth, tail-wagging, vocalization, etc., that serves the experimenter as a decisive indication of the absence or presence of an emotional state and of its negative or positive tinge.

The switching function of emotions is manifested both in the sphere of innate forms of behavior and in accomplishing conditioned-reflex activities, including its most complex manifestations. It is necessary to remember also that the evaluation of probability of satisfying a need may occur in man not only at the conscious, but also at the subconscious level. A clear example of subconscious prediction is intuition, where evaluation of approach to the goal or moving away from it is initially realized in the form of emotional "premonition of solution," which induces logical analysis of the situation that gave rise to the emotion (Tikhomirov, 1969).

The switching function of emotion is especially clearly apparent when motives compete, when a dominant need is isolated that becomes the vector of goal-directed behavior. Thus, in a battle situation, the conflict between man's natural instinct for self-preservation and the social need to follow a determined ethical norm is experienced by the subject as a struggle between fright and a sense of duty, between fright and shame. The dependence of emotion not only on the magnitude of the need, but also on the probability of its being satisfied, complicates the competition of coexisting motives greatly, and, as a result of this, behavior frequently seems to be preoriented to a less important, but easily attainable goal: "a titmouse in the hand" is preferable to "a crane in the sky." In the course of evolution, the constant threat of such preorientation necessitated the formation of a special brain apparatus capable of diluting this "achilles' heel" of emotion. At the level of human higher nervous activity, it stands before us as the physiological mechanisms of the will.

A partial, although qualitatively specific diversity of the switching function of emotions is their reinforcing function.

THE REINFORCING FUNCTION OF EMOTION

The phenomenon of reinforcement occupies a central position in the system of concepts in the science of higher nervous activity since it is precisely on the fact of reinforcement that the formation, existence, extinction, and features of any conditioned reflex depends. As reinforcement "Pavlov understood the effect of biologically significant stimuli (food, a harmful stimulus, etc.), that adds a signal significance to another nonessential stimulus that is combined with it in a biological relation" (Asratyan, 1971, p. 5). Developing the concepts of Pavlov, Asratyan proposed that the term "reinforcing reflex" reflects more completely and precisely the essence of the matter than "reinforcing stimulus" (Asratyan, 1971, p. 6). Numerous facts indicate that a conditioned reflex may also be developed by linking so-called indifferent stimuli, although the rate of closure of the conditioned connection, its stability and further fate, depend to a decisive degree on the species characteristics of the animal, the intensity of the stimuli, their sensory modality, and the order of combination (Schoenfeld, 1978).

We will note that "indifference" of stimuli must be treated very carefully. A stimulus that appears to be indifferent to an experimenter may be ecologically important for an animal of a certain species, not to mention that investigative need (curiosity) is exceptionally strong in many animals and makes "indifferent" circumstances "vitally important" (Berlyne, 1978).

As if perceiving all the contradiction and ambiguity in the term "reinforcement," Pavlov in his later informational works (for example, in the paper, "The Conditioned Reflex," written for the *Great Soviet Encyclopedia*) simply did not use this term, preferring to speak only of the coincidence of an indifferent stimulus with an unconditioned one. In the strict sense, the effect of the second stimulus in order of combination in time should be called the reinforcement because it is due to this stimulus that the first stimulus begins to elicit a reaction that was not natural to it before. Nevertheless, the biological significance of the second stimulus must not be disregarded even in modeling the conditioned connection by direct stimulation of the brain structures for the purpose of studying the cellular-synaptic mechanisms of closure. In the experiments of L. L. Voronin (1976), sensory stimuli (click, light) were connected with direct stimulation of the skin and elicited movement of the corresponding paw. When this procedure was combined with stimulation of the emotional structures of the hypothalamus, the development of a conditioned reflex was facilitated and the reflex was more stable.

The need to involve the brain mechanisms of emotion in the process of developing a conditioned reflex becomes particularly apparent in the case of instrumental conditioned reflexes where reinforcement depends on the reaction of the subject to a conditioned signal. Analyzing the nature of the development of instrumental reflexes from all aspects, W. Wyrwicka (1975) came to the conclusion that the direct reinforcement in this case was not satisfaction of any need, but obtaining desirable (pleasant, emotionally positive) stimuli or eliminating undesirable (unpleasant) stimuli. Depending on their intensity, on the functional state of the organism, and the characteristics of the environment, the most varied "indifferent" stimuli — light, sound, tactile, proprioceptive, olfactory — might be accepted. On the other hand, animals frequently refuse vitally necessary food ingredients if the food is not tasty. It was impossible to develop an instrumental conditioned reflex in rats when food was placed in the stomach through a tube (that is, bypassing the taste receptors), although such reflex was developed by introducing morphine into the stomach; morphine very quickly elicits a positive emotional state in the animal. The same morphine, because of its bitter taste, is not a reinforcement if it is administered by mouth (Cytawa and Trojniar, 1976). In another series of experiments, the authors developed an instrumental alimentary conditioned reflex in rats, and when it was stable they replaced natural food by introducing a nutritive solution into the stomach through a nasopharyngeal tube. The lever-pressing reflex was extinguished in this case, but was preserved if a 0.05% solution of morphine was introduced into the stomach (Trojniar and Cytawa, 1976).

We believe that the results of these experiments agree well with the data of Onioni (1975), who used direct electrical stimulation of the limbic structures of the brain as reinforcement for developing a conditioned reflex. When an external stimulus was combined with brain structure stimulation that elicits eating, drinking, aggression, rage, or fear, 5 to 50 presentations developed only the conditioned avoidance reaction and fear in a satiated cat. Conditioned reflex hunger could not be developed even under natural conditions: circumstantial signals of the situation in which rats were starved elicited fear and the conditioned avoidance reaction in them and not feeding behavior (Mowrer, 1960). Similar reactions were observed in Oniani's experiments when a conditioned stimulus was reinforced by stimulating the "aggression centers."

After 110 presentations of combined sound and light with stimulation of the drinking zone of the hypothalamus in goats, the conditioned signal did not result in drinking behavior, although reinforcing stimulation immediately elicits drinking (Milner, 1966). On the other hand, Fonberg succeeded in developing an instrumental conditioned reflex in dogs, reinforcing it with stimulation that induced a sated animal to eat. The author suggests that in these experiments electrical current activated not the hunger structures, but the engrams of characteristics of tasty food, and this persuaded the dogs to continue eating regardless of their satiated state (Fonberg, 1967).

According to Oniani, reinforcement may be stimulation only of those brain structures that under natural conditions are activated by external factors (fear), and not interoceptive impulses (hunger, thirst). Oniani explains the possibility of developing conditioned avoidance reflexes reinforced by stimulation of the "aggression centers" by the fact that the formation of natural conditions of aggression has an endogenous component (hormonal in mating action, hunger, etc.).

From our point of view, the results of these experiments once again indicate the decisive role of emotions in the development of conditioned reflexes. Fear has a clear aversive quality for an animal and is actively minimized by the avoidance reaction. Stimulation of the eating and drinking systems of the brain in sated animals elicits stereotypic acts of eating and drinking without involving the neural mechanisms of emotion, which excludes the development of conditioned reflexes. With appropriate localization of electrodes and parameters of current, stimulation of aggression centers generates an emotionally negative state which, like the emotion of fear, leads to the minimizing avoidance reaction. If aggressive behavior of cats is accompanied by involving the emotionally positive structures, then, on the basis of their stimulation, a conditioned reaction of self-stimulation can be developed, as was demonstrated by Waldman et al. (1976). Emotionally positive coloring of aggressive behavior can be observed under natural conditions. For example, in mice the instrumental conditioned reflex of pressing a lever can be developed very well if this action is reinforced by the appearance of another mouse in the cage which is soon attacked by the "lever-presser" (Connor and Watson, 1977).

Figure 6 is an attempt to present the role of emotions in the closure of a conditioned reflex. From the moment it was introduced, the conditioned reflex theory assumed a convergence of two stimuli: from the conditioned stimulus and from the stimulus that elicits the unconditioned reflex, for example the afferentation from the oral cavity when food enters the mouth (Fig. 6, I). At the same time, the significance of the "present functional state," food excitation, has been elucidated (Fig. 6, II); today we can consider it to be the result of stimulation of brain structures that are activated by the appearance of an appropriate need, the state of hunger. But neither afferentation from the

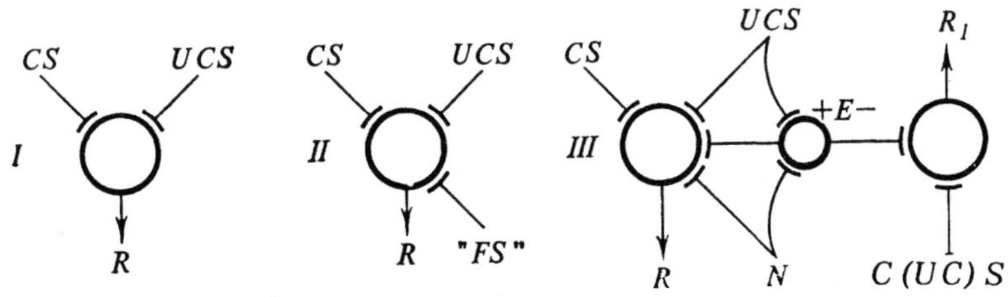

Fig. 6. Two- (I), three- (II), and four-factor (III) diagrams of the meeting of stimuli at the point of convergence in the formation of a conditioned reflex. CS) Conditioned stimulus; UCS) unconditioned stimulus; R) reaction; FS) functional state; N) need; E) emotion.

cavity nor hunger stimulation in themselves can play the role of reinforcement that ensures the formation of an instrumental conditioned reflex. Only integration of hunger stimulation and stimulation by a factor capable of satisfying this need, that is, the mechanism that generates a positive emotion, ensure the development of a conditioned reflex. In a different relationship of the converging stimuli, for example when food reaches the mouth of a sated animal and mechanisms of negative emotion are activated, the defensive avoidance reaction results (Fig. 6, III).

Participation of the neural mechanisms of emotions in the process of the development of any instrumental reflex makes the isolation of the phenomenon of so-called emotional memory highly relative. Evidently we can speak only of the greater or lesser force of an emotional reaction to a reinforcing stimulus such as occurs in the development of a conditioned reflex after one combination, or in the development of conditioned food aversion where reinforcement (poisoning of the animal) occurs several hours after the conditioned signal is perceived. As far as emotions are concerned that are present at the time the conditioned connections are made, they depend on the degree of actuality of the need that the given emotional reaction is based on. It has been demonstrated experimentally that 10 days after the first experiment, eight-year-old children were better at reproducing verbal material that coincided with the motive that was dominant in their personal hierarchy, whether it was hostility, leadership, curiosity, attachment, etc. (Moore et al., 1978).

The experimentally established role of emotions in the process of developing classical, and particularly instrumental, conditioned reflexes leads to the conviction that without consideration and further development of the neurophysiology of emotions, we can scarcely resolve the central problem of the science of higher nervous activity: the problem of the mechanisms of closure of conditioned connections.

COMPENSATORY (SUBSTITUTION) FUNCTION OF EMOTIONS

Being the active state of the systems of specialized brain structures, the emotions influence other cerebral systems that regulate behavior, the processes of perceiving external signals, the recovery of these engrams from memory, and the involuntary functions of the organism. Precisely in the latter case is the compensatory significance of emotions especially obvious.

The fact is that, as a rule, with the development of emotional stress, the magnitude of involuntary shifts (increased heart rate, elevation of blood pressure, release of hormones into the bloodstream, etc.) exceeds the actual needs of the organism. Evidently the process of natural selection found this excessive mobilization of resources expedient. In a situation of pragmatic indeterminacy (which is what is specifically responsible for the arousal of emotions), when the subject does not know what or how much he will need in the next few minutes, it is better to expend energy unnecessarily than to be without sufficient oxygen and metabolic "raw material" at the height of stressful activity, fight or flight.

But the compensatory function of emotions is far from limited to hypermobilization of the involuntary functions. The development of emotional stress is accompanied by a transition to forms of behavior and principles of evaluating external signals and reacting to them that are different from the resting state. Physiologically the essence of this transition can be defined as a return from precisely specialized conditioned reactions to reacting according to Ukhtomsky's principle of dominance. It was not by chance that Osipov termed "emotional" precisely the first stage of developing a conditioned reflex, the stage of generalization.

Pavlygina (1973) analyzed in detail the marks of similarity between the dominant and the conditioned reflex at the generalization stage, in their behavioral, electrophysiological (spatial synchronization of the electroencephalogram, elicited potentials, multisensory activity of the neurons, shift in the level of the constant potential) and microstructural characteristics. The most important trait of the dominant lies in its capacity to respond with the same reaction to a very broad circle of external stimuli, including stimuli that the subject had never experienced before. It is interesting that the ontogenesis seems to repeat the dynamics of the transition from the dominant to the conditioned reflex. Chicks that have just emerged from eggs begin to peck any objects that contrast with the background and that are of the same size as their beaks. Gradually they learn to peck only those that can serve as food (Hailman, 1967).

Considering the process of generalization at the first stage of the development of the alimentary conditioned reflex where a tone was used as a signal, Pavlov explained: "When the connection with the other tones proved in reality to be incorrect, the process of inhibition began. Thus, your real connection becomes more and more precise. The process of scientific thought is like this. All habits of scientific thought consist in, first, obtaining a more stable and more precise connection and, second, subsequently disposing of accidental connections" (Pavlov, 1973, p. 588). According to Ukhtomsky, the dominant "includes all that is necessary and unnecessary from which a selection is subsequently made of that which enriches experience" (Ukhtomsky, 1950, p. 28). Popper, who recently worked with Eccles, stresses a more important significant of just such a mechanism of acquiring new experience, new knowledge. To a book written jointly with Eccles, Popper contributed a chapter titled, "Criticism of the Theory of Unconditioned and Conditioned Reflexes." He writes: "I propose that organisms do not wait, passively, for repetitions of an event (or two) to impress or impose upon their memory the existence of a regularity or of a regular connection. Rather, organisms actively try to impose guessed regularities...upon the world ....Without waiting for repetitions (of events), we produce guesses, conjectures; without waiting for premises, we jump to conclusions. These may have to be discarded; or if we do not discard them in time, we may be eliminated with them. It is this theory of actively proffered conjectures and their refutation (by a kind of natural selection) which I propose to put in the place of the theory of the conditioned reflex ..." (Popper and Eccles, 1977, p. 137).

The theoretical concepts developed by Popper with respect to the activity of the brain are quite fruitful for understanding the mechanisms of creativity, and we will speak about this in a later chapter. In a number of essential points they are close to our own concepts (Simonov, 1966) of the role of "psychic mutagenesis" and "radar reflection" of external events (in this work, Popper uses the expression "projector"). But we cannot agree with Popper on the idea that the mechanism of forming hypotheses and their subsequent verification (selection) must be opposed to the theory of conditioned reflexes and must even replace it. The fact is that these two mechanisms not only exist and mutually complement each other, but they make up a multitude of mixed forms, as was observed in the transition of Ukhtomsky's dominant to Pavlov's conditioned reflex, and vice versa.

For the brain, these transitions are subject to the universal "law of inverse relations between reflexes," formed by Ukhtomsky (1966, p. 246). In its most complex and highest manifestations, this universal law is apparent in the fact that "between the dominant (internal state) and the given receptive content (complex of stimuli), a firm ("adequate") connection is established so that each of the contractors (internal state and external image) elicit and reinforce only each other" (Ukhtomsky, 1950, p. 169). This pattern was analyzed in the work of Beritov and Pavlov; it was studied in all aspects by Asratyan, who used the example of the interaction of direct and reverse conditioned connections.

Two-way conditioned connections are originally not equivalent. Since at each moment in time a living being is affected by a significant number of external stimuli, the reaction then depends to a decisive degree on the present "internal state" of the subject, determined by the real need. Ukhtomsky wrote: "Each time that the symptom complex of the dominant changes, there is a predetermined vector of behavior" (Ukhtomsky, 1950, p. 300). We termed a similar dependence the "radar principle," understanding it as a selective readiness of the brain to respond to the given stimulus when it appears in the environment and to actively seek this stimulus. Being an elementary unit of behavior, the "radar principle" implies an integration of at least two reflexes: a more or less specialized dominant and a conditioned (or unconditioned) reaction to an appropriate external stimulus. In an obvious sense, these hypotheses agree with the idea of Konorski on dividing all reflexes into two basic groups: a preparatory drive reflex and effecting (consummative) reactions (Konorski, 1970).

Therefore, in our opinion, the elementary unit of behavior (its "brick," its "measure," or its "quantum," in the terminology of other authors) is the system comprised of the scanning dominant and the effecting unconditioned (or conditioned) reflex. This is a point of view quite close to Asratyan's hypotheses about the conditioned reflex as a synthesis of two or several unconditioned reflexes, connected among themselves by direct and reverse conditioned connections. Our differences (pertaining more to terminology than substance) can be reduced to two points:

1) Asratyan believes that after the development of the conditioned reflex is complete, the system, consisting at first of *two* reflexes, may be considered as *one* conditioned conditioned reflex, as a new integral whole;

2) we believe that the reverse conditioned connection, having its origin in a dominant at an earlier stage of the formation of the conditioned reflex, is nothing other than a "specialized dominant" or a third stage of evolution of the dominant in Ukhtomsky's terminology. In other words, the specialized dominant should be compared not with a conditioned reflex as a whole, but only with a reverse conditioned connection.

From our point of view, two discoveries by two Soviet scientists, Ukhtomsky's dominant and Pavlov's conditioned reflex, are not simply close, related to each other, but they *complement* each other in a most important point in the development of the science of the activity of the brain. The dominant explains the active and creative nature of this activity, the conditioned reflex, the subtlety, efficiency, and adequate reflection of the environment. In the individual higher nervous (psychic) activity of the brain, the dominant and conditioned reflex occupy a place similar to variability and selection in the evolution of the world of living creatures.

If the process of consolidating a conditioned reflex is accompanied by a decrease of emotional stress and simultaneously by a transition from the dominant (generalized) reaction to a strictly selective reaction to the conditioned signal, then the appearance of emotion leads to a second generalization. "The stronger the need becomes, the less specific is the object that elicits the corresponding reaction," wrote Newton (1975, p. 89). Here the increase in need is more likely to increase reactivity to external stimuli than simply to increase motor anxiety. In an informationally impoverished environment, motor activity of hungry rats increased by only 10%, while under normal conditions it increased by a factor of four (Hinde, 1975, p. 279). An increase in emotional stress, on the one hand, extends the range of engrams drawn from memory and, on the other, decreases the criteria of "accepting a solution" in comparing these engrams with the present stimuli. Thus, a hungry person begins to perceive indeterminate stimuli as being associated with food (McClelland and Atkinson, 1948). It has been demonstrated experimentally that the type of response to a neutral slide in a series of emotional slides (changing the heart rate and plethysmogram of the head) depends on the degree of anxiety of the subject. The stronger the anxiety, the more frequently does the subject respond to the neutral slide as being averse (Hare, 1973). We believe the physiological basis for such a reaction to be the activation and reinforcement of the functional significance of reverse conditioned connections. In experiments with dogs, defensive stimulation of the animal leads to an increase in reactions between signals and objective manifestation of reverse connections in the system of motor defensive conditioned reflexes (Ioffe and Samoilov, 1972).

It is quite obvious that the hypothetical dominant reaction is purposeful only under conditions of pragmatic indeterminacy. When this indeterminacy is eliminated, the subject can turn into a "scared crow that is afraid even of a bush." This is why evolution formed a mechanism by which emotional stress and the characteristic type of reaction to it is dependent on the magnitude of the deficit in pragmatic information, and a mechanism of eliminating negative emotions as the informational deficit is reduced. Let us emphasize that emotion in itself carries no information on the external world; the lacking information is supplied by scanning behavior, and by perfecting habits, by mobilizing engrams that are in the memory. The compensatory significance of emotions lies in their *replacement* role.

As far as positive emotions are concerned, their compensatory function is realized through their effect on the need that initiates behavior. In a difficult situation where the probability of attaining a goal is low, even a small success (increase in probability) induces the positive emotion of enthusiasm that reinforces the need to achieve the goal according to the rule $N = E/(I_n - I_a)$, derived from the emotions formula.

In other situations, positive emotions induce living creatures to disrupt attained "equilibrium with the environment." Striving toward a repeated experiencing of positive emotions, living systems are forced to actively seek unsatisfied needs and a situation of indeterminacy where the information obtained might exceed the predictions made earlier. By the same token, positive emotions compensate for the inadequacy resulting from unsatisfied needs and the pragmatic indeterminacy that can produce stagnation, degradation, or a halt in the process of self-motivation and self-development. Later we will discuss the problem of the role of positive emotions in the differentiation of needs into two basic categories: the needs of necessity and the needs of growth; in physiology, the concepts of stimulation and desire and two varieties of motivation: negative and positive (appetite) correspond to these.

Thus far we have discussed the participation of emotions in the organization of individual behavior. Emotions have no less significance in the behavior of a group, a society, or a colony. It becomes all the more necessary to consider this problem since, according to modern concepts, the elementary evolving unit is not the organism, but a local population with its inherent reverse connections.

THE ROLE OF EMOTIONS IN REGULATING THE SIZE, DENSITY, AND QUALITATIVE COMPOSITION OF A POPULATION

When the density of numbers of individuals of any species (mouse, rat, lemming, or other species) exceeds a certain limit, there is a suppression of the reproductive function. Evidently, a hormonal mechanism of emotional stress is at work because we have found an increase in the weight of suprarenal glands in the animals. Sometimes we have also observed a picture of herd "madness" and mass suicide:

animals swim out to sea, lose themselves in deserts, or are washed ashore. It has been noted that abundance of food does not prevent emotional conflicts between members of the group; with excessive density of population, aggressiveness increases to the point that the animals begin to starve.

The increase in absolute numbers of individuals in a society leads to disruption of the hierarchy normal to the given species and to an increase in aggressiveness since it is precisely the hierarchy that limits and controls aggressiveness. In a group comprised of 10-14 mice, in 70% of the cases the dominants attack three aggressive subdominants closest to them in rank; this reduces the number of conflicts among the subdominants and stabilizes the group (Novikov, 1979). The group hierarchy is established gradually and, in monkeys, the behavior of the subordinate, not the dominating individuals, plays the decisive role in its formation and maintenance (Rowell, 1974; Dlag, 1977). Figuratively speaking, the hierarchy develops not because it is "established" by high-ranking animals, but because the subordinate behavior of other members of the society produces dominants.

If the tendency of mice to resettle does not meet with external obstacles, the high-ranking subdominants that resemble the older males emigrate first. At the beginning of settling new territory, aggressiveness yields to investigative activity in the mice, but later dominant individuals begin to be selected and a hierarchy is established in its past form (Poshivalov, 1977).

The role of emotional conflicts in regulating the size of groups living together may be observed also in races that live in a primitive communal structure. When the numbers in a population of a village of Yanomame Indians reaches approximately 80 individuals, the number of conflicts, intrafamily, and even more, interfamily, that have nothing to do with shortage of food, increases greatly. In an attempt to eliminate these conflicts, the village divides and creates a new settlement. Only the appearance of an external threat interrupts the internal conflicts and, at the same time, prevents dispersal.

Over the course of long evolution, emotions participated in regulating not only the size, but also the qualitative composition of a population. We saw this function of emotions in studying their effect on a healthy and pathologically changed heart (Vainshtein and Simonov, 1979).

Summarizing the data in the literature and the results of our experiments, we can evidently say that any positive or negative, sthenic or asthenic, strong emotions are not harmful to the healthy heart. The appeal to "guard your health," avoiding negative emotions is not only ethically unacceptable as an appeal to indifference and social passivity, but it has no basis from a purely medical aspect either.

The picture becomes essentially different when we consider the pathologically changed heart muscle and coronary vessels. Similarly to other severe functional burdens (and to a greater degree than many other burdens!) emotional stress can lead to dramatic decompensation for the existing peripheral defect. In these circumstances, most harmful are not the nonpositive and nonactively aggressive reactions with their characteristic sympathetic shifts, but the passive-defensive states of anxiety, depression, and feelings of guilt accompanied by symptoms of relative dominances of the parasympathetic section of the autonomic nervous system. The same conclusion may be found in the teachings of Orbeli on the universal adaptive-trophic effect of the sympathetic section of the autonomic nervous system; it contradicts the widespread version of the harmful significance of the "adrenergic" emotions of anger, indignation, or rage with their typical shifts of a sympathetic type.

More complex is the matter of chronic emotionally negative states arising in a situation of long-maintained conflicts at work, in daily life, or in the family. Clinical physiological studies indicate that this class of emotional states can have an effect on the cardiovascular system only in a certain category of persons of a specific constitutional psychological type (Friedman et al., 1969; Ganelina, 1975). If we consider concrete psychological traits of this type (haste in attaining a goal, impatience with the environment, inability to stop working and rest, etc.), then we will see that we are speaking not so much of emotions as of needs and motives. Among the "Sisyphean" or "stress-coronary: type there are almost no subjects with a clear dominance of materially biological or ideal (spiritual, creative-cognitive) needs. Most of them are, as a rule, hypersocial and occupy or strive to occupy a place in a group that is not appropriate to their natural abilities. The "leader" finding himself in the position of "leadership," or that of an ideal "leader," to whom circumstances gave the social role of "leader," these are typical examples of a situation that produces a "stress-coronary" personality. The negative emotions that arise in this case are not the primary cause, but only an indicator of motivational disharmony. Studying the personality features of patients suffering from stomach ulcers, duodenal ulcers, and chronic nonspecific ulcerated colitis, V. P. Belov (1971) came to the conclusion that for these persons, anxiety, irritability, hypersocial achievement, a painful sense of duty, and devotion to ethical standards were characteristic.

Bassin and Rozhnov (1975) are entirely correct in emphasizing that the main source of chronic emotional stress that arises from time to time in the life of a perfect man is not the notorious "information explosion," nor the ever more complicated technology and increased speed, and so on, but interpersonal conflicts which affect the health of persons of a specific constitution especially seriously.

Evaluating the whole array of data that we have accumulated thus far, we cannot isolate the version of heart pathology of neurogenic origin as a "disease of civilization" that appeared because man was made to suppress external manifestations of his aggressive instincts and to smile politely at an offender instead of shattering everything in his path. What kind of "disease of civilization" can we be speaking of if the mechanism of myocardial infarction was formed by evolution as early as in the fossil fish of the salmon family? As a working hypothesis, we are inclined to consider cardiovascular pathology of nervous origin as a result of long-term evolution of one of the mechanisms that maintain the stability and qualitative improvement of the population at the cost of eliminating poorly adapted individuals under certain conditions of existence of our early ancestors (Simonov, 1972). Gilyarov wrote: "In regulating phylogenetic changes according to the principle of complex feedback, a change arising in any link leads to reinforcing the original change. Such feedback both corrects phylogenesis and accelerates its flow" (Gilyarov, 1976, p. 75).

Our data on the adverse effect of passive-defensive states of the pathologically changed heart agree well with the results of the systematic studies of Arshavsky and Rotenberg (1976) and Rotenberg (1978). They demonstrated that various pathological states (experimental epilepsy, extrapyramidal disorders, arrythmia of the heart, anaphylactic shock, and others) are intensified by passive-defensive reactions of animals when they cannot seek a way out of the situation. Active seeking behavior, regardless of its positive or negative (aggressive, avoidance) emotional coloring, on the other hand, has a beneficial effect on those same forms of experimental pathology. Since passive animals are frequently better protected from external dangers (predators, attacks, etc.) than individuals with active seeking behavior, natural selection could result in an accumulation of passive cowards in the population, to their predominance, which would mean a regression of the species with its increasing stagnation. This danger of degeneration was averted by linking the inclination toward passive—defensive behavior with susceptibility to cardiovascular and certain other psychosomatic diseases. An extreme, but clear form of similar intrapopulational self-regulation are the suicidal tendencies of chronic depressive subjects.

Of course, we are far from thinking that the same mechanism operates in contemporary urbanized and congested human society. Such a hypothesis would indicate a vulgar reduction of the life of a human society to simple biology. We are speaking only of biological prehistory, of evolutionary prerequisites of the undoubted and proven fact that the degree of risk of cardiovascular diseases is not the same for persons of different psychological types.

From the position of the information theory of emotions, the approach to the role of emotions in the genesis of cardiovascular diseases of a nervous origin, in a practical sense, leads us to switch our attention from the psychoprophylactics of negative emotions to goal-directed fostering of needs and motives equally useful for both society and for the personality, for its harmonious development and health.

IMITATIVE BEHAVIOR AS AN EXAMPLE OF THE COMPENSATORY FUNCTION OF EMOTIONS AT THE POPULATIONAL LEVEL

The transition to imitative behavior is extremely characteristic for the emotionally stimulated brain. In essence this is a special case of dominant reaction to signals with small (problematic) probability of reinforcement, in the given case, to signals coming from other individuals. When the subject does not have the data or the time for an independent and solidly based resolution, he is left with following the example of other members of the community. To the extent that the expediency of the adaptive reactions is relative, imitative behavior is not very likely to be optimal. It has been demonstrated that the motivation of following the leader in selecting a door in a labyrinth is stronger in rats than their own experience. Rats without a leader select the correct door in 66% of the cases. Rats following a leader that has been taught to select the opposite door make the correct choice in only 40% of the cases (Konopasky and Telegdy, 1977). Under conditions of mass panic, imitative behavior may turn into real catastrophe. Nevertheless, in the course of long evolution, such behavior evidently was statistically advantageous and it was fixed by natural selection.

THE REINFORCING FUNCTION OF EMOTIONS AT THE POPULATIONAL LEVEL: THE PHENOMENON OF EMOTIONAL RESONANCE

It has been shown many times that animals are capable of reacting to external manifestations of an emotional state of another individual of their own species and sometimes also of another species. Moreover, these signals may play a reinforcing role in the development of instrumental conditioned reflexes in rats also (Rice and Gainer, 1962; Greene, 1969).

The avoidance reaction when a painful stimulus is administered to another individual was developed in 267 male adult white rats. In these experiments, we used the preference to be in a limited space that is ecologically characteristic for rats. In an apparatus constructed by Puchkov, an engineer, the floor of the Plexiglas "house" was a pedal that automatically switched on a clock and a painful electrical stimulation of the paws of another rat that was behind a thin, transparent partition permeable to sound (Fig. 7). Once a day the experimental animal was placed in the open, relatively spacious part of the apparatus for 5 min and the time that he remained on the pedal was recorded. For 10 days (and in series of experiments, 5 days) entering the "house" was not accompanied by painful shock to the other rat, while during the next 10 days every entry of the experimental animal into the "house" switched on a current of 1-2 mA. Shocking the "victim" continued for 3-5 sec at 5-sec intervals as long as the experimental animal remained on the pedal.

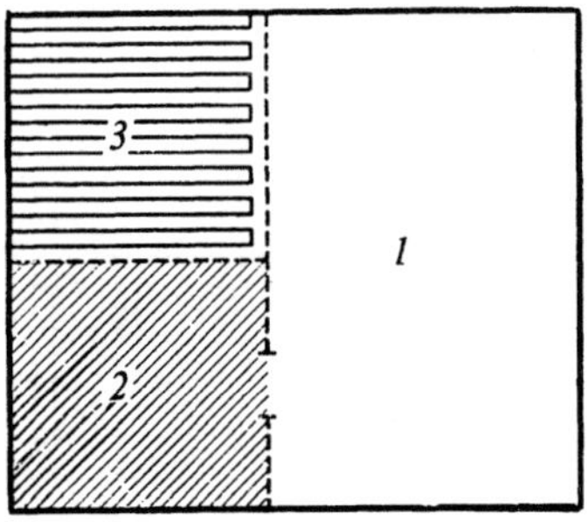

Fig. 7. Apparatus designed by Puchkov for the study of the avoidance reaction in rats painfully shocked by other rats. 1) Free space; 2) "house" with the pedal; 3) "victim's" space.

Specially designed experiments with sound and visual isolation of the rats showed that in a complex of signals of the "victim's" defensive arousal, a scream had decisive significance for the experimental animal. This is why we changed the partners at random, and the "victim" rats inclined toward the passive-defensive reaction of "freezing" with a hoarse or soundless vocalization were rejected and replaced by others. When the developed conditioned avoidance reaction was extinguished and the current was switched off, however, the "victim" rat remained in the chamber as before.

It developed that over the course of 2-3 (rarely 6-8) experiments, for 85 of the experimental animals (approximately 32%), the time the animal remained on the pedal became shorter, 1 min 30 sec, and the average number of entries into the "house" did not exceed 3.1 (see rat No. 13, Fig. 8). Some rats in this group simply stopped entering the "house," although they spent most of the time near the entry to the pedal. Among the remaining 182 rats, animals could be singled out that remained on the pedal almost all of the 5-min period, as well as rats that continually ran from the free space into the "house" and out again when the shocked "victim" screamed.

We were interested in three questions:

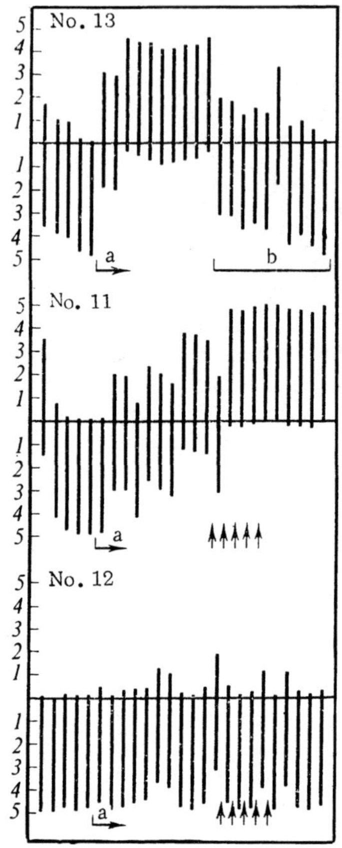

Fig. 8. Dynamics of developing an avoidance reaction in rats Nos. 11, 12, and 13. Abscissa: successive trials. Below the ordinate: time the rats remained in the "house" (min); above the ordinate: time outside the "house"; a) beginning of the development of the conditioned reflex; b) extinction. Arrows indicate when that rat was used as the "victim."

1) What are the characteristic traits inherent in other forms of zoosocial behavior of rats that differ in their reactions to the painful stimulation of a partner?

2) How and to what extent can the reaction of rats to a painful cry of another rat be changed?

3) Which sections of the brain must be damaged and, as a result, in what direction is this avoidance reaction changed?

The results of experiments cited to answer these questions are presented below.

Earlier (Simonov, 1976) we demonstrated that rats that develop the avoidance reaction with respect to a scream of pain without preliminary acquaintance with a painful stimulus are characterized by a high level of investigative activity in an "open field," absence of defecation and urination in an "open field" situation (an indicator of the passive-defensive reaction of fear), and a low aggressiveness when the paws of two rats are exposed to electric shock. Rats that do not show a capacity for developing a conditioned avoidance reaction, on the other hand, were relatively inactive in an "open field," were timid (judging by defecation and urination), and aggressive. The combination of these three qualities was most unfavorable for the development of a conditioned reflex.

In experiments set up by D. Z. Partev,* each of ten rats separately developed a conditioned defensive reflex to a bell reinforced by painful stimulation of the paws. A chamber with a grid floor was divided in half by a partition with a door. Electric current was sent to the grid of half the chamber 5-8 sec after a single sounding of the bell which then continued to sound for another 10 sec together with the painful stimulation.

After a stable defensive conditioned reflex had developed in all ten rats (80-100% reactions to the conditioned signal), 3-5 animals were placed in the chamber simultaneously. If the bell sounded at this time, the rats that had quickly run to the safe half of the chamber behaved differently. Some of them tried to reach the safe side as before, while others began to fight. Some of the rats, having reached the safe half, stood in the door and attacked the rats that were trying to save themselves from being shocked. We must emphasize

*Laboratory of Psychopharmacology of the Institute of Precise Inorganic Chemistry, Academy of Sciences of the Armenian SSR, Yerevan.

that the same animals do both, run away and fight. Even when the conditioned signal (bell) is presented to an aggressive rat simultaneously with an open door, the rat does not flee from the current, but runs in the exactly opposite direction in order to attack another animal. When the conditioned reaction of fleeing from a scream of pain was developed (before beginning experiments with group behavior) in a group experiment, after 120 presentations of the conditioned signal (bell), rats that were in the "house" for an average of 2.13 min registered escape to the safe half in 80% of the cases and fighting in only 14%. For those rats that had been in the "house" for an average of 4.03 min, the number of fights reached 65% and avoidance of electric shock was observed in only 46% of the cases. As far as "defense of safe territory" is concerned, this form of behavior was observed in both categories of rats in the same number of cases (6%). Partev's experiments demonstrated that the character of the reaction to painful stimulation of a partner represents a stable trait of the individual features of a given animal, regularly correlated with its behavior in a situation threatening it with painful stimulation; rats that are not very sensitive to the cries of pain of a "victim" are more likely to exhibit aggressive behavior.

Can the reaction of rats to a cry of pain of another individual be changed, and to what extent?

The 182 rats that remained on the pedal more than 1 min 30 sec were used as "victims" from 3 to 10 times in developing conditioned avoidance reactions in partners. This procedure resulted in decreasing the time the rats remained in the "house" in 14 of the animals, although it remained unchanged in 68 (see rats Nos. 11 and 12, Fig. 8). We might have assumed that applying the current would lead to the development of the usual defensive reflex when a limited space becomes the conditioned signal for a painful stimulation. Experimental facts contradict such an explanation. As soon as the conditioned reflex begins to be extinguished (that is, when the "victim" rat is no longer being shocked), even in the first trial the rats remain on the pedal longer than 4 min. This means that using an experimental animal as a "victim" does not result in the development of the usual defensive conditioned reflex, but increases the sensitivity to signals of defensive stimulation of another individual. Church obtained similar results earlier (1959).

However, using electric shock had this effect in only 42% of the total number of experimental animals. Only 68 of 267 rats (26%) continued to remain on the pedal longer than 3 min (an average of 3.77 min) even after being shocked. The question arose as to whether this "insensitivity" to cries of pain of other individuals could be explained by difficulty in developing the conditioned avoidance reaction, that is, a defect in the mechanisms of learning or acquiring new habits. We developed solid bases for such a hypothesis during Partev's experiments, where it became clear that rats that remained on the pedal less than 2 min reacted to the signal of electric stimulation with a conditioned defensive reflex in 81% of the times the signal was given for 11-14 days, and rats that remained on the pedal longer than 3 min, in only 61% of the times. This is why we were interested in the proposal of Dr. W. Wetzel* to use orotic acid, a substance that promotes consolidation of renewed conditioned connections.

With Dr. Wetzel, we set up experiments with orotic acid using ten rats. We dissolved 300 mg of orotic acid and 375 mg methylglucamine in 30 ml water and administered intraperitoneal injections of this solution at a rate of 1 ml per 100 g body weight. The ten control rats were injected with an 0.9% solution of sodium chloride also at 1 ml per 100 g body weight. The injections of the solutions were administered 1 h before the start of the experiments on developing a conditioned avoidance reaction.

Over a 5-day period all the rats developed the conditioned reaction of avoiding a cry of pain. During the next 5 days, two rats were placed in the compartment for the "victims" since we had demonstrated earlier that fighting in rats, provoked by painful stimulation of the paws, is a stronger stimulus than a cry of pain of one rat. From the 11th to the 15th day we carried out extinction of the established conditioned reaction.

Statistical processing of the results showed the inadmissibility of combining all experimental and all control rats into only two groups. Reliable differences could be obtained only by dividing each group into two subgroups:

---

*Institute of Pharmacology and Toxicology, Magdeburg, East Germany.

those animals that were and those that were not sensitive to a partner's cry of pain. In this case, the difference between rats that were given orotic acid and the control animals was reliable in rats that reacted to the cry of pain when one "victim" was shocked. Making the stimulus stronger by simultaneously shocking two "victims" masked the effect of the orotic acid, which became statistically significant again in extinction experiments. Extinction of the conditioned avoidance reaction reliably occurred more slowly in rats that had been given orotic acid and had earlier exhibited quite high reactivity to a partner's cry of pain.

Thus, we were convinced that injecting orotic acid promotes the development and fixing of a conditioned avoidance reaction in only those animals for which a partner's cry of pain is an adequately effective stimulus. Neither amplifying the signals for defensive stimulation by using two "victims," nor using a painful shock, nor the chemical effect of orotic acid had any effect on rats that did not initially react or reacted weakly to the cry of pain of another individual.

Together with Pigareva and Brazovskaya, we studied the change in the avoidance reaction to a cry of pain in rats after damage to various brain formations. To damage the frontal and cingulate areas of the cortex, we removed the appropriate overlying plate of the skull and carried out a thermocoagulation of the brain tissue with a Nichrome wire electrode. Coagulation of the entorhinal area of the cortex and subcortical formations was done by stereotaxic insertion of steel electrodes insulated with lacquer except for the tip, 0.1-0.2 mm in diameter (current, 2.5-3 mA for 20-30 sec). A neutral electrode was attached to the animal's tail. Stereotaxic coordinates were determined according to Fifkova and Marshall's atlas. The experiments were carried out 10-12 days after the operation. When the experiments were concluded, the brain was examined histologically (Nissl's stain). Every 20th section, 20-40 μm thick, was stained with cresyl violet.

All the sections of the brain that we studied can be divided into three basic categories:

1) brain formations which when damaged have no reliable effect on the avoidance reaction in rats: the cingulate and entorhinal cortex, hippocampus, septum, and mammillary bodies;

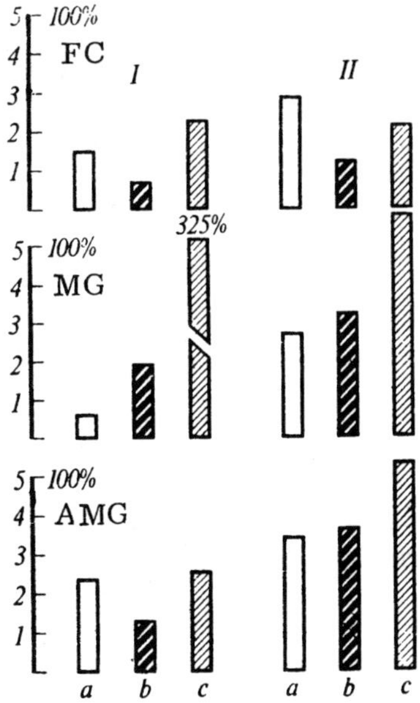

Fig. 9. Average time (min) that two groups of rats (I and II) remained on the pedal when a painful stimulus was administered to another rat. a) Before the operation; b) after the operation; c) change in time on the pedal, in %; FC) frontal cortex removed; MG) medial gray matter destroyed; AMG) amygdala damaged.

2) structures clearly affected by damage regardless of individual traits of the animal: the frontal area of the cortex;

3) structures, consequences of damage to which depend on individual traits of the animal before the operation: the amygdala, medial gray matter, and hypothalamus.

The consequences of damaging the frontal cortical area, the medial gray matter, and the amygdala in thirty rats are presented in Fig. 9. Each group of ten rats was divided into two subgroups, I and II, depending on sensitivity to a partner's cry of pain before the operation. Removal of the frontal cortex reduces the time the rat remained on the pedal in both the first and second subgroups of animals to practically the same degree (44 and 41%, respectively). After the medial gray matter was destroyed, the time on the pedal increased sharply in animals that were highly sensitive to a cry of pain (325%). In rats that remained on the pedal an average of 2.65 min it also increased, but only by 121%. Bilateral damage to the amygdalae decreased the time on the pedal by approximately one-half (53%) in rats of the first subgroup but left it practically unchanged in the second subgroup (105%).

The effect opposite to the consequences of amygdalectomy was observed after damage to the lateral hypothalamus. The time on the pedal was decreased for rats that had earlier remained in the "house" for a comparatively long time, and increased for those animals that had spent most of their 5-min exposure in the free space. In other words, after damage to the lateral hypothalamus, all rats became alike and spent approximately the same amount of time inside and outside the "house." Those rats habitually stood in the door of the "house" with half the body on the pedal and the other half in the free space.

Experiments with local damage to brain structures led to the following conclusions:

1. The conditioned avoidance reaction to a cry of pain depends on the preservation of no one section of the brain, but a whole series of brain formations: the frontal cortex, medial gray matter, amygdala, and hypothalamus.

2. Also, it has been incorrectly assumed that the conditioned avoidance reaction is accomplished by the brain as a whole because there are some structures that can be damaged with no effect on the forms of behavior that were studied. Among these, for example, are the entorhinal and cingulate cortex, hypothalamus, septum, and mammillary bodies.

3. Participation of brain formations in the learning reaction is closely connected with the functional specialization of formations that were discovered during the study of other forms of behavior: conditioned reflex switching of alimentary and defensive reflexes by Asratyan, or development of conditioned reflexes with partial (reliable) reinforcement, etc.

4. It is of interest that the effect of damage to some structures (medial gray matter, amygdala, and hypothalamus)

depends on individual characteristics of the animal before surgical interference. We may assume that it is precisely these structures that are the neuroanatomical substrate for the individually different reactivity of rats with respect to the signals of defensive stimulation of the partner, and for some other forms of behavior characteristic for the given animal.

Among the brain formations of the latter group, especially clear and unequivocal are the results we obtained by destroying the medial gray matter. After this section of the brain was damaged, the avoidance reaction deteriorated sharply in all rats that had previously reacted well to a partner's painful cry. According to data of a number of investigators, the medial gray matter is linked to transmitting pain afferentation and to integration of the reaction to emotionally negative (aversive) stimuli: sounds, smells, etc. It is possible that in the process of evolution, natural selection "used" those same brain mechanisms that are connected with perceiving averse stimuli, including pain stimuli, addressed to the *animal itself* for reacting to signals of a negative emotional state of *another* individual. These data, obtained in experiments with animals, help us understand the mechanism of the phenomenon that occurs when a person, being a witness to the suffering of another, experiences an almost physical illness: constriction in the heart region, a lump in the throat, nausea, and other somatic symptoms.

Preobrazhenskaya (1973) developed an instrumental conditioned motor avoidance reflex in dogs when the dog's partner was painfully stimulated. Two dogs were placed in a chamber on different stands a half meter apart. The hind leg of the "victim" was administered a shock of significant force that elicited not only local movement of the paw, but panting, whimpering, and squealing. The front paw of the "observer" dog was fastened to a lever. By raising the paw above a certain level, this animal could switch off the current going to the first dog. A 10-sec sound signal (a tone of 600 Hz) preceded the switching on of the current which remained on for 30 sec. If the dog raised its paw and switched off the current, the current stopped. A record was made of the dog's motor reactions, breathing, electrocardiograms, and electrograms of the dorsal hippocampus.

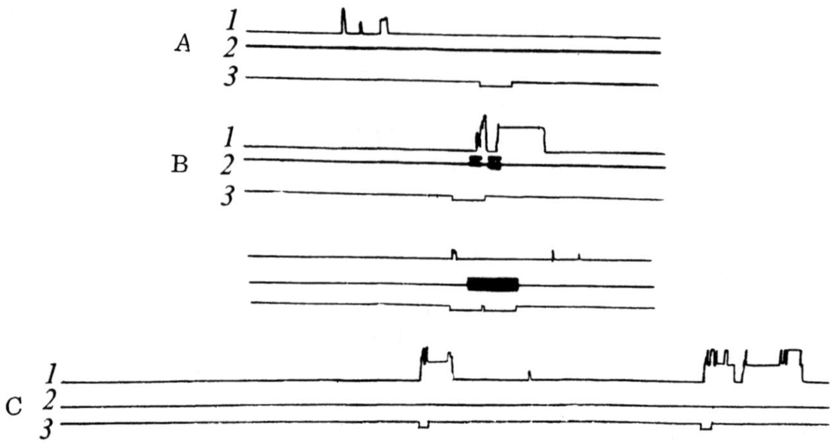

Fig. 10. Dynamics of the development of an avoidance reaction in dogs when a partner is painfully stimulated. 1) Raising of the paw by the "observer" dog; 2) current acting on the "victim" dog; 3) notation of the conditioned signal (after Preobrazhenskaya); A, B, C) sequential parts of the experiment.

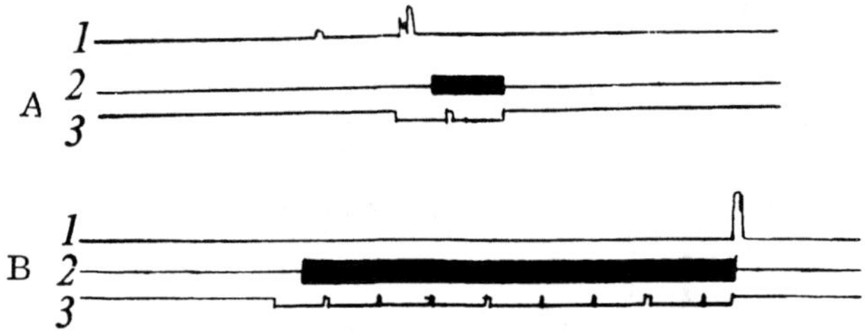

Fig. 11. Elimination of the conditioned avoidance reaction after transfer of the electrode to the "victim" dog. Notation as in Fig. 10 (after Preobrazhenskaya).

Three of six dogs developed the conditioned reflex (Fig. 10). It should be noted that the dog's "own" defensive reflex, developed earlier, did not facilitate the avoidance reaction when a partner was painfully stimulated if the sensitivity of the given animal to signals of defensive stimulation of another individual was low. From Fig. 11 it

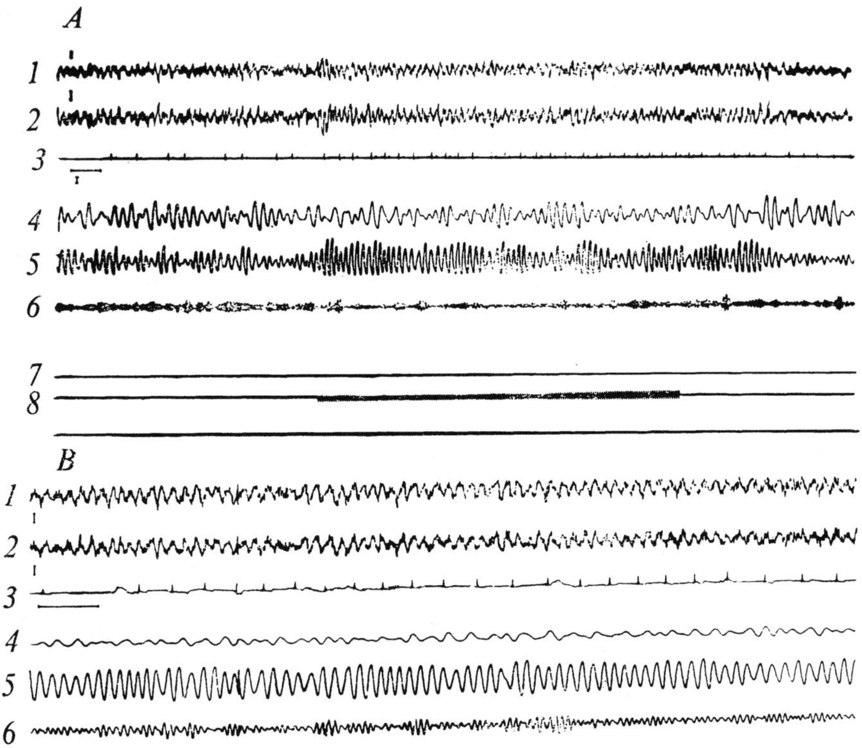

Fig. 12. Changes in the electrogram of the hippocampus and EKG with painful stimulation of the dog (B) or its partner (A). 1, 2) Electrogram of the hippocampus; 3) EKG; 4, 5, 6) delta, theta, and alpha: frequencies of the electrogram isolated by an analyzer; 7) notation of raising of the paw by the "observer" dog; 8) current applied to the "victim" dog (after Preobrazhenskaya).

is apparent that with the first applications of the conditioned signal after the electrodes were transferred from the paw of the "victim" to the paw of the "observer," there was still a short conditioned reflex raising of the lever that turns off the current. But soon the "observer" stopped reacting to the conditioned signal and to the signals coming from the partner.

TABLE 2. Average Value of Frequency of Heart Contractions and Amplitude of Integrated Theta Rhythm (in arbitrary units) in "Observer" Dogs (after Preobrazhenskaya, 1973).

Dog's name	Average frequency of heartbeat for 10 sec			Average of integrated theta rhythm		
	normal	during stimulation of partner	% of change from normal	normal	during stimulation of partner	% of change from normal
Laskovy	14.8	18.7	126.3	86.9	99.6	114
Belka	15.4	17.2	111.6	73.9	82.6	112
Snezhok	13.2	18.7	141	92.7	97.6	105

In dogs that were sensitive to the painful stimulation of a partner, it was possible to record objective traits of emotional stress in the form of increased heart rate and increased theta rhythm in the hippocampus (Fig. 12; Table 2).

Statistical processing of the data showed that the number of experiments in which changes were observed was reliable and fluctuated in different animals from 66 to 87%. These shifts lasted a very short time and returned to the original value very quickly after stimulation of the partner stopped. The behavior of the "observer" dogs in the intervals between the shocks was calm, and some dozed. Two of the dogs developed instrumental conditioned reflexes: elevation of the left front paw that turned off the painful stimulation of the partner, and pressing the lever which resulted in the "observer" getting food. To determine the relative strength of the two motivations, special trials were done with simultaneous stimulation of the partner and switching on the conditioned alimentary signal. It developed that, in most cases, the dog carried out the reaction that ended the defensive stimulation of the partner. Similar results were obtained in experiments with monkeys: of 15 macaque rhesus monkeys, 10 stopped pressing a lever if presentation of food was accompanied by painful stimulation of another individual (Masserman et al., 1964).

Thus, in some animal "observers," signals of defensive stimulation of another individual elicit a state of negative emotional stress that the animal strives to minimize, that is, interrupt or prevent. Our own experiments on rats and dogs, like the results of other investigators that included experiments on monkeys, showed that individual features of reacting to a cry of pain depend mainly on the need-motivational traits of the given individual and not on his capability for learning. This is why among animals at different stages of evolutionary development (rats, dogs, monkeys) there are individuals sensitive in different degrees to signals of the emotional state of another creature of the same species.

In man, the reactions to the emotional state of another have a qualitatively new and more complex character. It is difficult to agree with the hypothesis of co-experiencing as simple imitation, a direct reproduction of emotion on the principle: he saw a happy man and he became happy; he saw a sad person, and he felt sorrow. It is true that such a point of view is frequently applied even to art, considering it as a means of "transmitting feelings" from the artist to the viewer. Here an expression of feelings acts in an "infectious" way, and the viewer responds to the actor with a "co-experiencing understanding" as a result of which there is an "emotional understanding of what is taking place" (Yakobson, 1977).

But it is precisely art, especially the art of the theater, that daily refutes the belief that co-experiencing is imitation resulting from the celebrated "infectiousness of feelings." N. Plotnikov, People's Artist of the USSR, wrote: "It happens that an actress cries as it were 'real tears' as the director demanded at rehearsals. All the same, a viewer nudges his companion, gives him his binoculars, and says: 'Just look, she's crying! Really crying!' As if it were real life on the stage (an actress is indeed crying), but this is not art" (Plotnikov, 1971). It may be that only in early childhood do we find the mechanism of purely imitative production of emotions by a group of children without an explanation of why the first child cried or why a little girl overcome by laughter immediately has the whole group laughing. Later the mechanisms of co-experiencing become ever more complex.

In order to suffer, it is not enough simply to be a witness to the suffering of another person, as the partisans of direct "infectiousness" of emotion assume. The insensitivity and cruelty of children of a certain age are based on the incapacity of a child to connect external traits of another's state with their own similar state and expression characteristic for it. As we have proven above, even in animals, the animal's own experience of a painful action substantially affects its sensitivity to signals of defensive stimulation of another individual. Sympathy and empathy must be learned, and the development of this capability depends to a decisive degree on proper upbringing. Sukhomlinsky wrote: "The work of the soul is to suffer, to hurt with the suffering and pain of man, first of all that of the mother, the father, sister, grandfather, grandmother. Do not be afraid to expose a young soul to these sufferings; they are beneficial. Let a nineteen-year-old son spend a sleepless night at the bedside of a sick mother or father, let someone else's pain fill every corner of his heart. One of the most excruciating difficulties in education is to teach a child the work of love" (Sukhomlinsky, 1971, p. 4). And, in a different place, he wrote: "The art of endowing a child or youth with higher feelings and experiences is the art of co-experiencing" (Sukhomlinsky, 1979, p. 273).

No matter how important the capability to empathize (experience emotions similar to emotions of another), in itself it does not determine the character of action. L. N. Tolstoy and F. M. Dostoevsky distinguished passive, contemplative, and, therefore, fruitless love from active, efficacious love. Here we again see the law formulated by the information theory of emotions. The signals of the feeling of another person are only information perceived by the subject. As far as the actions of this subject are concerned, they will depend on the *need* that is dominant in the structure of the given personality. It may be a maternal need to help one's own child (or another child), or a complex social need to respond to an ethical standard that requires one to behave in a strictly determined way, or an egotistic need to not get involved and save oneself from unnecessary trouble. Each of these needs elicits its own series of emotions and its own chain of actions. Dostoevsky wrote: "Dreamlike love thirsts for the instant deed, quickly satisfied, and the attention of everyone. Here it actually comes to sacrificing life itself so that it would not drag on, but be finished more quickly, as on a stage, so that all those who saw it might praise it. Active love, on the other hand, is work and endurance, and for others, if you please, it is a lesson in itself" (Dostoevsky, 1958, pp. 75-76). Many years later, Eric Fromm wrote: "Productive love is incompatible with love that simply contemplates the life of the loved one: love includes activity, concern and responsibility for his development" (Fromm, 1960, pp. 100-101).

The task of bringing up a child is essentially the formation of the requisites (motives, stimulations) most valuable for the given community. "The work of the soul" in Sukhomlinsky's sense cannot be reduced to having the child simply feel some kind of emotional discomfort on seeing a person in pain or unjustly treated, he must not simply try to eliminate his own painful "co-experiencing," but must help and must experience the positive emotions that successful action directed toward easing another's burden brings.

This is a very brief review of the regulatory — switching, reinforcing, compensatory — functions of emotions at the individual and populational levels. Over the course of the whole chapter, we tried to show that these regulatory functions of emotions come directly from their reflective-evaluative function and are promoted by it. As distinct from the conceptions of "relation," "significance," "sense," and so forth, the information theory of emotions precisely and unequivocally defines that objective existing reality, that "standard" (if we may use the expression of Vilyunas) which has a subjective *reflection* in the emotions of man and the higher animals: need and probability (possibility) of its satisfaction. Precisely these two factors make events "meaningful" for the subject, give them "personal meaning," and move the subject not only to experience, but also to express, and to realize effectively his "relation" to the surrounding world and to himself.

Analysis of Criticism of the Information Theory of Emotions

During the 15 years of its existence, the information theory of emotions has been included in current scientific literature. In an editorial, "Activities of the Physiology Department," the journal *Vestnik Akademii Nauk SSSR* [*Bulletin of the Academy of Sciences of the USSR*] (1975, No. 11, pp. 7-8) published the following statement: "the Resolution (of the Presidium of the Academy of Sciences of the USSR) contains a list of the principal results of the scientific research activities of Soviet physiologists in recent years ... Specifically mentioned is the experimental confirmation of the information theory of emotions on which the principles of simulating emotional stress during surgery are based."

In the same journal, in connection with awarding the 1979 Pavlov Prize for the monographs, "The Theory of Reflection and the Psychology of Emotions," and "Higher Nervous Activity in Man. Motivational-Emotional Aspects," we read the following: "The information theory of emotions, one of the fundamental concepts developed in recent years, is a significant contribution to the creative development of the teachings of I. P. Pavlov on higher nervous activity. This theory has become the basis for setting up and resolving many very important problems of applied psychology" (Vestnik Akademii Nauk SSSR, 1979, No. 6, p. 151).

The formulation of the information theory was given a positive evaluation in reviews by Shingarov (1970), Gorfunkel' (1971), Shustin and Serzhantov (1974), and Smirnov (1977). Strongman, in his review monograph, "The Psychology of Emotion" (1973), and Izard, in his book, *Human Emotions* (1977), present the basic principles of the theory. It is used in the analysis of the nature of art (Lilov, 1977) and in attempts to simulate the functions of the brain (Gorsky, 1978).

There are some proposals to modify the "formula of emotions" in one way or another. Thus, Yankelevich (1965), analyzing the genesis of emotional stress in pilots, proposed basing a subjective evaluation of danger on the ratio of the number of crashes the pilot was aware of to the total number of flights of the given type. Attempting to unify the information theory with Anokhin's theory of the functional system, Kositsky (1977) modified the formula in the following way:

$$DS = G(I_n E_n T_n - I_a E_a T_a),$$

where DS is the degree of stress; G is the goal (a synonym of afferent synthesis); I, E, and T are information, energy, and time necessary for achieving the goal, and information, energy, and time available.

We have already said that predicting the probability of achieving the goal inevitably also includes the knowledge, habits, and energy resources of the organism as well as the time necessary and sufficient for the appropriate actions. Entering all of these (and many other) factors into a structural formula of emotions is, in our opinion, unnecessary. As far as the goal is concerned, it is always the function of need, and need (even its elementary variabilities) can be measured, but a "goal" cannot be measured. Introducing it into a formula is clearly unproductive.

The information approach to analysis of emotional stress under normal conditions and in the presence of pathology of higher nervous activity is used more and more frequently. In his book, *Information Neurosis*, Khananashvili writes: "A. M. Svyadosh believes, as I do, that an important condition for the development of neurosis in man is great significance of the signal, assuming that the information that affects the probability of satisfying need is significant" (Khananashvili, 1978, p. 71). As we have said earlier, Kharkevich (1960) is responsible for the concept of determining the pragmatic value of information according to the change in the probability of achieving a goal as a result of obtaining certain information. It is specifically this meaning of the term "information" that we used in the development of the information theory of emotions, making the concept "achieving a goal" an idea of satisfying a real need.

We believe that the situation described by Khananashvili as neurogenic represents a special case of a situation leading to negative emotional stress according to the information theory of emotions. To what extent this emotional stress can lead to neurotic derangement depends on other factors: on the duration of the given emotional state, on individual (typological) features of the subject, on the degree of asthenization of his nervous system, etc.

Since pathogenesis of the neurotic state always involves the brain mechanisms of negative emotions ("The psychology of emotions," noted Krechmer, "is the psychology of the human heart in general"), in 1966, he wrote: "Human neurosis is a classical 'informational disease' which requires adequate 'informational' methods of treatment" (Simonov, 1966a, p. 61). Developing this hypothesis as applied to experimental pathology of higher nervous activity, we emphasized that: "An animal is forced to carry out actions that in their scope, rate, and other characteristics are beyond his nervous system... Under natural conditions, the animal constantly changes the tactics of his adaptive behavior; it seeks methods of achieving a goal that are not only the most effective, but also the most economical for the nervous system. But in an experiment we limit the animal's selection of means and make it do work that exceeds the capabilities of its brain... Experimental neurosis in animals is simply the result of unsuccessful attempts to solve a difficult problem that is beyond their nervous system; it is always the result of a strong need to reach a solution brought about by stronger biological needs of a living being ... During the time of the famous Leningrad floods in 1924, neurosis increased in dogs with which Pavlov was working not because water came into the room, but because the dogs, locked in their cages, had no possibility of immediate escape" (Simonov, 1968, pp. 14-15).

It may be that Khananashvili's concept of the genesis of negative emotional stress will lead to experimental neurosis, contradicting factual data and theoretical hypotheses of the information theory of emotions. Actually, these always speak of the *deficit* of pragmatic information, while

Khananashvili emphasizes the significance of information overload of the brain in conjunction with a deficit of time allowed for its processing and reaching a solution. But this seeming contradiction is due to the ambiguity of the term "information."

THE TERM "INFORMATION" AS APPLIED TO THE STUDY OF EMOTIONS

We will mention only a few of the meanings of the term as it is used in modern literature. Here we find: an everyday concept of information as messages transmitted from system to system (living or automatic); a concept of information as negative entropy (negentropy), that is, a measure of ordering, organization, nonrandomness; a semantic value of information determined through a change in the thesaurus (the fund of knowledge); and, finally, its pragmatic value, the measure of which is a change in the probability of achieving a goal as a result of having a given communication. More precise knowledge of the state of the problem may be found in the works of Kolmogorov, Kharkevich, Bongard, Shreider, Menitsky, Wolkenstein, and others.

Let us consider a typical example of the development of emotional stress as a result of "information overload." During 40 sec of flight, 70 (!) different operations have to be accomplished. Every minute, the pilot must read 120-150 instruments (Mikhailov, 1977). At the moment of landing he must simultaneously keep track of the instruments, the operation of the motors, direction of flight, distance to the earth, etc. A beginner pilot (I know this from personal experience) literally "chokes" on the torrent of signals coming at him and finds himself in the situation of a very severe *deficit* of information necessary and sufficient for timely execution of the actions that control the plane. This results in very serious emotional stress: a sharp increase in heart rate, tremor, a convulsive seizing of the control knob, and a growing hazard of pilot error. The so-called "overload" turns into an information deficit and a decrease in the probability of achieving the goal.

A similar misunderstanding occurs quite frequently [see, for example, Bekhtel' (1968)]. Critics of the information theory of emotions for some reason like to cite the same example as if to disprove the theory. They say: "As long as a man is judged, he finds himself in a state of a deficit of information concerning his future fate. Then the verdict is announced. Indeterminacy decreased, the accused knows precisely what sentence threatens him. Have his negative emotions become weaker now? On the contrary, they have become stronger." This is understandable. It is true that his need was to escape punishment. When the verdict is announced, the probability of satisfying this need decreased critically, and negative emotions increased sharply. This example once again confirms the theory and does not disprove it.

It is another matter if the accused is striving for punishment, as it sometimes happens. Akutagawa Ryunosuke (1974), in her short story, "A Tale of Recompense for a Good Deed," tells of Poro Yasaburo who, being convicted in place of Jinkaya, is *glad* of his coming execution. By dying for Jinkaya, who had saved Yasaburo's father from ruin, he first repays him for the good deed and, at the same time, he avenges Jinkaya's refusal of Yasaburo's gratitude. Finally, dying under the name of the renowned thief, he takes on the fame of that thief in place of his own pathetic, destitute, inglorious existence. The happiness of the convicted man is the result of an increase in the probability of satisfying his three needs or, more precisely, one very deep need for justice in keeping with the norms adopted by the hero of the tale.

TRAITS OF SIMILARITY AND THE ESSENTIAL DIFFERENCE BETWEEN THE INFORMATION THEORY OF EMOTIONS AND ANOKHIN'S "BIOLOGICAL THEORY OF EMOTIONS"

At least three circumstances brought about this similarity. First and most important is the fact that evidently both conceptions properly reflected some aspects of an objectively existing phenomenon. Second is the fact that the author of the information theory belongs to a generation for which the books, speeches, and papers of Anokhin, together with works of other Soviet physiologists and physiologists of other countries, were an organic part of the formation of their own scientific world view. Finally, there is no doubt of the genetic similarity of the biological and information theories since they both belong to the Pavlovian trend in the science of the activity of the brain and come directly from the same ideational source: Pavlov's concept of the noncoincidence (nonconformity) between the internal stereotype constructed earlier and the changed external dynamic stereotype.

The most substantial difference between the theories can be reduced to two points. Anokhin's "acceptor of the results of an action" assumes the prediction of only a single content, the semantics of the goal, of the afferent characteristics of the goal object. In the introduction to the collection, *Systemic Organization of Physiological Functions* (1969, p. 10), we read: "As a rule, *complete* coincidence of the properties of the acceptor of an action with the signals coming in concerning the result of the action is always accompanied by positive emotions of a pleasant type that approve the success of the completed action. Conversely, *any* "nonconformity" is a source of unpleasant, biologically negative emotions that favor a rapid satisfaction of the arising needs. This representation, in accordance with which emotions make it possible for an organism to evaluate needs and their satisfaction, was the basis of the original biological theory of emotions developed by P. K. Anokhin" (author's emphasis).

In not one of Anokhin's works have we found mention of the fact that, together with content (semantics) of a goal, the brain always predicts the *probability* of its achievement. As far as our theory is concerned, this is a key point that has its reflection even in the very title, *information* theory of emotions. Introducing the category of probability of predicting (Feigenberg, 1963) immediately extends the limits of application of the theory to actually observed facts. The phenomenon of probability of predicting makes it possible to understand why emotions arise not only in the process of taking action (Anokhin's theory), but before any action begins as well, as happens in most cases. Secondly, predicting the probability of achieving a goal (satisfying a need) explains the mechanism of the development of positive emotions.

The treatment of this mechanism in Anokhin's work is most contradictory. In most of his work, positive emotions are spoken of as the result of *coincidence* of the acceptor of the action (afferent model of a result) with the afferentation that signals achievement of the result. But there is also the following reasoning: "...in the process of evolution, the factor of nonconformity between the goal set and the result obtained was linked to the development of a negative emotion where the nonconformity arose on the basis of failure to obtain vitally important factors. Conversely, if there is no reverse afferentation that signals a biologically negative action, then the nonconformity leads to positive emotions" (Anokhin, 1966, p. 29). The last case contradicts everything that has been said before. The action of the subject cannot be "biologically negative," since it is directed toward achieving a "positive result." If the author implies the action of an external harmful factor (for example, pain), then afferentation, signalling external harm, will not be "reverse." It is completely obvious that absence of predicting the probability of achieving a goal in the concept of an acceptor of an action excludes the possibility of *positive nonconformity* in the sense of an *increase* in probability in comparison with earlier prediction.

Is this a chance gap in the theory of the functional system and the biological theory of emotions that is organically connected with it? We believe that it is not. The theory of a closed, "circular" functional system represents a variation of the homeostatic approach to behavior for which survival, self-preservation, "equilibrium with the environment," and reduction of drive are not only the main, but the only factors that organize behavior. For this kind of a design, positive emotions are essentially *unnecessary*; the system can work on the basis of only one "penalty" (negative emotions), where elimination of the penalty (satisfying the need) is the reward. No attempt to somehow introduce positive emotions into the design of the functional system as an additional, auxiliary factor that facilitates the attainment of a beneficial result can be logically justified.

Anokhin and his successors ignored the fact that the presence of positive emotions stimulates living systems to actively *disrupt* an achieved equilibrium with the environment. Perhaps this happened because Anokhin did not consider all the diversity of the needs of man and the higher animals, including such diversity as the need to investigate (in man, the need to know), the need to take possession of new territory, new areas of activity in the sense of Vernadsky, the need for advancement in rank in a hierarchy, etc. It is not by chance either that the theory is called the "biological theory of emotions," limiting in advance the sphere of its application to strictly biological motivations (hunger, thirst, sex).

An answer to the question on the relation of our theory to Anokhin's theory can be formulated quite clearly: *the information theory of emotions represents generalization on a broader scale; Anokhin's biological theory enters into it as a special case.*

ARE THE LIMITATIONS THAT CRITICS APPLY TO THE INFORMATION THEORY OF EMOTIONS JUSTIFIED?

Many authors, referring to information theory, think it is necessary to point out its particular character. Reikovsky writes: "In psychological literature we find the opinion that the source of emotions is a discrepancy between the amount of information present and the information needed to solve the problem that confronts a person (Simonov, 1966). It follows from data considered here that this representation considers only some reasons for the development of emotions" (Reikovsky, 1979, p. 356). Unfortunately, after a most careful study of Reikovsky's book, we could not find "data" indicating any reasons for the development of emotions except for the presence of actual needs and evaluation of the possibility of their satisfaction.

Other critics do not bother at all to look for concrete examples. Dodonov: "...as distinct from P. V. Simonov, we do not see the possibility at this time of encompassing all emotions in a single 'measuring formula.' It is obvious that for each class of emotions, the 'formula' must be different" (Dodonov, 1978, p. 45). Exactly which emotions are not encompassed by the formula? How has it become "obvious," why "must" the formula be different for each class of emotions? We can only guess at this. Incidentally, why did Dodonov arbitrarily convert a structural formula into a "measuring" formula? The book contained not a word about this either.

But when critics of the theory give concrete examples of a contradiction between information theory and reality, their extremely simplified understanding of our conception is apparent. "P. V. Simonov's treatment of the role of emotions seems very limited to us since in real life, time and again, we come upon emotions that arise not only as a result of nonconformity between need and the possibility of satisfying it, but we also come upon the reactions to the subject's own actions (for example, joy elicited by resolving a difficult problem)," writes Putlyaeva (1979, p. 29). Excuse me, but the possibilities of satisfying a need depend primarily and mainly on the subject's own actions precisely. It has been demonstrated experimentally that when symptoms of emotional stress are recorded in members of a plane crew and the passengers, that is, in persons with an identical degree of risk in a complex flight situation, the frequency of heart contractions increases most in the pilot making the landing, on whose actions the attainment of the goal depends (Roscoe, 1978). The moment of resolving a difficult task is characterized by an increase in the probability of satisfying the need, and this leads to the positive emotion of happiness in the example given by Putlyaeva.

Very frequently claims against the information theory of emotions are explained by the arbitrary reduction of human needs to so-called biological needs; as a result of this, the information theory is then treated as exclusively "biological." The book by Rappoport, *Art and Emotion*, may serve as an example of this.

According to Rappoport, Simonov regards the origin of human emotions "only on the biological plane... They (human emotions) are undoubtedly determined by needs and the circumstances of their being satisfied, but very frequently these are needs not of a given subject, but of one social group of people or another, of humanity, nations, classes, a given collective, etc.... To connect these emotions with a deficit or surplus of information seems unconvincing... What is to be done with the whole complex and relatively independent work of the psyche...where should it be referred, to close or distant interactions? How can its origin, development, and attainment of its exceptional complexity and richness be explained? All of these questions cannot be resolved if we remain on the platform of the biological theory of emotions" (Rappoport, 1968, pp. 101-104).

It is necessary to explain that needs of society may elicit emotions in a specific subject, but they will be represented in the system of his own individual needs, motives, and interests. "'History' is not some kind of special personality that uses man as a means for achieving *its* goals. History is *nothing other* than the activity of man pursuing his purposes" (Marx and Engels, *Works*, 2nd edn., Vol. 2, p. 102). It is precisely the character of the needs, including the higher socially determined and spiritual needs, that gives emotions their qualitative specificity. It is illogical to contrast the character of a need that gives rise to one emotion or another with the universal mechanism of forming emotional states, their dependence on the possibility of satisfying them, etc.

We have spoken earlier about the fact that, depending on the factor of time, an emotional reaction may acquire traits of a rapidly developing affect or a rigidly maintained attitude. In close interaction with an object (with food, the source of pain, etc.) which can be extended or interrupted, but which can no longer be prevented, emotion appears in the form of an emotional tone of feelings. In all of the cases mentioned, the internal organization of the emotion is similar. Even pain, according to Waldman and Ignatov (1976), has two components: perceptive or informational (location, character, modality, novelty, the possibility of becoming weaker), and a truly emotional component (degree of suffering, endurance). Parygin does not want to agree with this universality of the principle of the formation of emotional reactions; for him the information theory presents "...basically a very vulnerable, even simply erroneous conceptual model of emotions. In our view, it is completely groundlessly identified with the much more complex psychic formations to which experience and the psychic state, as a whole, the psychic mood of man, belong" (Parygin, 1971, p. 141). What is to be done? The "psychic state of man as a whole" and his "psychic mood" have actually been described much more precisely and completely by Tolstoy and Dostoevsky than by the psychology of feelings.

THE EXPEDIENCY OF EXPRESSING THE INFORMATION THEORY IN THE FORM OF A "FORMULA OF EMOTIONS"

Many critics object to using "formula of emotions" since it is not quantitative in the strict sense. Foreseeing this, we emphasize each time that our formula represents a *structural model* in an extremely short and graphic form that demonstrates the internal organization of emotions. Lomov has developed a very sound base for the expediency of such a model. "One can isolate several approaches to using mathematics in psychology. The simplest is the so-called discursive approach, which consists essentially of substituting mathematical symbols for a natural language. Normal language frequently is not quite adequate for expressing economically and precisely the whole complexity of some of the ideas developing in science. In this situation, the use of symbols may replace long discussion. It may serve as a unique kind of mnemonic medium, an easily remembered code.

"An example of the discursive approach may be the familiar 'formula' of emotions proposed by P. V. Simonov: $E = N(I_a - I_n)$. It expresses very well the basic idea of the author, but is completely unsuitable for concrete computations. The author does not disclose the nature of the dependencies of which we are speaking and does not supply measurements that would make it possible to come to a quantitative evaluation of the related phenomena" (Lomov, 1971, p. 34).

While being in agreement with Lomov in his evaluation of the discursive approach, I cannot agree with the latter part of this citation.

It is understood that we do not have universal units of measuring needs, emotions, and the pragmatic value of information. Nevertheless, a real possibility exists for experimental confirmation of the formula in the simplest and, therefore, most empirically measurable situations. For example, we can measure the need for food by the duration of food deprivation within certain limits, and we can evaluate the probability of satisfying this need through the probability of reinforcing conditioned signals with food. Thus, in experiments with dogs, Mekhedova (1969) demonstrated that the degree of emotional stress, which was judged according to frequency of heartbeat, depended both on the need (duration of food deprivation) and on the probability of reinforcement. With identical probabilities, the emotional stress differed after a one-day deprivation and a three-day deprivation. On the other hand, with identical duration of deprivation, the frequency of heartbeat reliably increased when there was a transition from constant to probable (partial and random) reinforcement of the conditioned signals. In our own experiments with development of human conditioned defensive reflexes over time (see above), we measured the deficit of pragmatic information through the total number of errors made by the subject in the process of learning.

At present, the possibility of "concrete computations" and "qualitative evaluation" depends more on the successes of applied mathematics than on the experimenting psychologist.

Anisimov and Raibman, with our participation, applied the so-called game methods, specifically minimax methods, to the study of human emotional reactions (Simonov et al., 1978). These methods make it possible to determine not the exact value (magnitude) of emotion, but only the probability of one value or another of emotion. With a similar, but more exacting approach, not in an isolated experiment but in many studies, a regular dependence of emotions on degree of indeterminacy becomes apparent and, therefore, has the character of statistics. An analysis of experimental material showed that with one and the same need, when indeterminacy increased, the probability of strong emotional reactions (heart and galvanic skin reactions) increased, and the probability of absence of emotional reaction dropped.

We are firmly convinced that further improvement in experimental techniques and methods of processing factual data will make it possible to modify the formula of emotions so that it will reflect not only the qualitative-functional dependencies, but also the quantitative. Moreover, the productivity and prospects of our structural model can by no means be reduced to this potential possibility.

We disagree categorically with Lomov on the point that the information theory of emotions "does not disclose the character of the dependencies of which we are speaking." Let us remember that the formula very graphically demonstrates the dependence of the positive and negative emotions on the increase ($I_a > I_n$) or drop ($I_n > I_a$) in the probability of satisfying the need. But the formula reflects even more complex relations.

It agrees with the formula $N = E/(I_n - I_a)$. Actually, emotion increases need. It has been experimentally demonstrated that fear of pain increases the feeling of pain and decreases the pain threshold. On the other hand, a feeling of happiness and enthusiasm, even if it arises after a small success, increases the need to achieve a final goal. But too high or too low a probability of achieving a goal has a depressing effect on the need. Something that is very accessible stops being desired and loses its fascination. A pessimistic prognosis engenders a state of hopelessness. Antoine de St. Exupery writes about a pilot who had crashed: "...beginning with the second day, the greatest effort was made not to think...the situation was already very hopeless, to have the courage to go on, he had to reflect less on his situation" (St. Exupery, 1957, p. 104).

The mechanism of predicting the possibility of satisfying a need in its turn is subject to the effect of emotions and need since $(I_n - I_a) = E/N$. Negative emotion makes an unfavorable prediction even more pessimistic. A positive emotion promotes a reevaluation of actual achievements ("giddiness from success"). As far as need is concerned, its increase makes the subject overcome even a low probability of achieving a goal. On the other hand, a strong need is inclined to minimize an increasing probability: when need is strong, a gain seems somewhat less significant. We assume that a fluctuation of the "level of aspiration," described by Lewin and his followers, depends to a significant degree on the mutual influence of the mechanisms of need (motivations), emotions, and predictions of the possibility of achieving a goal.

In the most general form, we may say that with an identical magnitude of need, man will more willingly strive for a goal when the task is difficult, but its resolution possible. This rule ideally corresponds with the maximum of positive emotions according to the formula $E = N(I_a - I_n)$. Gantman (1971) studied the dependence of satisfaction through activity (positive emotional state) on the difficulty of a task and the "knowledge—aptitude" complex. It developed that satisfaction is linearly dependent on motivation (that is, on N). Like an excessively difficult task, an overly simple task with adequate knowledge and aptitude has a negative effect on satisfaction through activity. The exceptional complexity of the phenomenology of emotions consists in the fact that needs, emotions, and mechanisms of prediction, affecting one another, continue to depend on factors that cannot be changed by them. This is why the determination of the quantitative ratios, of which Lomov was speaking, is still clearly a problem that is beyond us. But as far as qualitative functional dependencies are concerned, the information theory of emotions has demonstrated its productivity and conformity to empirically observed facts many times. In the next chapter we will try to show how the information theory necessitated a radical review of a whole series of positions that were traditional for modern psychology.

In their joint paper, Lomov and Ivanitsky (1977) considered the case where two concepts, the psychological and the physiological, come to similar conclusions. They write: "As a result, a seemingly unique equation can be constructed that will make it possible to express the psychological concept through physiological characteristics (or conversely). To construct such a formula, it is necessary that both theories should be, as it were, focused on identical experimental facts" (Lomov and Ivanitsky, 1977, p. 953).

The formula of emotions is just such an "equation," constructed by us in 1964.

ON THE SO-CALLED "VALUE" OF EMOTIONS

The information theory considers need and emotion as being closely connected, but by no means as phenomena that can be reduced to one. This point of view is probably generally accepted today.

Leont'ev wrote: "Emotions are not motives." Emotions "do not carry information about external objects," but they "reflect relations between motives and the realization of activity that responds to these motives" (Leont'ev, 1971, pp. 16-18). The Dutch philosopher, Strasser, answering the question, "What is emotion?" emphasized: "The term 'emotion,' definitely is not a synonym for the terms 'fascination' or 'need.' Hunger, thirst, need to sleep, pain, and other deprivations may be a cause of emotions, but they are not in themselves emotions. Moreover, emotion is not motive" (Strasser, 1970, p. 301). Neuropharmacologists are also in agreement with philosophers and psychologists: "...neurochemical substances make it possible for us to separate the emotional state from the motivational state. These data provide no basis for identifying the neurophysiological mechanisms as being the basis for both processes" (Waldman et al., 1976, p. 39).

It would seem that this question might be considered as answered, but, according to Dodonov (1978), emotion is also present in the function of evaluation when a person strives directly for experience. In this case, emotions themselves are the motive that "draws" the subject to activity. We have spoken before about the capacity of emotions to affect the needs they generate and the prediction of the possibility of their satisfaction. Correspondingly, the role of emotions is very great *in the transformation* of human needs, in the organization of their personal hierarchy. Positive emotions will encourage and emphasize the needs they accompany. Negative emotions, arising in connection with chronic lack of satisfaction of definite needs, frequently lead to a replacement of those needs by motives of the first (positively colored) group. Thus, a person troubled by lack of satisfaction of his needs (and he may not even be conscious of some of those needs) turns to alcohol, a source of easily achieved satisfaction.

But the independent value of emotions and their capacity to motivate behavior in a given case appear to be an illusion. Striving for "experiencing positive emotions" cannot explain why a given person strives precisely toward one source of satisfaction, happiness, or good fortune and not another. Freud understood this when he called for an attempt to find the moving forces of human behavior "beyond the principle of satisfaction." When Dodonov classified "emotional tendencies of a personality" as a striving for experiencing altruistic, communicative, glorious, etc., emotions, he is only contrasting the subject's orientation toward his preferential satisfaction of certain *needs*.

Striving to experience negative emotions for their own sake ("I want to live! I want to suffer" — Lermontov) appears to be the same kind of illusion. This cry of the soul of the poet is evoked by his lyrical hero's feeling of an absence of significant and inspiring vital goals. Recognizing the sense, the purpose of his existence is a very important human need. "Without a firm understanding of why he is alive, man will not consent to live and will sooner destroy himself than remain on Earth, even if he has all the things he needs" (Dostoevsky). The presence of not only positive, but also negative experiences is evidence for the subject that he has desires, strivings, goals, that is, that he is alive with a life worthy of man. One must not take Lermontov's lyrical hero literally: he would not be satisfied with just any kind of life, and he would not want to endure just any kind of suffering. In exactly the same way seeking danger and risk is not controlled simply by the attraction of negative emotions, but by a more complex system of needs for social self-confirmation coupled with a personal need to overcome the obstacle that we call pain.

The idea of the intrinsic value of emotions and their capacity to motivate behavior distracts the investigator from the necessity of analyzing what is hiding behind emotions and, what is most important in the modern study of man, from analyzing the sphere of needs and motives.

We have considered a number of the most typical critical notes on the information theory of emotions. An encounter with the facts and contradictions of theoretical concepts is a most important event that prompts the development and improvement of a theory or giving it up if new facts refute the theory as a whole. Over the course of 15 years, my colleagues and I have been literally hunting such facts in scientific literature and in life. Unfortunately, we have not been able to find any substantial contradictions thus far, just as we have not been able to find theories that can respond more precisely and persuasively to the problem of the patterns, internal organization, and functional significance of emotions.

At present the information theory of emotions has no alternatives that can compete with it.

The Physiology of Emotions

Our purpose here is to review all the physiological changes accompanying the emotions of man and the higher animals that have been studied thus far. Such reviews are easy to find in the literature (for example, see Lindsley, 1951). We will consider only the changes in those physiological functions, the dynamics and mechanisms of which have become more clear due to the information theory.

THE EFFECT OF EMOTIONS ON THE HEART

Patterns of cardiovascular shifts that accompany emotionally colored reactions of man and animals can be understood only if we consider these shifts as involuntary components of integral behavioral acts. Recording of arterial pressure during stimulation of various structures of the hypothalamus in rabbits showed that each behavioral reaction of the animal corresponds to its own type of pressure change in the carotid artery. Orienting—exploratory behavior is accompanied by a slow increase in pressure with a longer latent period after the beginning of stimulation. A short latent period followed by a rise in arterial pressure is characteristic for aggressive—defensive reactions, and a drop in pressure accompanies a state of general depression of the experimental animal, behavior of the passive—defensive type (Kozlovskaya and Waldman, 1972).

Observations of this kind served as a basis for considering changes in the function of the cardiovascular system affected by emotions as a means of providing energy for prospective or imminent motor activity. But reducing the adaptive significance of emotions to an involuntary-energy "servicing" of the working muscles does not seem possible. Definite changes in the autonomic functions were also observed in types of motor activity that did not involve the nervous apparatus of the emotions. Moreover, involuntary shifts during emotions are excessive, as a rule, and clearly exceed the real energy expenditures. A future important competition elicits stronger involuntary and hormonal shifts in athletes than training exercises with physical stress exceeding the effort that the athletes expend during competition. In a state of immediate readiness for physical stress, the immediate volume of blood increases by 66% in water polo players and by 22% in marksmen in comparison with the normal average. A competitive situation increases the immediate volume by 85 and 74%, respectively (Dashkevich, 1970).

Greater involuntary shifts can be recorded when there is emotional stress that is not at all connected with physical effort. In simultaneous translators, the frequency of heart contractions sometimes reaches 160 beats/min while a significant physical stress (60 hops in 30 sec) results in a pulse rate increase in the same persons that does not exceed 145 beats/min (Karimova, 1968). A sensitive indicator of emotional stress is the amplitude of the T spur on the electrocardiogram; changes here depend less on physical stress than on pulse frequency (Frolov and Sviridov, 1974; Rusalov, 1979). Punch and King believe that changes predominantly reflect the sympathetic influence on the heart while frequency of heartbeat is regulated by the activity of two sections of the autonomic nervous system (Punch and King, 1976).

Changes in the value β obtained with an approximation of the initial segment of the T spur of the bell-shaped curve are presented in Fig. 13 (see Frolov and Sviridov, 1974) before the beginning of training on a centrifuge immediately before the experiment and with acceleration equal to 3 and 5 units. For comparison, the same figure includes changes in the R–R interval, also in percents of the initial value. During the prestart state, the β index rises markedly and later, at the 3- and 5-unit overloads, it changes little. Pulse frequency increases monotonically over the course of the whole experiment. These data indicate that the amplitude of the T spur may serve as an indicator of emotional stress even under conditions of overwork (within certain limits, to be sure), while the frequency of heart-

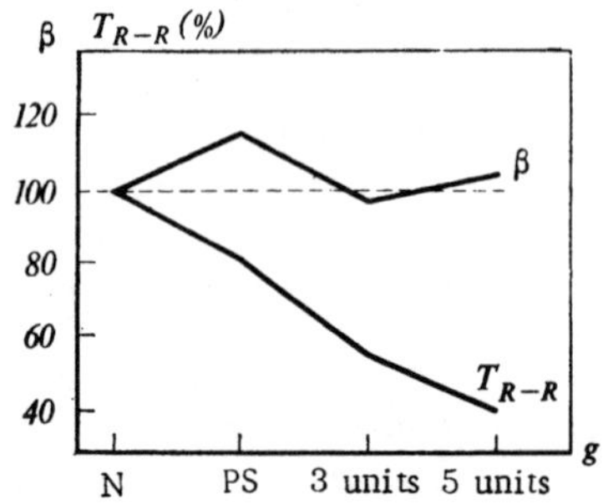

Fig. 13. Changes in the β indicator and the R—R of the EKG in the normal state (N), in the prestart state (PS), and with acceleration of 3 and 5 units (after Frolov and Sviridov).

beat no longer is an indicator of only the degree of emotional stress of the subject.

The phenomenology of involuntary shifts during emotional reactions of higher animals and man is least of all like the massive, generalized energy supply during battle or flight as was believed by investigators in the past, at the beginning of this century. In many cases, we have found that involuntary shifts were dependent on unusually precise intellectual operations done in the brain. For example, the degree of emotional stress in a person who is faced with a dangerous task depends on his subjective evaluation of the degree of danger through a comparison of the total number of such operations that he knows about with the number of operations that have had an unfavorable outcome (Yankelevich, 1965). Involuntary shifts are minimal in first parachute jumps and in jumps by masters of the sport, but the reasons for these two phenomena are different. Making a first jump, a person has not yet experienced the real degree of danger and the strength of the feelings that develop. In the second case, the experience of the master guarantees him a successful jump. In agreement with the information theory of emotions, in both the first and second case there is a deficit of pragmatic information; in the novice it is connected with the absence of prediction, and, in the master, with adequate information necessary for effective action.

Even in normal horizontal flight in a fighter plane with no clear signs of physical stress, the frequency of heart contractions of the pilot, who is responsible for carrying out the task, increased to 90 beats/min, in breaking the sound barrier to 100, and during refueling of the plane to approximately 115 beats/min when the normal is 65-70. Objective symptoms of emotional stress become even more obvious in the presence of any complications in flight. During an incident in the lunar module of the American spaceship Apollo 10, Astronaut Cernan's pulse rate doubled and reached 129 beats/min. Similar changes were also recorded in the electrocardiograms of members of Apollo 13 when there were problems in the fuel supply system. A feeling of responsibility and striving to achieve socially significant goals are so strongly developed in man that they lead to emotional stress even in situations where nothing directly threatens the life and welfare of the operator. During the time the lunar vehicle was approaching its landing and at the beginning of its travel on the moon, pulse frequency of the members of the team on Earth reached 130-135 beats/min, and breath holding, 15-20 sec.

Numerous investigations have shown that the orienting—exploratory reaction, which is based on a tendency to prolong contact with the external stimulus and to determine more precisely its physical characteristics and significance for the subject (Pavlov's "what is it?" reflex), is accompanied by decrease in heartbeat. The orienting—defensive reaction with its characteristic readiness for preventive breaking off of contact with a new stimulus (Pavlov's "biological caution reflex"), on the other hand, increases the heartbeat rhythm (Lacey et al., 1963). Exploratory or defensive types of reactions, with the autonomic components characteristic for them, depend not only on the degree of novelty and other parameters of the stimulus, but also on individual features of the subject. For example, a timid subject responds to a neutral signal among emotionally colored signals as he does to emotionally negative signals, with an increase instead of a decrease in heart rate (Hare, 1973).

In the first chapter, we cited our own data and data from the literature that indicate that changes in frequency of heartbeat, without regard as to whether we are speaking of an increase or decrease in the rate, depend on how strong the need (motivation) is and on the decrease (increase) of probability of satisfying this need at a given moment. Changes in heart activity are the most promising objective indicator of the degree of emotional stress in man in comparison with all the other autonomic functions under two conditions: 1) if we are dealing with an adequately expressed emotional stress; and 2) if this state is not accompanied by physical stress. But, in the latter case, the involuntary shifts that occur with emotions clearly exceed the energy expended by the organism, demonstrating a special example of the compensatory function of emotions. Facts indicate that emotional stress develops in a situation of pragmatic indeterminacy when the character, scope, and duration of future actions is not clear. In such a situation, changes in the autonomic functions of the organism cannot be precisely adapted to motor activity. Evidently the process of protracted evolution has demonstrated the expediency of a preventive surplus mobilization of involuntary energy resources in those cases where the prediction of the scope of future motor exertions is difficult. This expediency was fixed by natural selection.

To what extent does heart activity reflect not only the degree (dimensions) of emotional excitation, but also its "sign," positive or negative coloring?

Bovard (1961, 1962) believed that positive emotions are connected with activation of structures of the frontal and lateral hypothalamus, accompanied at the periphery by shifts of a parasympathetic type. Negative emotions, on the other hand, are connected with the posterior and medial sections of the hypothalamus and are manifested in sympathetic effects. These two systems are in reciprocal relation and the balance between them is fixed genetically and is regulated by nuclei of the amygdala complex.

However, Gellhorn (1948) had already demonstrated that, as a rule, the development of emotion leads to a simultaneous excitation of both the sympathetic and parasympathetic sections of the autonomic nervous system, which are frequently synergists. One and the same emotional reaction frequently appears as such a "sympathetic" shift as increase in heart rate and such a "parasympathetic" shift as increase in electrical resistance of the skin. The interaction of the sympathetic and parasympathetic effects is complicated by the dynamic coexistence of two tendencies, one of which is directed toward the involuntary-energy supply of the given emotional reaction, and the other toward preserving and reestablishing homeostatic constants (Gellhorn, 1960). In the language of modern control theory, we can say that, in the presence of emotions, shifts in the involuntary functions represent a combined system of control where the self-organizing part based on the principle of negative feedback provides a defense—compensatory correction to the phylo- and ontogenetically determined program (Khayutin, 1967).

The dynamics of human sexual arousal may serve as a clear example of the complex interaction of the sympathetic and parasympathetic effects in an emotionally positive state. Although there are sympathetic shifts in the initial stage of arousal (increase in blood pressure), at this stage activation of the parasympathetic system is dominant. After a time, the sympathetic effects of tachycardia and hyperventilation become dominant. The "sympathetic peak" alternates with a phase of parasympathetic hypercompensation. Signs of simultaneous increase in the activity of two sections of the autonomic nervous system are encountered much more frequently than reciprocal relations, and instances of relative dominance of one of the sections by no means indicate a complete dominance. Although the dynamics of involuntary shifts depend to a certain degree on motor activity, these shifts cannot be reduced to an autonomic "accompaniment" of the motor system. A high degree of emotional excitation of one of the sexual partners may elicit a greater shift in the autonomic system (acceleration of the heartbeat to 170 beats/min) in the other partner without any movement. Thus, the dynamics of involuntary shifts in sexual arousal have a complex internal structure that is not directly correlated with motor activity of the subject.

In man, both joy and sorrow are accompanied by activation of the sympathetic section; in sorrow, shifts in the cardiovascular system are more characteristic, and for joy, changes in respiration. Symptoms of excitation of the sympathetic section in the form of increased pulse rate, increased blood pressure and temperature, and decreased salivation and electrical resistance of the skin are characteristic for many negative emotions. In addition, there are signs of activation of the parasympathetic section in the structure of these reactions. The degree of participation of the sympathetic and parasympathetic effects depends on the character of the given negative emotion. Actively defensive—aggressive reactions of monkeys are accompanied by an increase in heartbeat; passive reactions, by bradycardia (Dzheliev et al., 1963). The effect of emotions on the human heart is similar: agressive reactions, like reactions that have a positive coloring, are realized against a background of increased pulse rate, while passive and depressive reactions have a tendency to slow the heartbeat (Theorell et al., 1974).

Thus, the analysis of data in the literature brings us to the conclusion that the sympathetic and parasympathetic sections of the autonomic nervous system are involved in the realization of both negative and positive emotional states. Any emotional reaction is characterized by its own type of interaction of the sympathetic and parasympathetic influences. In each specific case of emotional stress, that particular combination of sympathetic and parasympathetic effects results which was most expedient and became fixed by natural selection. The so-called "self-regulation" of the cardiovascular system has only the secondary significance of a factor that limits excessive deviations in the process of emotional mobilization of the involuntary-energy resources of the organism.

In Fig. 14 we present a diagram of the dynamics of activation of the sympathetic and parasympathetic sections of the autonomic nervous system as positive and negative emotional stresses develop. The diagram is based on a classification of basal emotional states that will be discussed in the last chapter. It is important to emphasize that, in the process of realizing emotions, both synergism and reciprocal sympathetic and parasympathetic effects on the autonomic functions of the organism can be observed. We admit that this is a rough diagram and requires further refinement.

ELECTROENCEPHALOGRAM CHANGES DURING HUMAN EMOTIONAL REACTIONS

The degree of emotional stress is frequently considered as a phenomenon identical with the levels of waking. According to this concept, emotional arousal occupies an extreme position in the continuum of waking, diametrically opposed to deep slow-wave sleep and coma. A similar view of the nature of emotional arousal, reinforced by the discovery of the function of the reticular formation of the brain, was most fully embodied in the "activation theory of emotions"

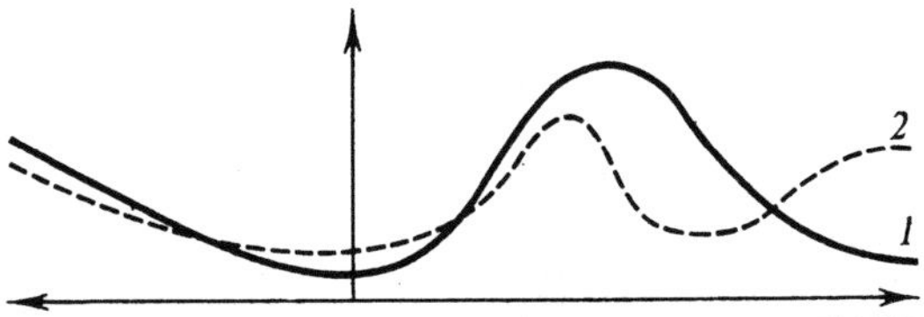

Action				
Contact interaction	Satisfaction	Comfort	Dissatisfaction	Aversion
Display	Joy	Calm	Anxiety	Grief
Defense	Courage	Weakness	Active fear, panic	Passive fear, stupefaction
Battle	Enthusiasm	Imperturbability	Rage	Frenzy, prostration

Fig. 14. Diagram of interaction of the sympathetic (1) and parasympathetic (2) sections of the autonomic nervous system according to the increase in emotional stress.

of Lindsley (1951). But there is factual evidence of multiple examples of a clear dissociation between the degree of emotional excitation, if we consider the shifts in involuntary functions, and the level of waking diagnosed according to the total electrical activity of the brain. In the experiments of Frost and his colleagues, expectation of painful stimulations led to shifts in the frequency of heartbeat and electrical resistance of the skin without reliable changes in the alpha rhythm on the electroencephalogram (Frost et al., 1978). In a state of fear, with the perception of emotionally colored words when taking an exam, not a decrease, but an increase in alpha rhythm, an increase in its amplitude and an increase in the alpha index, were observed.

The question of the correlation of the involuntary and EEG signs of emotional excitation was subjected to systematic analysis in the experiments of Rusalova (1979). From Fig. 15 it is clearly apparent that emotional stress, judged according to increased heart rate, may be accompanied in one and the same subject by both a drop and exaltation of the alpha rhythm. How do these two situations differ? In the first case, the subject expected a real painful stimulation of the skin of the forearm. In the second case, he was given instructions to imagine a painful stimulation at the end of a decreasing count on a tape recorder.

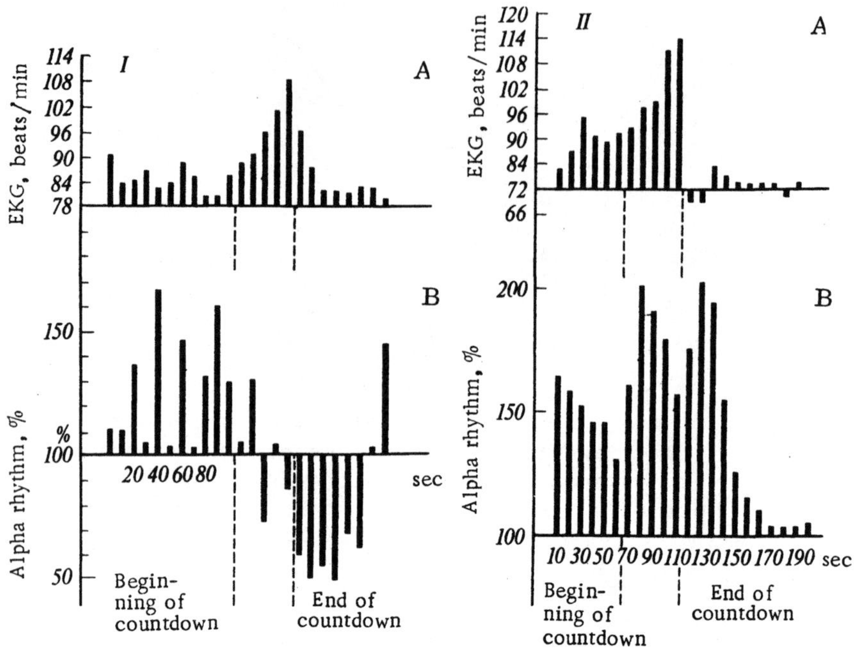

Fig. 15. Dynamics of changes in amplitude (B) of alpha rhythm (as indicated by the integrator pen) and frequencies of heart rhythm (A) after instructions, during the countdown, and after the countdown. Alpha rhythm (11 Hz) is expressed in percent of the normal rhythm assumed to be 100; I) actual expectation of pain; II) imagined expectation of pain (after Rusalova).

We have said before that an emotional reaction may be the result of both the arrival of information from the external environment and the recovery of traces of earlier impressions from the memory. Many experiments set up by Rusalova (Valueva), as well as data found in the literature, are deficient in that depression of the alpha rhythm is characteristic for situations in which the attention of the subject is turned toward the external environment. If the subject concentrates mainly on traces preserved in the memory, even a high degree of emotional excitation will not result in depression of the alpha rhythm, but will frequently be accompanied by its elevation. Such a conclusion agrees well with the concept of the alpha rhythm as an electrophysiological correlate of the mechanism that quantifies the flow of afferentation entering the brain (Walter, 1954). Nunu and Osselton (1974) demonstrated that brief visual stimuli are not perceived if they are presented during certain phases of the alpha rhythm. They believe that the alpha rhythm is correlated with the activity of the "nervous catch" that periodically interrupts the flow of information to the brain.

The question may arise as to why, when there is a strong flow of afferentation and a great need for the "catch" to work, the alpha rhythm disappears or is depressed. Here we must not identify the activity of the quantifying mechanism with the expression of its electrophysiological correlate. An alpha rhythm that records well when the eyes are closed and everything is peaceful and quiet is the "idling" of the quantifying mechanism which, incidentally, exists also in persons who have no expressed alpha rhythm in the EEG. What has been said is also true for the dynamics of the theta rhythm, which we will now consider.

One of the EEG symptoms of emotional excitation is an increase in the theta rhythm with an oscillation frequency of 4-7 Hz. With analyzers of the EEG frequency spectrum, theta rhythm was recorded in healthy persons in the presence of negative (Suvorova, 1975) and positive (Walter, 1953; Valueva, 1967) emotions. In children engaged in activity with positive emotional coloring, the theta rhythm was expressed better in the right hemisphere of the cerebrum, particularly its frontal areas (Denisova, 1978). For an understanding of the functional significance of the theta rhythm, the data of Brown (1971) are of interest; he demonstrated the subject's own alpha, beta, and theta rhythms in the form of different colors on a screen. The subjects were asked with which subjective state the colors corresponded. It developed that, for the theta rhythm, thinking about plans, indeterminacy of a mentally analyzed situation, change in the subject of thought, resolving technical and everyday problems, and daydreams were characteristic. An increase in percent content of theta rhythm in the EEG spectrum agrees with a decrease in the human subject's vigilance with respect to external signals (Beatty et al., 1974).

In order to evaluate the functional significance of EEG changes in the presence of emotions, we will consider a hypo-

TABLE 3. Change in the Electroencephalogram Predicted by Volterra's Theorem

Change in number of elements		Change in oscillation		Physiological state
Excitation	Inhibition	Amplitude	Frequency	
No change	Decrease	Did not change	Increased	
Decrease	No change	Did not change	Slowed	
Decrease	Decrease	Increased	Did not change	
Increase	Increase	Decrease	Did not change	
Significant increase	Increase	Decrease	Increased	Depressed alpha rhythm
Increase	Significant increase	Decrease	Slowed	Slow sleep
Significant decrease	Decrease	Increased	Slowed	Exaltation of alpha and theta rhythms
Decrease	Significant decrease	Increased	Increased	Rapid, high-amplitude activity

thetical mechanism of rhythmic fluctuations of the biopotentials of the brain. According to the hypothesis of Andersen and Eccles, inhibiting neurons play an important role in the formation of these fluctuations (Anderson and Eccles, 1962). This provides a basis for applying the theorem of Volterra (1976), concerning the regular changes of amplitude and frequency of oscillation in a system comprised of two types of functionally antagonistic elements, to the interaction of excited neural microstructures and the neural microstructures that inhibit their activity (Table 3).

To what extent does the picture presented in the table agree with the physiological facts? Least open to argument, perhaps, is the mechanism of classical depression of the alpha rhythm that is determined by an increase in the number of excited and inhibited elements with a predominance of the increase of the former. Quite unexpected may be the fact that the pattern characteristic for slow sleep is also promoted by an increase of the excited and inhibiting elements, but the number of the latter increases to a greater degree than the number of the former. Moreover, recent data provide no basis for rejecting this conclusion. An increase in the activity of the cortical neurons and the reticular formation during sleep leads us to consider sleep more as the result of a reorganization of the interaction of neural elements than as a state of "diffuse inhibition" of the cortex and subcortex in the old understanding of this term. Some authors ascribe important significance in the genesis of slow sleep to an increase in the activity of the mechanisms of reflexive inhibition.

High-amplitude slow oscillations indicate a decrease in the number of both excited and inhibiting elements with a relative predominance of the latter. A decrease in the number of excited elements, but with a predominant decrease in inhibiting microstructures, also occurs during rapid, high-amplitude activity. Applying the theorem of Volterra to the rhythmic bioelectrical activity of brain structures not only gives us the prerequisites for mathematical simulation of the EEG, but also makes us look anew at the internal neuronal mechanism of a number of typical changes in the electroencephalogram.

If in the genesis of the alpha rhythm corticothalamic relations are of decisive significance, then the theta rhythm is connected with corticolimbic interactions. The appearance of the theta rhythm in the EEG of a person in a comatose state can be considered a result of the activity of the phylogenetically old limbic structures against a background of deactivation of less stable neocortical formations (Grindel' et al., 1974).

Thus, the alpha rhythm is a "sensory" rhythm connected with the transmission of information from the external world. It is not by chance that it is expressed most clearly in the visual sections of the neocortex since, in man, vision is the basic channel for obtaining information about the external environment. The "emotional" theta rhythm, "limbic" in origin, evidently is related in some way to the "evaluative" activity of the brain mechanisms. The temporal parameters of the alpha and theta rhythms agree well with such a hypothesis. According to data of the psychophysics of perception, the first 100 msec are needed to reflect the physical characteristics of the stimulus in the structures of the brain and to form its "neural model." In the next 100 msec, the brain compares the model with engrams extracted from the memory. The result of the computation is available in 200-300 msec, and preparation for reaction begins if the stimulus present requires a response (Lomov and Ivanitsky, 1977). The duration of the first stage corresponds

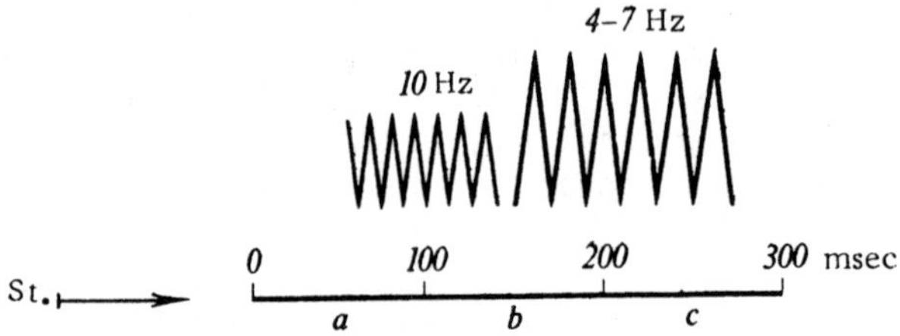

Fig. 16. Diagram of comparison of the temporal characteristics of EEG alpha and theta rhythms with the process of perceiving an external stimulus (St). a) Formation of the neural model; b) comparison of the model with engrams extracted from memory; c) beginning of formation of a reaction depending on the results of the comparison.

with the temporal characteristics of the alpha rhythm. The duration of the processes of computation and "reaching a decision" (150–250 msec) are identical to the frequency of the theta rhythm (Fig. 16).

We assume that strengthening of the theta rhythm in the presence of emotion cannot be reduced to a simple activation of the neocortex by the limbic structures. The situation of pragmatic indeterminacy characteristic for emotions requires a stronger mobilization of the engrams preserved in the memory and their comparison with signals coming from the external environment. It is quite probable that the theta rhythm is the electrophysiological correlate of the mechanism that *quantifies the flow of engrams extracted from memory* in the same way that the alpha rhythm is connected with the mechanism that quantifies the flow of information from the external environment. Such a hypothesis would explain very well why the theta rhythm is so characteristic of the electrical activity of the hippocampus in many species of animals; we will discuss this in the following chapter.

What was said above does not mean that each time we record the theta rhythm we observe the process of engram extraction: in a woman about to give birth, in a comatose patient, etc. It refers specifically to cases of pathology. When manual controls are damaged in a car and two wheels are missing, a motor that continues to work no longer seems to be the source of movement through space. On the other hand, the arrival of external information and actualization, the extraction of information that the subject has are *two fundamental processes* of functioning of any neural network. This is why we are correct in thinking that the presence of the alpha and theta rhythms in many brain formations indicates not only the similar level of their excitation, but also the similarity of the working processes that are taking place in them. The functional significance of spatial synchronization according to theta rhythm was established in the laboratory of M. N. Livanov (1972) and is evidence of this.

Information theory, disclosing the complex internal structure of emotional states and the presence in this structure of need—motivation and information components, makes it possible to analyze more adequately the changes in the EEG in the presence of emotions without identifying these changes with a scale of fluctuations in the levels of waking. At first these fluctuations were explained by the activating effect of only one reticular formation of the brain stem, then gradually the number of activating (as well as deactivating) systems began to grow. The more complex construction and interaction of the activating systems cannot be compared with the "integral" extended concept of emotion that can still be found on the pages of textbooks and handbooks.

EFFECT OF EMOTIONS ON ACTIVITY (USING THE PROCESSES OF PERCEPTION AS AN EXAMPLE)

In its principal characteristics, this effect is subject to the well-known Yerkes—Dodson law that postulates an optimal level of stress for each specific type of work (Yerkes and Dodson, 1908). A decrease in emotional tonus as a result of the subject's low need or completeness of information (monotonous, stereotyped activities) results in drowsiness, loss of vigilance, omission of significant signals, and slowed reactions. On the other hand, an excessively high level of emotional stress disorganizes activity, produces a tendency toward premature reactions, reactions to extraneous signals that are not significant (false alarms), and to primitive actions such as trial-and-error methods. A detailed analysis of the interaction of the sensory and extrasensory factor in perception, like analysis of the problem of reflection of these factors in the structure of elicited electrical potentials of the brain, is available to the

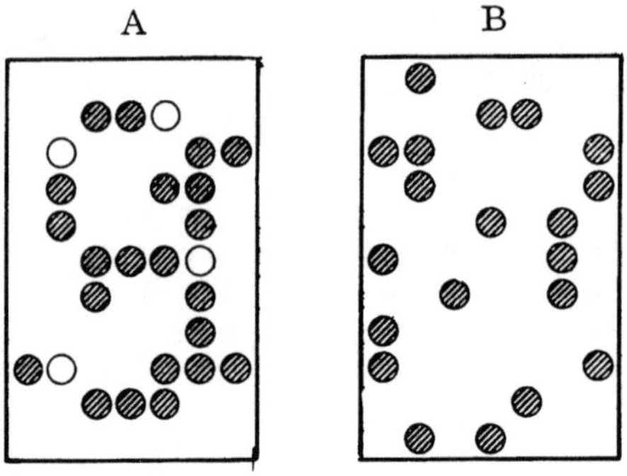

Fig. 17. Samples of visual images presented for recognition: A) the number "9"; B) noise (after Frolov et al.).

reader in a book by Ivanitsky (1976). The patterns of change in human efficiency of perception with an increase in emotional stress, and the kinds of errors made will be illustrated by the results of the experiments of Frolov, Evtushenko, and Sviridova.

Five male adults participated in the experiments; they were preliminarily trained to recognize visual images against a background of noise. The objective index of the degree of emotional stress was the standardized sum of electrocardiographic parameters, the average duration of the R-R interval, and the amplitude of the T spur. The selected index is notable because of its reliability and convenience of recording under natural conditions of human activity. As the stress factor precipitated (parachute jump), the standardized sum of EKG parameters changed unidirectionally in most cases.

The perceptive activity of the operators was studied at several stages as the parachute jump drew near: immediately after boarding the plane (Fig. 18A, I); at takeoff (II); during ascent (III); during jumps of other parachutists (IV); and directly before the jump (V).

The tachistoscopically presented visual images were the Arabic numerals 0, 2, 3, ... to 9. Each symbol consisted of 20 dark elements in a framework containing 7 × 11 cells. Noise was the masking of the symbols with random in-

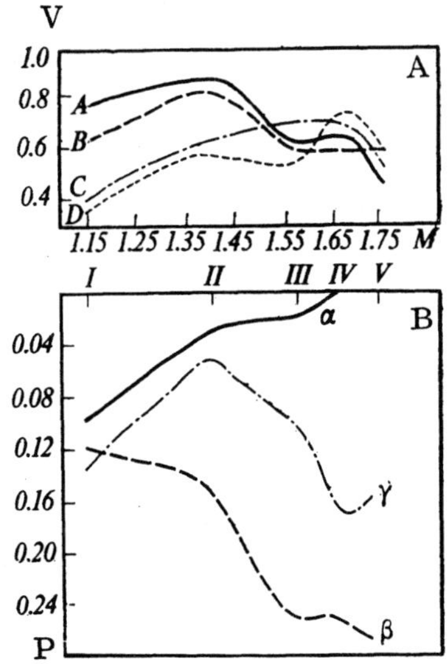

Fig. 18. Efficiency of activity (A) according to recognition of visual images by subjects A, B, C, and D at stages I-V of preparation for a parachute jump and change in probability of errors (B) of different types. Explanation in the text.

terference: light spaces in the contour of the symbol and additional dark elements in the field. The noise level varied from 10 to 30%. At each stage of the experiment, the subject was presented with ten frames of symbols; the number of frames containing the masked digits was equal to the number containing uniform "pure" noise. Examples of the visual images are presented in Fig. 17: A is the digit masked by noise (light circles in the contour are the result of interference); B is pure noise. Distribution of the frames within the series was random. The exposure time for each frame was 2 sec. Recording of the electrocardiogram and results of the subject's activity was done with an airborne tape recorder.

Data from processing this material are presented in Fig. 18A and B. In Fig. 18A, the abscissa is the averaged standardized sum of EKG parameters (M) at various stages of the experiment (I-V). Under normal conditions (before boarding the plane), M = 1. Along the ordinate are the values representing the efficiency of recognizing visual images (V),

$$V = \frac{0.1}{N} \sum_{j=1}^{N} \sum_{i=1}^{K} \theta_{ij},$$

where θ = 1 in the case of correct identification, 0 in the case of incorrect identification; K is the number of cases where θ = 1 in a series; N is the number of the series at a given stage of the experiment. Each of the four curves in Fig. 18A represents the work of one subject under emotionally complicated circumstances and demonstrates the presence of clear maximums in the curve of efficiency. The location and expression of the maximum under identical conditions of the experiment characterize the individual differences of operators A, B, C, and D, the degree of emotional stability of each of them, and the individual interrelation of motivations connected with the activity of perceiving visual images and the imminent parachute jump.

Probability of errors (P) of various types during the work of operator B is presented in Fig. 18B. It is apparent that an increase in degree of emotional stress is accompanied by a decrease in errors such as "omission of a signal" in which the subject identifies the digit as noise (α), and by an increase in the number of "false alarms" when the subject identifies noise as a digit (β). The number of erroneous identifications of a symbol (the subject identifies the digit presented as a different digit) decreased initially, then increased (ν).

Using mathematical time series apparatus makes it possible to predict the dynamics of errors of the first and second type according to the subsequent increase in emotional stress (Frolov and Luzhbin, Fig. 19). As a result of these computations, we developed curves of prediction whose average deviation from actual values did not exceed 10%.

These experimental observations indicate that even when emotional stress is connected with motivation extraneous to the work being done by a person, this stress does not have an unambiguous disorganizing effect. A moderate degree of

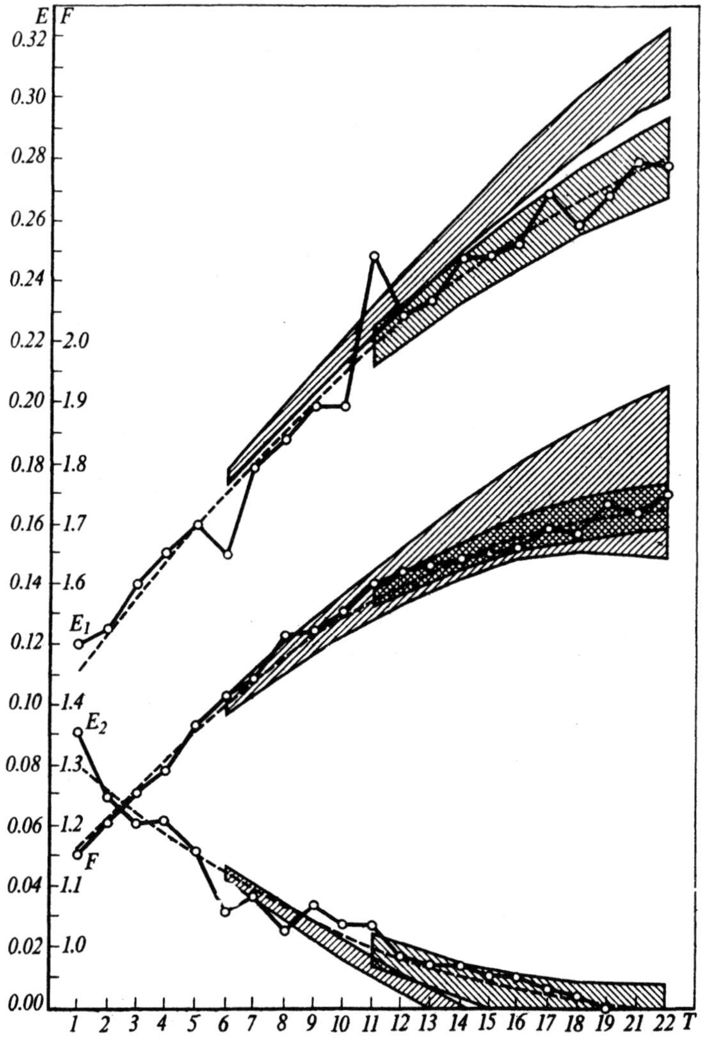

Fig. 19. Predicting probability of error of the false alarm type (E_1) and omission of a signal (E_2) according to the increase in emotional stress (F) indicated by changes in the EKG (after Frolov and Luzhbin). Explanations in the text.

emotional stress can increase the efficiency of activity and decrease the number of errors made by the subject. The beneficial effect of emotions is evident, particularly when the emotions are connected with the specific activity itself and are based on the need that motivates the activity of the subject. A special series of experiments showed that introducing a combined reinforcement of success and failure in the form of reward and punishment could increase the efficiency of recognizing masked visual images with respect to both rate and correctness of identification by 15%.

Of theoretical and practical interest is the patterned character of errors made by the operator as the degree of emotional stress increased. With a decrease in precise distinguishing of similar signals and an increase in the number of false alarms (the subject identifying noise as an objectively nonexistent digit), there is a decrease in the number of erroneous omissions of a signal. Such changes in perceptive activity can scarcely be explained just by a fluctuation in the level of vigilance. We believe that the basis for the regular change in perceptive activity is a transition from precisely specialized conditioned reflex behavior to reacting according to a type of Ukhtomsky's dominant where many events in the external environment become significant for the subject. The transition to a broadly generalized dominant reaction, characteristic of the emotionally excited brain, must be taken into account in the evaluation of the dependability of an operator. An emotionally excited operator maintains a high level of vigilance (capacity to react to a significant signal) for a comparatively long time, but he begins to perceive signals that are not objectively significant as being significant.

From the position of the information theory of emotions, exceptionally important in the study of the effect of emotions on activity is the question as to whether the emotion is related to the need that motivates the given activity or whether it developed as the result of another, competing need. Many authors considering the problem "emotion and activity" simply ignore this difference. Others prefer to speak of the emotional stress of the operator only in the presence of secondary motivation (fear for one's life, concern for prestige, etc.). When the need to carry out a task is dominant, these authors believe that the stress is no longer emotional, but "operational" (Naenko, 1976).

The question of the dependence of results of activity on the genesis of the emotional state of the subject has been specially studied by Rusalova (1979). In experiments with 24 subjects, the absolute auditory threshold was determined: the subjects had to say "I hear" every time they heard a sound. In the second series ("neutral background"), a flash of light marked sound signals that the subject missed. In the third series of experiments, determination of thresholds was done with a painful punishment for missed signals (negative emotion depending on failure in the activity studied). Then the subjects were divided into two groups of 12 persons each. Before the beginning of the experiment, Group A heard, as if by chance, a conversation of two experimenters who gave a favorable evaluation of qualities of the subjects that were not relevant to the given activity (positive emotional background). The subjects in group B heard negative remarks about themselves that were also irrelevant to the task (negative emotions based on a secondary need). At the end of the experiments, the thresholds were again determined in a situation with a neutral background.

The dynamics of changes of the average value of auditory threshold in all of the subjects are presented in Fig. 20. Introducing a light flash following a missed signal decreased the thresholds, but painful punishment increased auditory sensitivity even more. Emotions not related to the activity being carried out had a strong and diametrically

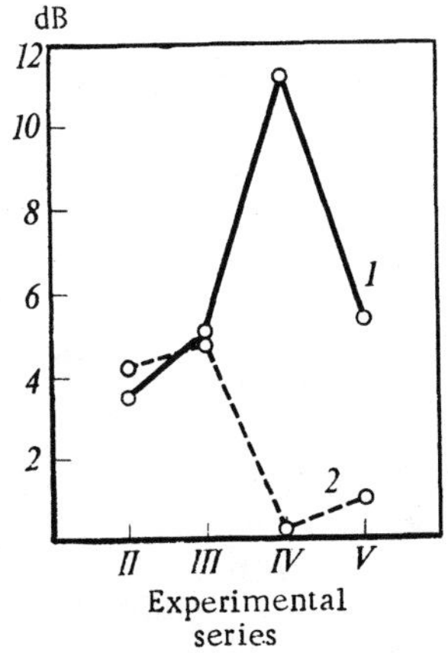

Fig. 20. Differences in threshold intensities of sound computed according to relation to the background (in decibels of damping by an attenuator). 1) Group A; 2) group B (after Rusalova).

opposed effect: a negative emotional state was accompanied by a rise in the thresholds, a positive state by a significant drop. The results of Rusalova's experiments lead to the conclusion that the effect of emotions on activity depends on the character of the need served by the given emotional state. Positive emotions are relatively nonspecific: we all know from personal experience that a good attitude has a beneficial effect on work efficiency even when it is caused by factors that are not related to the work (good news, fine weather, etc.). As far as negative emotions are concerned, their motivational source is very important with respect to the kind of effect they have on activity. As experiments and direct observation have shown, the effects may be exactly opposite.

The quality of the needs that are responsible for one emotional state or another acquire a particularly important significance when we move on to emotions that arise on the basis of complex socially determined motivation.

Valueva (1969) and Gryzlova (1976) recorded the changes in auditory thresholds and frequency of heartbeat in two series of experiments; in one case, omission of a sound signal was followed by an electric shock to the wrist of the subject and, in the second case, by a shock to his partner. Judging by the degree of emotional stress according to the change in frequency of heart contractions, of the 20 subjects in the experiment, 14 (70%) disclosed a high degree of anxiety in the situation where they themselves were threatened with punishment. Three subjects registered an equal degree of anxiety for their partners and for themselves and, in the other three, the frequency of heart contractions was maximum when the partner was punished. These differences are not great, but they are statistically significant (P = 0.01).

In a study of the auditory thresholds of 27 other persons, the thresholds dropped in a situation where the partner was punished, but in 9 subjects (30%), they were the same as when the painful shock was administered to the subject himself.

But even these comparatively elementary situations involved the exceptional complexity of dependence of the final physiological shifts (changes in thresholds of perception of sound signals, frequency of heartbeats) on the whole aggregate of personal factors that determine the subject's reaction. Thus, a comparison of the results of measuring thresholds with an analysis of the subjects on the basis of Cattell's questionnaire showed that the subjects that were most sensitive to the situation where their partner was punished for errors they committed were: a) well in control of their behavior; b) adequately oriented in the environment; c) concerned about their results; d) rigorous in carrying out their social responsibilities; and, e) showed a high degree of anxiety and a predisposition to socially determined frustration (Gryzlova, 1976).

We believe that in the widely recognized experiments of Milgram (1974), two-thirds of the students continued to increase the electric shock to partners, regardless of the (imitation) cries of pain that these partners produced, not because of any personal inclination toward cruelty, but because of the nature of the instructions (voluntariness of the experiments, importance of the experiments for science, etc.). When the instructions were changed, resulting in a change in motivational attitudes, the results were substantially different.

The dependence of thresholds of perception on the nature of the motives is also disclosed in the experiments on recognition of neutral or emotionally charged words. Tachistoscopic presentation of these words showed that the duration of exposure of emotionally charged words necessary for reading them may be either greater or lesser than that required for neutral verbal signals (Bruner and Postman, 1947). Thus far it is not entirely clear as to whether we are dealing with subconscious reactions to emotionally significant words or whether the subjects are reluctant to respond when an "unpleasant" word appears on the screen (Whittaker et al., 1952). The fact that the need to respond verbally is not indifferent to the subject is indicated by the experiments of Begleiter and Platz (1969). Retarded components of potentials elicited by "forbidden" words were expressed more strongly than those elicited by neutral words. These shifts were reinforced if the subject had to repeat the words, including the emotionally charged words, after they were presented.

In the systematic studies of Kostandov (1977), the thresholds of recognition of emotionally significant words in persons who had committed illegal acts were higher two-thirds of the time and lower one-third of the time than thresholds of recognition of emotionally neutral verbal stimuli. We believe that the deciding significance for the shift in the threshold in one direction or the other has a motivational character that generates emotional stress. Dominance of motives of self-preservation, fear of exposure, and punishment included mechanisms of "psychological protection" and an increase in thresholds of perception characteristic for these mechanisms. If motives of anxiety for other people or feelings of repentance and guilt were dominant in the subject, these were accompanied by an increase in sensitivity and decrease in the thresholds. A rare coexistence of motives of the first and second type makes it entirely possible for thresholds to fluctuate in both directions in the same subject in the course of a single experiment.

SPEECH AND MIMICRY

Excitation of brain structures responsible for the realization of emotion has a selective and precisely specialized effect on the muscular apparatus of interspecific (in man, interpersonal) communication: on the mechanisms of speech and vocal and mimetic reactions. In emotional expression, the compensatory and reinforcing function of emotions is clearly apparent on the populational level. The compensatory role of emotional expression is apparent in the everyday fact that as human speech becomes more emotional, the less effectively the logically understandable content of what was said acts on a partner. We do not feel the need of resorting to emotionally charged speech if the listeners share the conviction of the logical arguments we present. The fewer logical arguments we have, the less time for argumentation and, finally, the less confidence that the content of an important communication will be fully appreciated by the listeners and will elicit the reaction we need, the more emotional will our speech become. In other words, the emotional coloring of speech depends to the same degree on the degree of need and evaluation of the possibility of its being satisfied as any other objective manifestations of degrees of emotional stress. In a study of the speech of pilots in crash situations, it was established that the dominant frequency of the voice of the pilot who could avert the crash by his actions increased by only 12%. In passive observers of the approaching crash, it increased by 45% (Sulc, 1975).

Emotional stress is manifested in a whole series of speech characteristics, including: 1) average length of speech segment delivered without a pause; 2) speed of articulation and its fluctuation; 3) latent period of speech reactions; 4) catches in speech, manifestation of indecisiveness; 5) duration of interval between increases in frequency of the basic tone; 6) variety of words used; 7) number of gestures; 8) incomplete sentences; 9) errors, slips of the tongue, etc. (Nosenko, 1978). No less characteristic for emotions are changes in voice and intonation patterns of speech. With respect to evolution, changes in voice represent the oldest mechanism for expressing emotions. This is borne out experimentally by the established capacity of man to correctly recognize the emotional tone of sound signals produced by monkeys. It developed that man's evaluations correspond well with the behavioral situation in which the sound signal was recorded, whether the signal was orienting, emotionally positive, actively negative (anger) or passively negative (sorrow, fright, anxiety), or neutral (Gershuni et al., 1976; 1977).

Recently a strong interest has developed in analyzing the voice as an objective index of the emotional state of a man carrying out the responsible activity of a cosmonaut, pilot, or flight controller (Luk'yanov and Frolov, 1969; Taubkin, 1977; Williams and Stevens, 1969, 1972; Older and Jenney, 1975; Kuroda et al., 1976). There are a number of reasons for this interest. An evaluation of the state of a man according to his voice does not require attaching special monitors to his body, which not only burden the subject, but turn him, psychologically, into an object to be observed with all the undesirable consequences of that situation. A recording of ordinary radio communications can be used to record and subsequently analyze speech intonation (Fig. 21). Second, simultaneous acoustical and computation technique makes it possible to supplement the auditory analysis with instrumental (ideally, automatic) evaluation of a person's emotional state. Third, the speech signal shows less effect of physical stress than do the involuntary functions.

Changes in frequency of heartbeat and the relevant formant instances in the voice of the cosmonaut A. A. Leonov at various stages of training and real flight in space are presented in Fig. 22. It is apparent that changes in pulse at the two stages (preparation to exit into open space, 4, and at the moment of returning into the lock chamber, 7) were

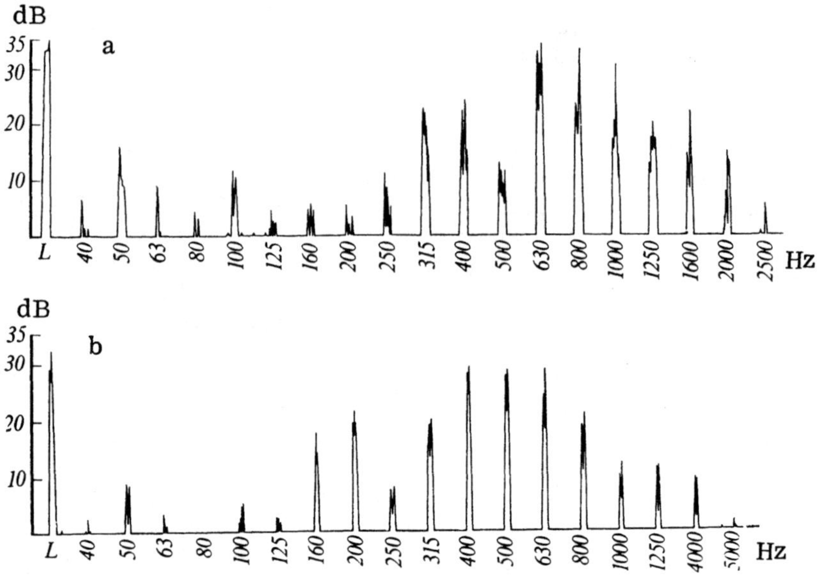

Fig. 21. Spectra of the sentence, "I am Almaz," spoken by A. A. Leonov at the "exit" stage of flight (a) and during training (b) (after Luk'yanov and Frolov).

stronger during training than in actual flight. Can it be true that the emotional stress of the cosmonaut was more significant on Earth than in space? An analysis of the intonational characteristics of speech shows that this is not so. As far as increase in frequency of heartbeat is concerned, during training it was the result of purely physical stress and the necessity of moving about in a heavy pressure suit meant for weightlessness.

The perceptions of emotional coloring of speech depend on personality traits of the man and on his own emotional state at the given moment. The emotions of another are recognized best by a person who is, according to his characteristics, the "dependent" type. In these people, Catrell's questionnaire detected traits of dependence, anxiety, conformance, and increased sensitivity. In disclosing the emotional coloring of a voice, the phenomenon of "psychological defense" may also be disclosed: patients in a state of depression determine the intonational traits of a depressed state less reliably than traits of other emotions (Korneva, 1978).

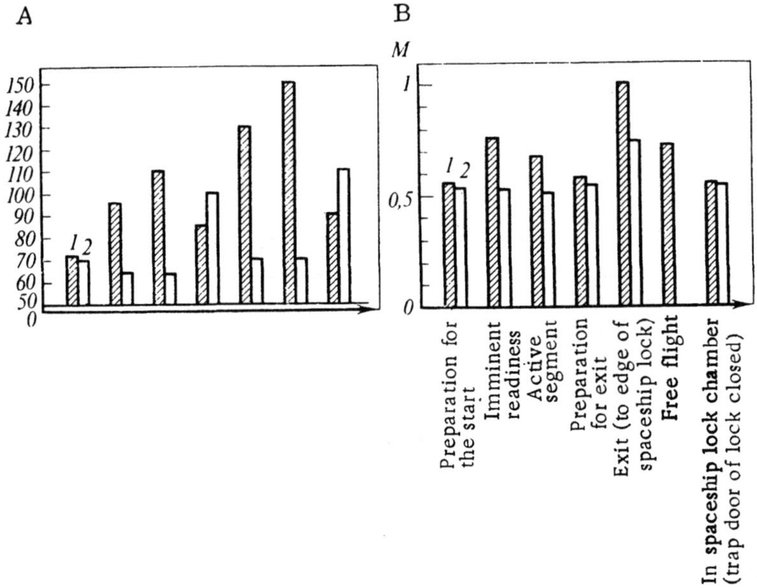

Fig. 22. Changes in pulse frequency (A) and in the acoustical characteristics of the voice (B) in the cosmonaut A. A. Leonov at various stages of flight (1) and during training (2) (after Luk'yanov and Frolov).

A person's own emotional state affects his ability to produce emotional mimicry although mimicry is one of the voluntary motor reactions. Schwartz made an electromyogram (EMG) of facial muscles in healthy subjects and in patients in a state of depression. When these patients thought of events connected with sadness and anger, they produced mimicry typical for these emotions. But they could not mimic expressions of happiness, and a mental image of a "normal day" situation was accompanied by mimicry similar to sadness (Schwartz, 1975). These and similar experiments show that using mimicry as a voluntarily controlled means of social intercourse did not free it completely from its involuntary components. Careful electromyographic analysis indicated that a mental representation of an emotionally colored situation produces mimicry more like natural emotions than a simple, facial "representation" of joy, sorrow, and similar emotions (Schwartz et al., 1976).

Thus, mimicry represents a complex "merging" of voluntary, trained, and involuntary emotional components. In experiments that Rusalova (1979) set up with Izard (USA) using professional actors, the EMG of mimetic facial muscles with mental representations of emotionally colored events corresponded to the natural emotions. The greatest activity of m. depressor anguli oris (smile) was observed in joy; of m. venter frontalis (raising of the eyebrows), in fear; of m. masseter (clenching of the jaws), in anger; and of m. corrugator supercilii (frowning), against a background of sadness. Control subjects (not actors) were able to produce only the EMG picture of happiness while all negative emotions elicited a strengthening of the activity of the same mimetic muscles (frowning).

Attempting a brief review of the data pertaining to the emotional coloring of speech and mimicry, we can say the following. The long process of socialization turned the voice and mimicry into a means of nonverbal communication that man uses not only for communicating his state, but also for masking this state from other members of society. Nevertheless, an adequately precise instrumental analysis can disclose components in emotional expression that are not subject to voluntary control. This makes the voice and mimicry a very important and promising objective index of the emotional state of man, which is of great interest to engineering psychology, medicine, and other clinical areas.

On the theoretical plane, we are once again convinced that speech and mimicry not only *express* the subjective experiences of man, but also *reflect* objective factors of the situation that gave rise to a given experience: presence of need and prediction of the possibility of its being satisfied. Even when mimicry or the coloration of speech does not correspond to the real emotional state of the subject, they are conditioned by some other need and will be all the more convincing, the stronger the need. A second very important condition for a convincing external expression of emotions is the capability and skill of the person in transforming his real need into motives of behavior of the personality he is portraying. Thus, the artistic need of the actor to solve his own "superproblem," the need to recognize and convey to the viewers something important about the world in which we live, serves as the source of the emotions of the specific character. But we will speak of this later.

Neuroanatomy of Emotions

The methodology of direct stimulation of the brain with electrical current through previously implanted electrodes is of enormous significance for disclosing and analyzing the brain structures that are directly responsible for the development and realization of emotional reactions (Hess, 1968). Successes in stereotaxic neurosurgery made the use of this method of diagnosis and treatment possible, and this opened the way for comparing the effects of stimulation with verbal responses of patients about their emotional state (Sem-Jacobsen, Heath, Delgado, Bekhtereva, Smirnov, et al.). The zones of stimulation that elicited emotional reactions of various intensity and stability in patients are presented in Fig. 23, taken from the work of Bekhtereva (1971).

The best summary of data obtained through stimulation in diagnosis and treatment can be found in the monograph of Smirnov (1976).

Summarizing the results of his own observations and information found in the literature, Smirnov notes that when the nuclei of the amygdala are stimulated, the patient indicates the development of a state of fear, anger, or rage, and rarely satisfaction. Stimulation of the septum, on the other hand, is accompanied, as a rule, by euphoria, delight, sexual arousal, and a general improvement in mood. When the frontal and posterior sections of the hypothalamus are stimulated, there is a reaction of anxiety and rage, and when the structures of the midbrain are stimulated, a broad spectrum of emotions ranging from anger and stress to sexual arousal with a definite positive coloring. As distinct from

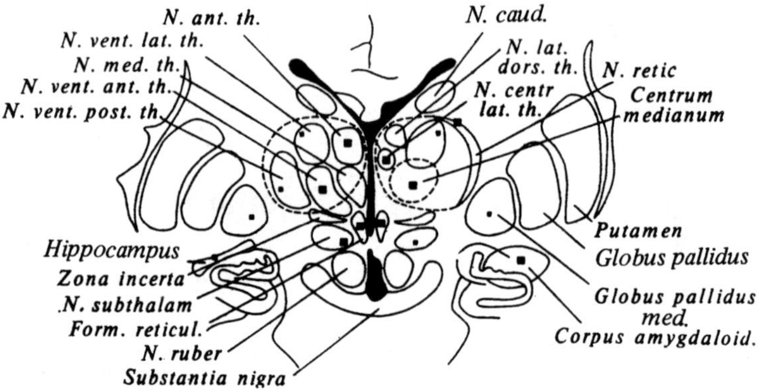

Fig. 23. Diagram of the human brain. Large black squares indicate zones where stimulation elicits strong and stable emotional reactions; small squares indicate the zones where stimulation elicits less strong and stable emotional reactions (after Bekhtereva).

the brain structures mentioned, stimulation of the hippocampus is not accompanied by fear or range or satisfaction. There is only confusion in recognition, temporary loss of contact with the doctor and, episodically, fear in the form of a secondary emotional reaction of the subject to the confusion in his surrounding world.

States of heightened activity or inactivity result from stimulation of the mesencephalic section of the stem and nonspecific thalamus. Activated states have a positive emotional tone, or, more rarely, are actively negative (anger, malice, but not melancholy or sadness). Inactivated states are characterized by calm and indifference. Feelings of unusual "lightness of body" or its "heaviness" which accompany these two functional states could not be directly related to changes in the muscle tonus of the vestibular functions.

In addition to the emotional states mentioned above, Smirnov's patients mentioned brief reactions that developed at the moment of electrical stimulation. These include: a feeling of confusion, perplexity (mesencephalic sections of the stem, subthalamus, reticular thalamic nucleus); fear, whose cause is not known to the patient or which is connected with an emotional reaction to somatic changes (limboreticular system); satisfaction in the form of pleasant, but not always precisely qualified feelings; unmotivated joy developing with stimulation of the midcenter of the thalamus, the globus pallidus, and the mesencephalic section of the stem.

For many years, neurophysiologists tried to find that section of the brain which is most responsible for the development of emotional states: the hypothalamus (Hess, Gellhorn), the thalamus (Cannon and Bard), the hippocampus (Beritov, Peipets, and Brady), the reticular formation (Lindsley), and so on. This tendency was reflected even in the naming of the theories: "thalamic," "hypothalamolimbic," "activating." A later modification of this approach to the problem of localizing emotions are the concepts of McLean (1970). He believes that stereotypic forms of behavior are represented in the hypothalamus and are, as a rule, accompanied by emotions (reactions of defense, attack, seeking, obtaining), and that motivations of one kind or another coincide with the upper sections of the brain: the amygdala, needs of self-preservation (hunger, defense, etc.); the septum, continuation of the species and sex; the cingulate and prefrontal cortex, zoosocial, group, and gregarious motivations; individual acquired experience is accumulated in the neocortex of higher vertebrates.

However, results of experiments with direct electrical stimulation of brain formations, like experiments with their destruction, give no basis for considering any one structure as a local "center" for the emotions of fear, rage, satisfaction, etc. Even a complete surgical isolation of the hypothalamus in cats (Ellison and Flynn, 1968) did not result in elimination of defense and alimentary reactions and emotional coloring characteristic for them. Evaluating the situation that developed, Waldman wrote: "In essence, attempts to represent emotions, like other psychic functions, topographically in the brain are an echo of localizationism ... The problem of the 'emotional substrate' at present may be resolved definitely only with respect to the topography of integrative centers of zones of emotionally expressive phenomena" (Waldman, 1972, p. 14). Smirnov agrees with this point of view: "...it would be difficult to name the brain structures that are responsible exclusively for emotions... For this reason, we agree completely with A. V. Waldman (1972) that the neurophysiological study of emotions and emotional behavior should not be directed to finding structural elements of emotions but that it should be based on a systemic principle" (Smirnov, 1976, p. 166).

Isaacson expresses similar views in his recent works: "There is no single anatomical formation for individual behavioral functions...there is no one behavioral function that can be matched to anatomical formations in such a way that these functions would be useful in any circumstances and under all external conditions" (Isaacson, 1978).

While we understand the complete validity of disappointment with the results of the search for "point" localization of structures that produce emotions, neither can we return to the diffuse concepts of emotions as functions of the "brain as a whole," as traces of "cortico—subcortical relations." With all the complexity of the problem, experimental neurophysiology of emotions would not be justified in rejecting the fundamental principle of "fitting the dynamics to the structure," left to us by Pavlov.

Today it is impossible to find an investigator who would think of the neural "centers" of emotion in the form of a limited segment of nerve tissue. Everyone who tries to consider the organization of the cerebral substrate of emotions speaks without fail of the system, of the widely branched constellation of neural formations represented at various levels in the brains of higher animals and man.

The concept of a dominant center as a "functional organ," as a system, is especially close to the neurophysiology of emotions that we link with the name of Ukhtomsky. Rusinov writes: "The dominant center is that constellation suggested by A. A. Ukhtomsky, that is formed as a system in the course of ongoing activity of an organism at all levels of the central nervous system in its various places, but with a primary center in one of the sections and with variable significance of the functions of separate components of the system" (Rusinov, 1967, p. 200). Ukhtomsky particularly emphasized that a factor that determines the temporal integrity of the "functional organ" is the achievement of a certain adaptive result. He wrote: "With the term 'organ' we have been used to connecting a concept of a morphologically constituted, statistically stable formation. This is not necessarily the case. An organ may be any temporary combination of forces *capable of accomplishing a specific end* (Ukhtomsky, 1950, p. 279; author's emphasis). Later Anokhin energetically developed the idea of the result as a system-forming factor.

The systemic approach, however, is productive only if we indicate more or less definitely the concrete elements that comprise the given system, the functional significance of each of these elements, and the rules of interaction of the elements with each other when the system functions as a whole. As "elements" we understand not hypothetical "blocks" of logical circuits, but real brain formations, that correspondence of dynamics to structure that Pavlov considered to be a fundamental principle of his materialistic theory. Unfortunately, it is just this last requirement that was critical for the neurophysiological base of a whole series of very beautiful and logically elegant concepts. In other words, any concept that pretends to explain the principles of organization of behavior must be comparable to the anatomical construction of the brain since both the first and the second were formed in the flow of a single evolutionary process.

In recent years, attempts have been made to isolate one conglomerate or another of anatomically and functionally interconnected brain formations to which we could attach not a separate fragment of goal-directed behavior, but an adequately universal behavioral function. Nebylitsin (1968, 1971) believed that the neuroanatomical basis for particular properties of the nervous system are analyzers (visual, auditory, touch, etc.). As far as general properties are concerned, they may be divided into activity and emotionality. The first depends on individual traits of functioning of the frontal reticular complex of the brain structures; the second, on the frontal limbic complex. Ilyutchenok isolated the emotiogenic system as including the following sections of the brain: the amygdala, the zona incerta, the peri- and paraventricular nuclei of the hypothalamus, and the central gray matter. Destruction of any of these formations, according to data of that author, makes it impossible to develop a conditioned reflex in rats after one combination, which is evidence of damage to the emotional component of reinforcement (Ilyutchenok, 1979). The similarity of the defect that appears when any link of complex of brain structures is damaged was the basis also for isolating the "systems of the frontal brain" described by Cherkes (1978). This system includes the associative cortex, the neostriatum (caudal nucleus), the hippocampus, and the amygdala. "This is the complex of structures that is responsible for the organization of those forms of behavior that are the most complex in a given species of animals" (Cherkes, 1978, p. 147). Unfortunately, the idea of "most complex" for a form of behavior of a given species is somewhat vague.

Douglas (1972) proposes to distinguish two basic systems of the brain: the analyzing (neocortex, specific nuclei of the thalamus, hippocampus, and amygdala) and the motivational (brain stem, hypothalamus, and nonspecific nuclei of the thalamus). He emphasizes the significance of mutual effects of these two systems on each others' activity. But even in this scheme the role of each of the structures mentioned is not made specific: it is simply not enough to say that the system "analyzes the more important stimuli" without explaining the principles of this analysis. The question of the relation of the amygdala to the system of analyzing structures also seems quite debatable to us since the amygdala is very closely connected with the functioning of the hypothalamus.

In his later works, Luria (1978) described three basic functional blocks of the brain: 1) the block that regulates tonus and waking (reticular formation and frontal sections of the cortex); 2) the block that receives, processes, and preserves information (primary, secondary, and tertiary zones of the cortex); 3) the block that programs, regulates, and controls activity (prefrontal sections of the frontal cortex). When we analyze the scheme of functional organization of the brain proposed by Luria, a whole series of questions arises. What role in this organization do the subcortical formations, other than the reticular formation, play? How are the functions of the "blocks" interconnected, that is, what processes of receiving and processing information affect the programming of activity, how does activity affect reception, processing and preservation of information, and how do the first two affect the regulation of tonus, etc. Moreover, Luria's scheme flows maturally from his general neuropsychological concepts from which need, motives, and emotions are practically excluded.

As far as chapters of textbooks and handbooks that describe the morphological substrate of needs and emotions are concerned, as a rule they simply enumerate the effects observed when the frontal sections of the neocortex, hippocampus, amygdala, and the hypothalamus are damaged or electrically stimulated without indicating the principal features of function of each of these formations or the specifics of their "contribution" to the organization of behavior. We assume that the reason for this situation is the absence of a general concept of integrated activity of the brain that could be matched to its anatomical structure.

Our own approach to this problem was determined by the information theory of emotions according to which needs, actions, and emotions not only represent phenomena of higher nervous (psychic) activity that are independent and not identical to each other, but of necessity must have their own morphophysiological substrate. Such a point of view has been confirmed by the results of many experiments.

MORPHOLOGICAL BASES OF NEEDS, MOTIVATION, AND EMOTIONS. THEIR RELATIVE INDEPENDENCE

In the diagram of the frontal section of the brain of a rat in one of the works of Olds (Fig. 24), the structures connected with biological needs for food, water, and a sexual partner look like islands against a background of brain tissue, the direct stimulation of which produces an emotionally positive, emotionally negative, or mixed effect. Stimulation of the brain of a cat from the posterior nucleus to the supraoptical in the lateral part of the hypothalamus below the filiform nucleus provokes an attack on a rat without external manifestations of rage ("cold" attack). An attack

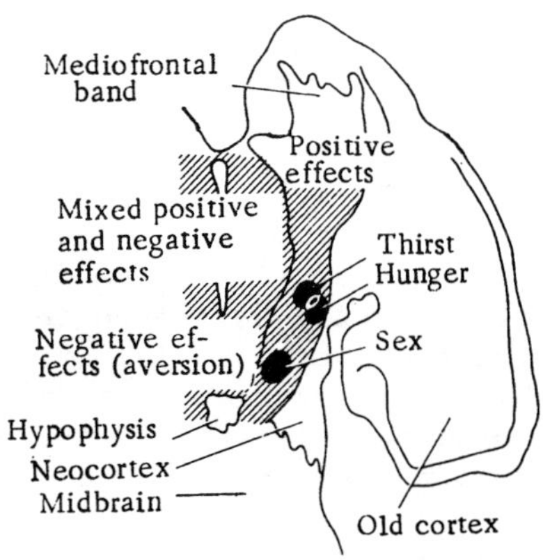

Fig. 24. Diagram of a rat brain with indication of zones which showed motivational and emotional effects when electrically stimulated (after Olds).

with rage can be observed when the electrode is moved in a medial direction. Rage without attack occurs with stimulation of the fornix at a point lying above the filiform nucleus (Wasman and Flynn, 1962; Flynn, 1967).

With electrodes located in the same place in the lateral hypothalamus of rats, the threshold of activation of motivational structures, judged according to effect on processes of eating, drinking, and copulation, was significantly lower than the threshold of emotional positive reinforcement, self-stimulation (Huston, 1971, 1972). Stimulation of the lateral hypothalamus with long bursts of stimuli led to greater need for milk than stimulation with short bursts, but the rats preferred the latter type of stimulation. Consequently, motivational and reinforcing (emotionally positive) systems are separated in the brain, although their simultaneous excitation was observed in self-stimulation (Ball, 1969). Pharmacological analysis also indicates different mechanisms for needs and emotions. Injecting disulfiram variously decreases the level of noradrenaline in the brain of rats, eliminates motivational effects of stimulation (eating, drinking, gnawing), increases the frequency of self-stimulation, and lowers the threshold of self-stimulation (Mikhailova and Cheresharov, 1979). According to data of Borisenko (1977), phenamine and cocaine facilitate self-stimulation of the hypothalamus and the septum, and depress eating and drinking reactions of the animal at the same time.

Up to this point, in speaking of the anatomical substrate of needs, we had in mind the actualization of natural needs of the animal for food, water, etc. As far as the phenomenon of self-stimulation is concerned, it is a mechanism that induces the animal to press the pedal repeatedly and is evidently connected not with hunger, thirst, etc., but with trace excitation of structures of emotionally positive reinforcement activated by the current. The short duration of this trace excitation also explains the comparative ease with which the reaction is extinguished when it is not reinforced and the necessity of "primer" stimulations in animals trained to press a pedal (Deutsch and Howarth, 1963). Even in his early works, Olds compared the phenomenology of self-stimulation not with hunger, but with striving for tasty food. Rats can stimulate structures of hunger and thirst, but only in the presence of food and water in experimental conditions when the high probability of satisfying natural needs guarantees the development of positive emotions in the process of eating and drinking (Morgan, 1969; Mendelson, 1970). On a solid basis, Cytawa proposes that we distinguish the system of "excitation" of the hunger, thirst, or pain type from the system of "desire" such as striving for repeated activation of structures of positive emotions. The activity of systems of "desire" is not identical with the mechanism of emotionally positive excitation itself ("satisfaction") that arises at the moment of reinforcement. It is Cytawa's opinion that dopaminergic structures predominate in the "desire" system, and noradrenergic in the "satisfaction" system (Cytawa, 1979). As far as intermittent stimulation is concerned, depending on location of the electrode and parameters of the current, it can be due to both adaptation to the action of the current and to involvement of mechanisms of negative emotions (Zvartau and Patkina, 1974; Grigor'yan, 1978).

We believe that the experiments done in our laboratory by Mikhailova and Sarkisova support the relative independence of the mechanisms of needs, motivations, and emotions. In the experiments, these authors used a gradual increase in intensity of stimulating current, used before by Waldman, Kozlovska, Huston, and other investigators.

Monopolar steel electrodes with an end diameter of 70 μm were inserted into the lateral preoptical area and into the lateral hypothalamus of 22 white, male rats (coordinates according to the König and Klippel atlas: A, 7.0; L, 1.8; H, 3.5; A, 3.0-3.5; L, 1.5; H, 3.5). During stimulation, there was a pedal for self-stimulation in the chamber and goal objects for eliciting specific motivations: food (sunflower seeds or oats evenly distributed on the floor), drink (bowl of water), material for gnawing (piece of chalk or wood), sex (a female rat). Stimulation was a rhythmic current (right angle, monophasic impulses, frequency, 100 Hz; duration, 0.1 msec; intensity, 0-1.0 mA) as well as constant current from 0 to 70 μA. Consuming reactions (eating, drinking, gnawing) were recorded with myograms of the chewing muscles. Latent periods of reactions and the probability of their appearance, that is, the ratio of the number of stimulations that elicited these reactions to the total number of stimulations, were computed. The reinforcing (emotionally positive) effect of the current was evaluated according to the frequency of self-stimulation. The rats had free access to food and water before the experiment.

In all cases, only those zones were stimulated which were capable of producing the self-stimulating reaction when affected by a current of adequate strength. It developed that when these zones were polarized by gradually increasing, constant current and when they were stimulated by rhythmic current of increasing intensity, the behavioral reactions always had an identical sequence. Weak stimulation elicited a generalized seeking activity without reference to the goal objects in the chamber: food, water, individuals of the opposite sex, etc. Only when the intensity of stimulation was increased did these external stimuli become effective: the animal began to eat, sometimes drink, gnaw, etc. When the rhythmic current or the constant current was further intensified, the reaction of self-stimulation developed.

If two different points in the hypothalamus were stimulated, a similar sequence of events followed, that is, two stimulations of "seeking intensity" resulted in the consuming reaction: most frequently, eating; less frequently, drinking, gnawing, etc.; and two stimulations of "motivating intensity" could elicit the self-stimulation reaction (Fig. 25). When one of the points was stimulated sufficiently to elicit self-stimulation, motivated behavior was depressed due to the stimulation of the second point. White (1973) observed termination of natural alimentary behavior with stimulation of the amygdala capable of eliciting self-stimulation. The experiments of Mikhailova and Sarkisova (1977) disclosed a methodical preference for the use of constant current in comparison with rhythmic current. Stimulation of two points with rhythmic current resulted in a strengthening (increasing the frequency) of the self-stimulation reaction. A weak cathode polarization of one point inhibited self-stimulation of the second center, but an increase in the intensity of the constant current increased self-stimulation. We must note that the inhibiting effect is the result of an intensity of constant current that elicits goal-directed, motivated behavior in isolated application.

The observed transformation of effects is difficult to explain by a nonspecific supplementary activation of "motivational—reinforcing" structures because stimulation of emotionally negative (eliciting flight) zones of the reticular formation of the midbrain inhibits the reaction of self-stimulation (an effect investigated in detail earlier by Mikhailova, 1975), but stimulation of emotionally neutral zones of the hypothalamus has no effect at all on self-stim-

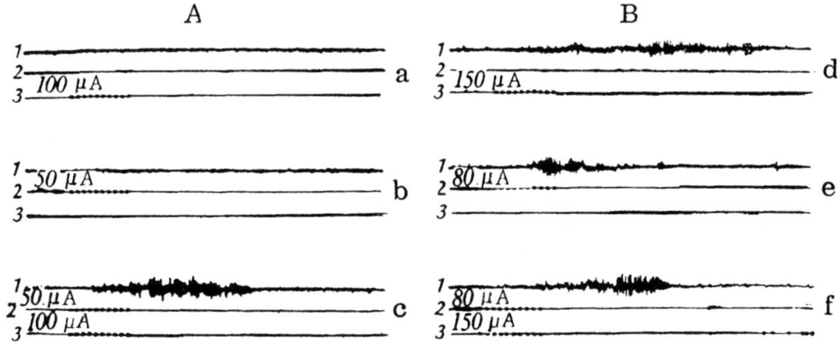

Fig. 25. Results of single stimulation of two points of the hypothalamus of a rat with a "seeking" intensity of the electrical current (A) and with "motivating" intensity (B). 1) Myogram of chewing muscles; 2, 3) stimulation of the first and second points. Deviation of line 2 in fragment c records self-stimulation (after Mikhailova and Sarkisova).

ulation. Only stimulation of emotionally positive structures of the reticular formation capable of independently causing even weak self-stimulation, can be integrated with the "seeking," "motivating," and "self-stimulating" stimulation of hypothalamic structures.

We think that simulation experiments, which we mentioned above, will reproduce the sequence of events characteristic for the organization of natural behavior (Fig. 26). A weak stimulation with electric current activates the system of brain structures that represents the need substrate. The process of actualizing a need that has not yet been transformed into motivation is manifested externally as generalized agitated seeking. Only an increase in the stimulation by increasing the intensity of constant or rhythmic current results in activation of those structures that store the engrams of external objects capable of satisfying the given need. As a result, external stimuli become effective and the motivated animal begins to eat, drink, gnaw, etc. However, a further increase in current is necessary for activation of the structures of emotionally positive reinforcement, and the animal transfers to self-stimulation of the brain in the absence of natural satisfaction of any need.

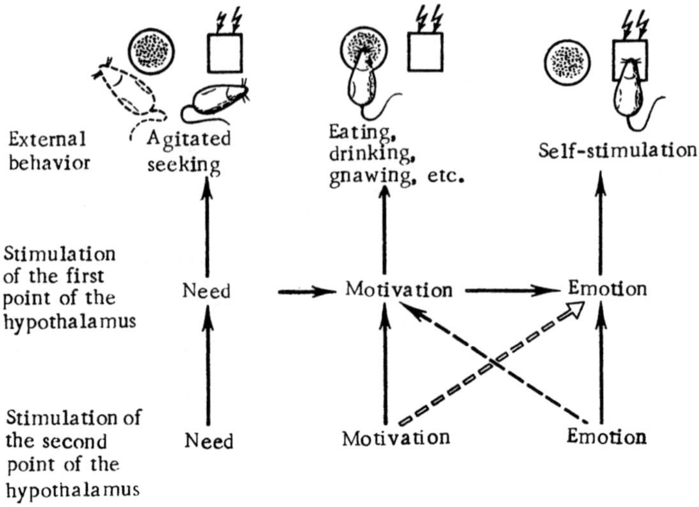

Fig. 26. Diagram of effects of simultaneous stimulation of two points of the hypothalamus. Solid arrows indicate cumulative effects; dotted arrows indicate inhibiting effects of stimulation with rhythmic and constant current (thin arrow) and with constant current alone (double arrow).

It must be understood that we do not think of the structures of need, motivation, and emotion as being linearly located in contiguous sections of the brain tissue and that electric current of increasing intensity sequentially engages these structures one after the other. We are saying that the system of structures necessary and adequate for actualization of need is more simple and contains fewer elements than the system that provides for goal-directed motivation of the animal. And the whole complex of morphophysiological organization of behavior (need + motivation + emotion) suggests the additional involvement of the neural apparatus of emotions also.

In order to understand the effects of stimulating two points on the hypothalamus with electric current of different intensity, it is expedient to remember the data obtained in the study of mechanisms of natural alimentary behavior by Shuleikina, Olds, and others.

As Shuleikina demonstrated (1971), hunger excitation (actualization of the need for food) arises primarily in the reticular nuclei of the pons and medulla oblongata, and includes the central gray matter of the midbrain, the nonspecific nuclei of the hypothalamus, and the dorsal hippocampus. In order for the actualized need for food to be transformed into goal-directed seeking of food, the structures of the neocortex, the amygdala, and "positive elements" (Shuleikina's terminology) of the medial hypothalamus must be involved.

Let us note that the structures of the hypothalamus begin to function actively at the food-seeking stage initiated by hunger excitation. Neurons that respond with changed activity to the sight and smell of food and to conditioned signals representing food can be found in the lateral hypothalamus of hungry monkeys (Mora et al., 1976). Also in the lateral hypothalamus, there are neurons that are activated by other needs as well: thirst or a state of morphine withdrawal in rats (Olds, 1977b).

Yet an animal comes into contact with food and begins to eat, an act realized by the synchronizing system of the lower section of the brain stem, thalamus, orbital cortex, and lateral hypothalamus. From the oral cavity and then from the stomach come neural impulses that signal the future alleviation of hunger. It has been known for a long time that such afferentation terminates the act of eating long before true "tissue" satiation. This process, later called "sensory satiation," was clearly described by Pavlov in 1910-1911: "The delivery of a small amount of food into the stomach temporarily terminates or weakens the action of the food center...The situation would be bad if excitability of the food center decreased only when the organism's need for liquid and solid food materials was completely satisfied, since a constant result of such condition would be overeating, an excessive filling of the stomach with food" (Pavlov, 1973, p. 108).

In the very beginning of eating, the delivery of food still continues to activate the "positive" neurons of the medial hypothalamus, but as satiation progresses, there is an activation of "negative" neurons that have an inhibiting effect on the neurons of the lateral hypothalamus earlier stimulated by hunger. Feeding then ends.

We agree with Shuleikina's opinion that the conclusion on localization of a "hunger center" in the lateral hypothalamus and a "satiation center" in the medial oversimplifies the true situation. We are inclined to connect the structures of the lateral hypothalamus predominantly with processes of food motivation at all its stages, from hunger excitation that provides the reactions of the neurons of the lateral hypothalamus to conditioned signals, the sight and smell of food, to the state of satiation. As far as "positive" and "negative" elements of the medial hypothalamus are concerned, changes in their activity form a basis for referring these elements to the neural mechanisms of *emotion*, positive during approach to food and at the beginning of the act of eating, and negative, which are activated as food is eaten.

We will now return to the analysis of experiments with electrical stimulation of the hypothalamus. A weak stimulation evidently imitates that hunger excitation that, under natural conditions, enters the hypothalamus from the reticular nuclei of the pons and the medulla oblongata. This excitation must be reinforced by increasing intensity of electrical current or stimulation by a different "food" point (and not any or all points) in order to activate engrams of food objects and produce the act of eating. In the process of eating, neural elements are excited which generate an emotionally positive state, but this excitation again is insufficient for a transition to artificial stimulation of the emotionally positive structures with an electric current. Only further strengthening of the current or summation of two "motivating" stimulations leads to food being exchanged for self-stimulation. We will once again emphasize that the phenomenon of artificial reinforcement is by no means the result of increasing motivating stimulation. It is not the stimulation of the motivation structures that is summarized, but the simulation of the emotionally positive elements, since the transition from eating to self-stimulation occurs only with stimulation of those points that can each elicit the reaction of self-stimulation if the strength of the electrical current is adequate.

The transition to self-stimulation gradually terminates the feeding behavior of the rat (a corresponding inhibiting effect is represented in Fig. 26 by the fine dotted line). This effect once again indicates that the direct reinforcing factor of instrumental reflexes is not the satisfaction of some need, but maximizing a positive (or minimizing a negative) emotional state. The inhibition of the reaction of self-stimulation by the stimulation of motivation structures was detected only when a constant current was applied (in Fig. 26 it is indicated by the double dotted arrow). From our point of view, this depressing effect shows that the basis for the phenomenon of self-stimulation is precisely the activation of structures of positive emotions. Depending on the degree of hunger excitation, identical afferentation of impending satiation (or its simulation by stimulation of the appropriate brain structures with an electrical current) can be either adequate or inadequate for activating positive emotions. In the latter case, reinforcing motivation leads to stimulation of emotionally negative elements and depresses the reaction of self-stimulation.

We have emphasized more than once the fact that any emotion is realized not by a "center" point, but by a constellation, a system of structures located at various "levels" of the brain. Developing the theoretical concepts of Sherrington, Magnus, and Pavlov, and considering his own data, Asratyan (1959) formulated a concept about the multitude of branches of the central part of the arch of the unconditioned reflex, each of which passes through various sections of the central nervous system, including the cerebrum (Fig. 27). The next step in the development of this kind of concept will evidently be to focus on the problem of the specific "contribution" of any one representation of this reflecting system to the production of an entire biologically expedient reaction. Two variants are possible here; we have presented them schematically in Fig. 28.

According to the first point of view (Fig. 28, I), each of the needs (hunger, thirst, sex, etc.), like each of the emotions (fear, rage, satisfaction), has its own "representations" at various levels of the central nervous system, including in the amygdala, the hippocampus, and the neocortex of the cerebrum. According to the second point of view (Fig. 28, II), integration of the somatic and autonomic components specific for the given emotion is apparent only at a definite, comparatively low level (in the hypothalamus?). As far as such brain formations as the hippocampus, amygdala, and, most of all the neocortex, are concerned, it is not separate needs and emotions that are represented in them, but *operations* needed for the genesis of various emotional states.

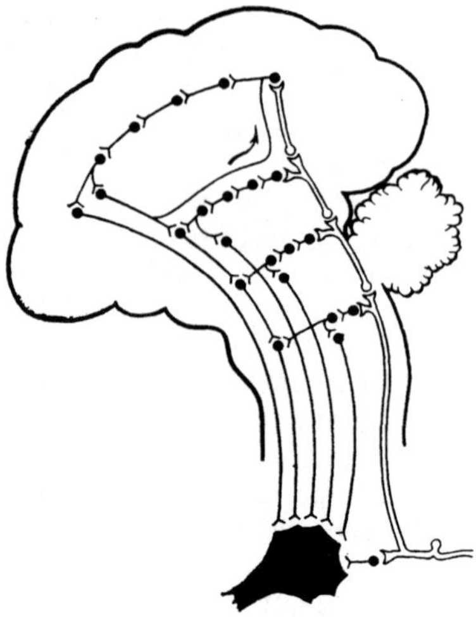

Fig. 27. Diagram of a "multilevel" structure of an unconditioned reflex (after Asratyan).

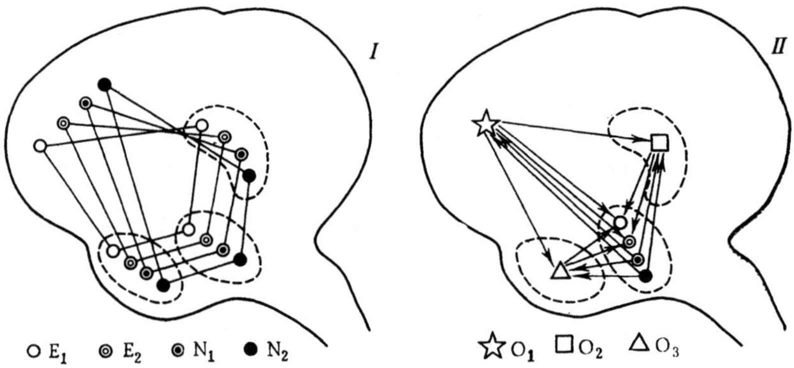

Fig. 28. Two possible variants of the functional organization of brain mechanisms of needs and emotions (I and II). E_1, E_2) Emotions; N_1, N_2) needs; O_1, O_2, O_3) operations.

The essence of these operations is determined by two factors that have a decisive significance for the organization of any behavior: the presence of actual needs and the possibility of satisfying them by interaction with the external environment depends on their relation to the needs of the organism, and all of these stimuli can be divided into two basic categories: stimuli with a high probability of being reinforced by factors that directly satisfy a need, and stimuli with a low probability of reinforcement. Among the actual needs, in their turn, there are the most pressing, dominant needs that require immediate satisfaction, and subdominant needs existing dynamically with the dominant or competing with it.

Experimental data obtained in our laboratory or found in the literature indicate that the interaction of the four brain formations that play a decisive role in evaluating signals coming from the environment and selecting reactions corresponds precisely to such a representation of the organization of behavior. Here we have in mind the frontal section of the neocortex, hippocampus, amygdala, and hypothalamus.

SIGNIFICANCE OF THE FRONTAL NEOCORTEX FOR ORIENTATION OF BEHAVIOR TO SIGNALS OF HIGHLY PROBABLE EVENTS

On the basis of the direct participation of the frontal sections of the neocortex in processes of motivation and emotions taken together with the established features of anatomical connections, some authors consider the frontal area as a neocortical continuation of the limbic system (Nauta, 1964). In man and primates, the connections between the neocortex and the hippocampus proceed from the frontal poles and the inferior parietal lobe. The prefrontal cortex in rats is the only neocortical area that is innervated from the ventral section of the skull and the amygdala. Like the mediobasal nuclei of the thalamus, the prefrontal cortex is not directly involved in the sensory or motor functions of the brain (Divac and Kosmal, 1978). As distinct from the neurons of any other sections of the cortex, only the neurons of the prefrontal section are activated by stimulation of self-stimulation points in rats (Rolls and Cooper, 1973).

In the mediobasal sections of the frontal cortex there is evidently an integration of signals from the internal environment of the organism based on the motor activity of the animal. Thus it is precisely the frontal cortex that controls, to a significant degree, the animal's seeking the means to satisfy his organic needs (Luria, 1962). This is why removing the frontal cortex has a definite influence on the mechanisms that motivate behavior. Thus, in lobectomized dogs, the identification of a dominant need is disrupted. If an intact animal has two levers for obtaining food and water, it gets water several times in a row, and then proceeds to get food; lobectomized dogs frequently move to the second lever after a single reinforcement (Uryvaev, 1978). We must note that such an effect evidently depends not only on the balance of two motivations, but also on a defect in the evaluation of reinforcement, which we will consider later. Damage to the orbital sections of the frontal cortex disrupts the zoosocial behavior of rats (Koeb, 1974). Bilateral removal of the lobes in monkeys results in a decrease in contact with other individuals and a weakening of investigative activity. Intact monkeys make fewer contacts with individuals that have been operated on (Deets et al., 1970).

When the frontal lobes are damaged, the emotional sphere of man is disrupted more severely than when other cortical areas are damaged, including the temporal. Two symptoms most typical for patients with "frontal" ailments are the syndrome of aspontaneity with manifestions of emotional dullness and indifference, the syndrome of lack of inhibition with overtones of euphoria that is completely inconsistent with the actual state of the patient. In both cases, emotions connected with activity, with social relations, and with creativity are disrupted. Emotions arising on the basis of primitive tendencies may even become stronger (Dobrokhotova, 1968). It is precisely in the frontal sections that electroencephalogram features characteristic for persons with a stable domination of positive or negative emotions are found. In the EEG of persons with happiness as a dominant, the alpha rhythm and slow components are well expressed; in the EEG of persons with anger as a dominant, beta activity predominates (Kovalev et al., 1976).

According to the concepts of Pribram (1961) and Luria (1962), the analytical—synthesizing activity of the posterior sections of the neocortex form the program of action while the frontal sections compare this program with the actual course of its implementation. Damage of the premotor sections of the brain does not result in a disintegration of the program of action, but disturbs its motor structure, leading to defects in kinetic organization (Luria, 1966).

The role of the frontal cortex in the processes of perception is also quite specific. With exposure to visual stimuli similar in configuration, but different in sense, the elicited potential in man was the same in the visual cortex, but differed in subsequent components of the frontal sections (Johnston and Chesney, 1976). Pribram suggests that the frontal cortex that is included in the structure of the frontolimbic system of the forebrain is connected with the function of calling attention to the stimulus and with organizing readiness for action (Pribram, 1975).

Discussing the problem of the role of the frontal sections of the neocortex, we cannot avoid the problem of the functional asymmetry of the cerebral hemispheres of man, all the more so since this problem is directly related to the neurophysiology of emotions.

Pavlov, in proposing his idea of the presence among people of representatives of the "artistic" and "intellectual" types, could scarcely expect that in the near future this idea would receive confirmation from the morphophysiological aspect. Following the pioneering studies of Sperry with patients with a severed corpus callosum, the number of works on the functional asymmetry of the brain began to expand like an avalanche. Today we know that the left hemisphere (in right-handed people) is connected with speech, abstract—conceptual thinking and mathematical capabilities, while the right operates through perceptually direct images and spatial perception and is connected with musical abilities and talent for synthesizing. When the right hemisphere is damaged, perception of space and time is disrupted. This becomes clear if we take into account that operating with abstract concepts does not require time "markers" (a table was a table in the time of Pushkin, and remains a table after even a hundred years). Concrete impressions of an event or an object or person we meet, etc., must be ordered in time, otherwise we lose the possibility of orienting ourselves to the sequence of events. On the basis of an example of a concept developed by Dobrokhotova and Bragina (1975), the right hemisphere is connected with the past and present, and the left is turned toward the future, the prediction of which has a probability character, and the future itself may be changed to a significant degree by the real actions of the subject.

The functional asymmetry of the brain has a great influence on the processes of perception and memory. When a text with content that was inconsistent with the intonation was presented to the left ear, 29 of 36 healthy persons gave preference to the intonational coloring. Listening with the right ear resulted in 21 of 36 subjects orienting their evaluations toward the content (Safer and Lekenthal, 1977). If the characteristics of elicited potentials are considered, then the right hemisphere is dominant in the process of recognizing a drawing. The ability of precise verbal description of the picture seems to involve the left hemisphere. The latent period of the elicited potentials in this hemisphere is markedly decreased, and their amplitude increases more than in the right hemisphere. After recognition is concluded, the asymmetry of the elicited potential disappears (Zenkov and Panov, 1976). In experiments with voluntary and involuntary memorization, the subjects were asked to distribute cards with printed words according to numbers and memorize how many words begin with the same letter and how many words had two, three, or four syllables, etc. (voluntary memory). At the end of the experiment they were asked to recall what the words were (involuntary memory). It developed that in patients with damage to the left hemisphere, predominantly voluntary memory was affected, and in those with right-hemisphere impairment, involuntary memory (Luria and Simernitskaya, 1975). The authors concluded that the right hemisphere ensures the "lower, involuntary, and subconscious forms of organization of any (including speech) psychic activity" (Luria and Simernitskaya, 1975, p. 417). Actually, even speech, if it is automatized, becomes a function of the right "nonverbal" hemisphere. It is not entirely clear why the involuntary and subconscious forms of psychic activity are defined as "lower." We know, for example, that the role of these forms in the creative activity of the brain may be exceptionally great.

Many facts indicate the predominant "emotionality" of the right hemisphere. Even Pavlov indicated the greater emotionality of concrete perceptual images in comparison with abstract concepts. The characteristics of functioning of the right hemisphere also agree with its anatomical cortico-diencephalic connections, while the left hemisphere, more than the right, is connected with activating stem formations (Dobrokhotova and Bragina, 1977). An unrecognized (tachistoscopically presented) emotionally charged word results subsequently in a one-sided activation of the right hemisphere

(Kostandov and Arzumanov, 1980). From the study of elicited potentials to neutral and emotional unrecognized words, the authors concluded that the right hemisphere plays a dominant role in the genesis of "nondistinct" emotions, the cause of which is not clear to the subject. It was noted that with emotional stress the frequency of movement of the eyeballs to the left increases, indicating the activation of the right hemisphere (Schwartz et al., 1975; Tucker et al., 1977). Emotionally charged activity of children (drawing, construction, etc.) is accompanied by a strengthening of the theta rhythm on the EEG of the right hemisphere, especially in its frontal areas (Denisova et al., 1978).

In a presentation of photographs of persons mimicking happiness, sorrow, anger, or in a peaceful state, recognition of emotions occurred more quickly if the photographs were presented in the left visual field (Suberi and McKeever, 1977). Other authors found no difference in recognition of emotions in tachistoscopic presentation of photographs of neutral, happy, and sad faces at a distance of 5° to the left or right from the fixation point (Buchtel et al., 1976). According to their data, the right hemisphere surpasses the left if the objects carry an unequivocal sign of classification. The dominance of the left hemisphere is evident in conflicting situations when it is necessary to decide into which category the classified object should be placed. A very clever experiment that disclosed the great emotionality of the right hemisphere as compared to the left was set up by Sackeim and Gur. Pictures of persons in different emotional states were made up of only the left halves and only the right halves. Most of the viewers evaluated the emotional expression as being more intense when they were presented with the left-side photographs. This indicates the expression of emotions depends to a greater degree on the right hemisphere (Sackeim and Gur, 1978).

In conclusion, we would like to consider the predominant connection of the left hemisphere with positive emotions, and the right with negative emotions. After unilateral electroconvulsive episodes occurring in the course of therapy in patients with inactivated right hemispheres, there was a shift of the left hemisphere toward negative emotions. This fact made it possible to explain a depressed state hypothetically by the predominance of the subdominant tonus of the hemisphere, and a maniacal state by a heightened dominant tonus (Deglin, 1973). Further observation showed that when the right hemisphere was switched off, the mood of the patient improved only when alpha rhythm was dominant in the left hemisphere. A good expression of alpha rhythm in the EEG of the right hemisphere also accompanies cases of worsening of mood after inactivation of the left hemisphere (Deglin and Nikolaenko, 1975). In other words, switching off one of the hemispheres does not unequivocally result in predominance of positive or negative emotions. Nevertheless there is a certain tendency here. Thus, by showing films of different content to the right and left visual fields (using a contact lens), it was established that the right hemisphere is predominantly connected with evaluating the neutral and the horrible, and the left with perceiving the pleasant and the mixed (Dimond et al., 1976). These authors believe that the right hemisphere can be considered as a substrate for subconscious motives. Patients with damage to the right half of the brain are affected differently by humor than are those with damage to the left half (Cardner et al., 1975).

With what is this nonuniform relation of the hemispheres to positive and negative emotions connected? Of course, it would be naive to think that the "centers" of positive emotions are to be found in the left hemisphere and the "centers" of negative emotions in the right. The situation is more complex than that. One of the most convincing explanations is that of Zenkov (1978). Switching off the left hemisphere renders the situation incapable of being verbalized, incapable of being understood by the subject, and, therefore, frightening, unpleasant, and emotionally negative. Switching off the right hemisphere, on the other hand, simplifies the situation, elucidates it, and this leads to positive emotions. Zenkov wrote: "Emotional effects arising with differentiated effects on the hemispheres of the brain are the result of informational processes, and not of strictly emotiogenic mechanisms" (Zenkov, 1978, p. 745). Here we must pause and establish why switching off the right hemisphere simplifies the surrounding world for the subject: obviously not because of a better understanding of the whole actual complexity of the situation, but because of a narrowing and unifying of the spheres of needs and motives, simplifying the requirements that the subject makes of the environment. A "magic transformation of the world" takes place, to use the expression of Jean Paul Sartre, but not as a result of a change in the world itself, rather because of a change in the subject perceiving that world.

Such a proposal agrees well with clinical observations that indicate that patients with damaged left hemispheres are preoccupied with their state and are anxious about it, while patients with damaged right hemispheres are unconcerned and are frivolous (Bragina and Dobrokhotova, 1977). This dissociation is expressed especially notably when the frontal lobes of the brain are unilaterally damaged on either the right or left side. When there is a defect in the medial sections of the right frontal lobe, the emotional component of recognizing his own state is disrupted and positive emotions develop that are not at all appropriate for the patient. A defect in the left lobe results in disruption of thinking, but the patient preserves the ability to evaluate his own state (Filippycheva and Faller, 1978). A paradoxical situation develops: preservation of verbal, logical thinking is combined with totally inadequate evaluation of the patient's own state. Patients, having lost the "higher" (abstract-conceptual, verbal) apparatus, conduct themselves more sensibly and appropriately than those who retain it.

The fact is that the right hemisphere, particularly its frontal sections, more than the left, is connected with the need-motivation sphere which has the initiating role in processes of goal formation. This process consists of two basic components: actualizing the need, "objectivizing" it, and aiming at the external object capable of satisfying it. The left hemisphere plays the leading role in the process of "objectivizing." Figuratively speaking, the right hemisphere is more closely tied to generating goals, and the left to their concretizing and specifying the *means* of achieving those goals. A person without a left hemisphere preserves goals, but remains without means. A low probability of achieving goals follows from this, and as a result negative emotions, confusion, anxiety, and depression develop. A person without a right hemisphere has a complement of means, clearly exceeding his narrowed and simplified goals. This results in a surplus of positive emotions, euphoria, a feeling of imaginary well-being.

Thus, an analysis of emotional consequences of damaged right and left hemispheres, first, convinces us once again of the informational nature of these emotional shifts and second, indicates the evaluation of the probability of attaining a goal (satisfying a need) as an important function of the neocortex, specifically its frontal sections.

Mekhedova (1968, 1971, 1974) developed conditioned alimentary reflexes in dogs, reinforcing the conditioned signal: 1) 5 g meat 100% of the time; 2) 50 g meat 100% of the time; and 3) 5 and 50 g of meat in random order in a 1:1 ratio. It developed that in the last series of experiments a specific average amount of saliva was produced that corresponded to the objective probability of reinforcement of the conditioned signal with food. Moreover, precisely the latter situation was accompanied by an increase in emotional stress, which was measured according to change in heartbeat frequency.

After surgical removal of the prefrontal area of the frontal sections of the cortex, the dogs lost the ability to react appropriately to the probability of food reinforcement of the conditioned signal: with random feeding of 5 and 50 g of meat, the same amount of saliva was secreted as in constant reinforcement with a larger (50 g) portion of meat (Fig. 29). At the same time, the signs of emotional stress in the transition from constant reinforcement to random reinforcement also disappeared.

The results of Mekhedova's experiments make it clear why conditioned signals have the same effect on lobectomized dogs as triggering signals (Andreev, 1969), although the probability of reinforcement of the conditioned signal is much less in comparison with the triggering signal. According to some data, the caudate nuclei, together with the frontal sections of the neocortex, participate in the process of identifying signals with a high probability of reinforcement. Bilateral disruption of the heads of caudate nuclei disrupts proper selection of the bowl where the food is placed. It is assumed that the caudate nuclei facilitate the inhibition of secondary elements of perception and, by the same token, the identification of the main element (Ungher et al., 1966). On the other hand, the significance of the evaluation of probability of reinforcement for the genesis of emotional stress is a good explanation of the difficulties that the investigator experiences in attempting to generate experimental neuroses in lobectomized dogs (Shumilina, 1950) and monkeys (Dzhalagoniya, 1972). Lobectomy makes complex situations less conflicting for animals, including making it easier for a rat to choose between an open space, ecologically aversive for rats, and the reaction of fleeing reinforced by painful stimulation of another individual. After coagulation of the frontal section of the

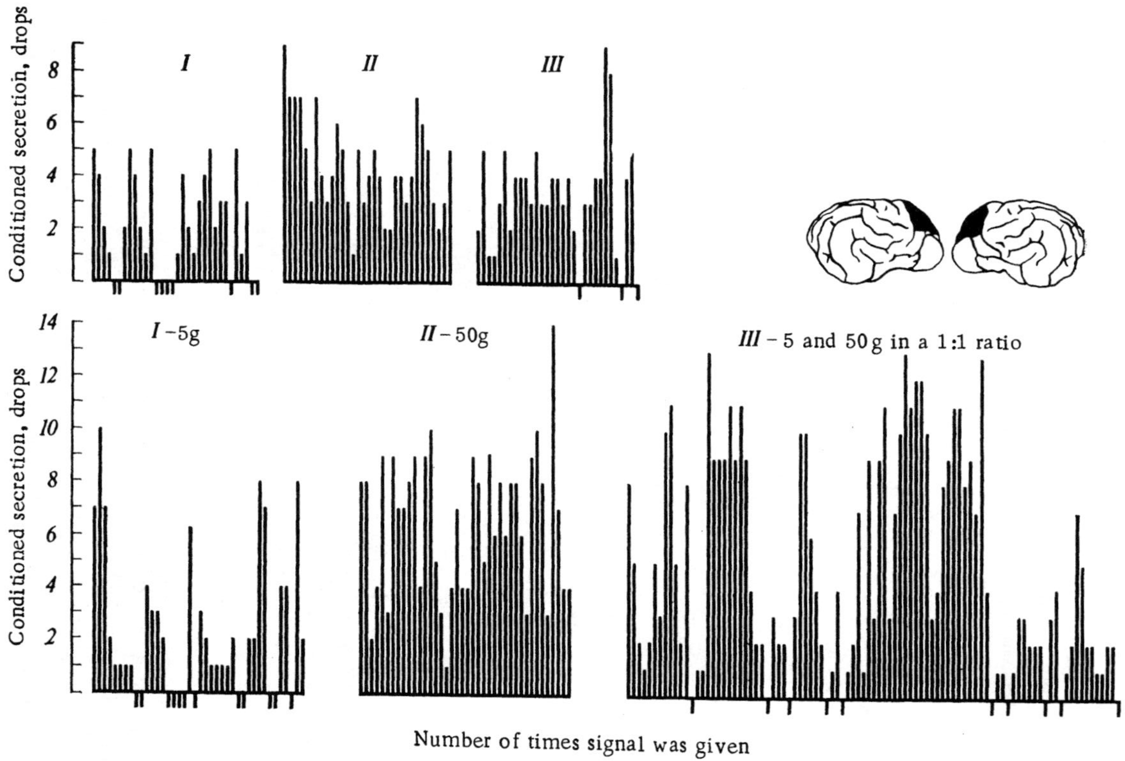

Fig. 29. Conditioned reflex secretion of saliva (drops) with constant reinforcement with 5 g meat, 50 g meat, and random reinforcement with 5 and 50 g of meat with a 0.5 probability. Above: before the operation; below: after removal of the dorsolateral sections (see diagram) of the prefrontal area of the cerebral cortex of a dog (after Mekhedova).

cortex, the reaction of fleeing did not change in only one of the nine rats. All the rest recorded a significant improvement in reaction: the time that they remained in the "house" on the pedal that switched on painful stimulation of the partner was definitely shortened. This effect did not depend on individual characteristics of the animal before the operation: it was observed in both the rats that remained on the pedal a long time and in the animals that were highly sensitive to the signals of defensive stimulation of another individual. Damage to the cingulate and entorhinal cortex in a control group of seven rats had no patterned effect on this form of behavior. Since, in the experiments of Krushinsky, the appearance of food was most probable from the side of the screen that corresponded to the direction of movement of the trough, lobectomy substantially disrupted the extrapolation activities of cats (Adrianov et al., 1978).

The function of evaluating the probability of any event is quite specific precisely to the frontal lobes: disruption of probability prediction is found only in a group of patients with damage to the frontal, and not the temporal, parietal, or occipital sections of the cerebral hemispheres (Bazhin et al., 1970). These data form a basis for assuming serious defects in the functioning of the frontal sections of the brain in schizophrenic patients. In carrying out a task of identifying emotional mimicry, these patients consider as significant signs that are considered nonessential by healthy persons because of the low probability of their being confirmed (Bespal'ko, 1976). Bespal'ko wrote: "The mechanisms of probability regulation in their very nature are evidently closer to the emotional-evaluative side of the psyche (and this is specifically the base on which conditioned reflexes are developed). At the same time, they have less effect on the formal-logical and verbal level, which evidently serves to preserve the formal constructive capabilities in schizophrenia, as Yu. F. Polyakov noted" (Bespal'ko, 1976, p. 1832).

We emphasize that, judging from the experiments of Mekhedova, the "probability defect" appears in dogs when the dorsolateral, and not the mediobasal, sections are removed. If we take into account the close connection of the mediobasal sections of the frontal cortex with the "visceral brain," with the structures of actualization of need for food, water, sex, etc., then we may hypothesize that even within the limits of the frontal neocortex there is a different participation of the brain formations in the evaluation of informational (dorsolateral sections) and motivational (basomedial sections) "components" of emotional excitation. It is interesting to compare the results of Mekhedova's experiments with Nauta's data (1964) on the fact that the dorsal part of the frontal cortex of monkeys has closer morphological connections with the hippocampus, and the ventral with the amygdala. As far as man is concerned, evidently the frontal sections of both hemispheres participate in evaluating the probability of achieving a goal; the predicting activity of the left hemisphere receives the reflection in the second signal system and becomes aware of it, and the "right hemisphere" prediction takes place at the subconscious, intuitive level and first makes itself felt in the form of an emotional reaction to the result of prediction.

Thus, the orientation of behavior to signals of highly probable events is accomplished by the frontal sections of the neocortex with a consideration of the significance of these signals and their relation to the needs that are dominant at the given moment. At the same time, there is an elimination or inhibition of reactions to signals with a low probability of reinforcement. It is obvious that it is only because of such a strategy that behavior is appropriate to reality and leads to the achievement of an adaptive effect.

In special cases, however, in situations that are not clear, when the brain does not have precise information for organizing action to satisfy an existing need, another tactic of reacting is required that also includes reactions to signals with a low probability of reinforcement. It developed that the hippocampus was the structure that was needed for reactions to signals of that kind.

PARTICIPATION OF THE HIPPOCAMPUS IN REACTIONS TO SIGNALS OF LOW-PROBABILITY EVENTS BY REGULATING THE SELECTION OF ENGRAMS WITHDRAWN FROM MEMORY AND THE PROCESS OF COMPARING THEM WITH PRESENT STIMULATION

In experiments on rats, Pigareva (1978) studied the phenomenon of conditioned reflex switching of different reflexes according to Asratyan (1938). The same triggering signal, a bell, was attached to food in the morning, and to a painful electrical stimulation in the evening. It develop-

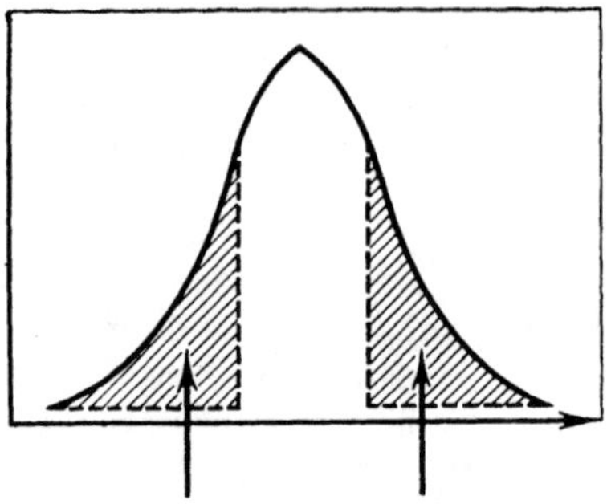

Fig. 30. Diagram of the results of hippocampectomy. Abscissa: signals; ordinate: probability of reinforcement.

ed that in hippocampectomized rats, switching was developed in 3-6 days of experimentation while intact rats could not develop switching even after 30 experiments. This paradoxical result cannot be easily explained by a simple defect of memory since the hippocampectomized rats preserved the conditioned reflex connections between the reaction and both the triggering signal and the more complex conditioned stimulus, the "switcher" (the time of day). Investigators have noted many times that disruption of the hippocampus in rats does not decrease their ability to develop new conditioned reflexes, but makes it more difficult for them to exclude secondary signals from the total flow of information (Rickert et al., 1978); at the same time, hippocampectomized rats are not inferior to control rats, and may even surpass them in distinguishing reinforced signals from nonreinforced signals (Means et al., 1970). The essence of the change in the working of the brain in Pigareva's experiments is that the behavior of a rat deprived of the hippocampus begins to be oriented only toward a highly probable event: for example, only toward obtaining food in a "feeding" apparatus. After the hippocampus is disrupted, behavior ceases to be complicated by the influence of low probability events such as painful stimulation during the morning "feeding" situation (Fig. 30).

Such a hypothesis required direct experimental confirmation. In the development of conditioned motor reflexes in rats with various probability of reinforcement with food, Pigareva established that, as distinct from the control ani-

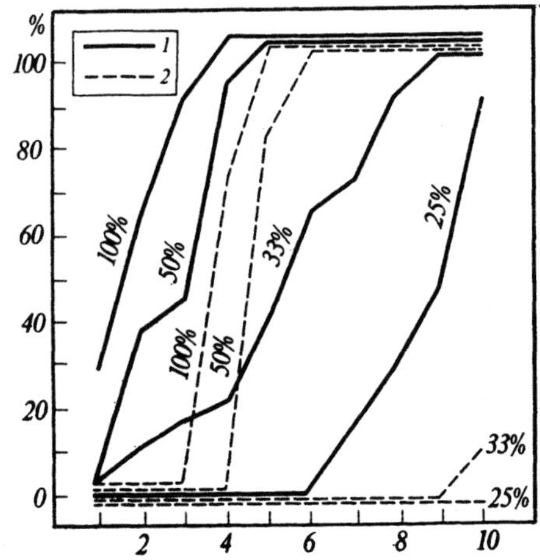

Fig. 31. Conditioned motor alimentary reactions of intact rats (1) and hippocampectomized rats (2) with various probabilities of reinforcement. Ordinate: percent of correct reactions in the experiment; abscissa: days of the experiment (after Pigareva).

mals, in the course of ten experimental days, the hippocampectomized rats were unable to develop conditioned reactions only when randomized reinforcement with food occurred in 33 and 25% of the presentations of the conditioned stimulus (Fig. 31). Indications of the special sensitivity of hippocampectomized rats to situations with a low probability of reinforcement may also be found in the literature (Kimble and Kimble, 1970; Jarrard and Becker, 1977). It becomes clear why, in the experiments of Stevens (1973), hippocampectomized rats differentiated the arm of the labyrinth with reinforcement 70 and 30% of the total number of trials more quickly than intact animals. Also clear is the fact, noted by many authors, of the predominant participation of the hippocampus in the early stage of developing conditioned reflexes when the brain had not yet accumulated enough statistical data and probability of reinforcement of a conditioned signal remained problematical (Morrell et al., 1960). According to the data of Segal and Olds (1972), in the development of a conditioned alimentary reflex, neurons of the hippocampus are the first to be involved in the process of integrating stimulation from the conditioned (sound) and reinforcing (food) stimulus.

For a long time, the hippocampus was thought to play almost the leading role in the genesis of emotional states. It was suggested that it is precisely in the hippocampus, the "heart of the limbic system," that integration of the somatic and involuntary components of emotion is completed by the addition of subjective experience. These hypotheses were not, however, confirmed by facts. Bilateral damage to the hippocampus has practically no effect on an animal's aggressiveness, on the reaction of flight when another individual is painfully stimulated, or on sexual and maternal behavior. Strong negative emotions are preserved in patients with bilateral insult to the hippocampus (DeJong et al., 1969). We believe that the results of the experiments of Pigareva and Weinstein will help to answer the question as to the role of the hippocampus in the genesis of emotional stress.

We noted earlier that the development of switching of defensive and alimentary conditioned reflexes in intact rats is accompanied by clearly expressed autonomic effects: urination, defecation, pilomotor reactions, and increased respiration rate. A neurotic state, ulceration of the skin, developed in some animals; in these animals it was impossible to develop switching of different conditioned reflexes. In hippocampectomized rats, these autonomic symptoms were absent.

For a more objective analysis of the changes in autonomic functions during the process of developing a conditioned reflex switch, a special series of experiments with electrocardiogram recording was set up with five hippocampectomized and four intact rats. In a chamber divided by a partition into two identical sections, different (alimentary and defensive) reflexes conditioned to the same sound stimulus were switched. The development of the defensive conditioned reflex (two-way escape) was followed by 10-15 trials during which the alimentary conditioned reflex was fixed (opening the cover of the trough). The switch was a flickering light turned on 1 min before the first presentation of the sound signal accompanied by painful stimulation. The flickering light was on during the whole "defensive" part of the experiment. In the first half of the experiment, ten presentations of the sound (at intervals of 1-3 min) were reinforced with food; after the flickering light was turned on, ten presentations of the sound stimulus were reinforced by an electric current (0.8-1.0 mA) administered through the wire floor if the rat did not run into the adjacent part of the chamber within 5 sec.

The electrocardiogram, motor reactions of the animal, and points at which the stimuli were applied were recorded by an automatic apparatus. For the electrocardiogram recording, several days before the experiment silver electrodes were implanted in the rats through an incision in the hip and attached to a muscle. An insulated wire attached to the electrode was passed under the skin with a probe to the head where it was fastened to the surface of the skull together with a neutral electrode.

There was no substantial difference in the general behavior and conditioned reflex activity of the intact rats and the hippocampectomized rats while the alimentary conditioned reflex was being developed. On the average, the frequency of heart contractions in the hippocampectomized rats was somewhat lower than in the intact animals; the frequency was 345 and 385 beats/min, respectively.

When the defensive reinforcement was administered to the intact rats, together with the involuntary reactions described above — intensive defecation during presentation of the sound stimulus and during the intervals between signals, urination, piloerection, and increased respiration rate — there was a significant increase in frequency of heart contractions. Averaged data reflecting the dynamics of frequency of heart contractions when a painful stimulus was administered and during motor activity are presented in Fig. 32. It is apparent that the presentation of the sound-conditioned signal in the first experiment resulted in a decrease in frequency of heart contractions in intact animals, while the flickering light, as well as the alimentary motor reaction, returned this index to the original base level. After a painful stimulation, there was at first a sharp rise, then a certain decrease in frequency of heart contractions. These data are presented more graphically in Fig. 33, where the frequency of heart contractions is expressed in percent of the base, assumed to be 100%. It is apparent that the sharp increase in this index occurs after a painful electrical stimulation (2 and 10 sec after the current is turned on).

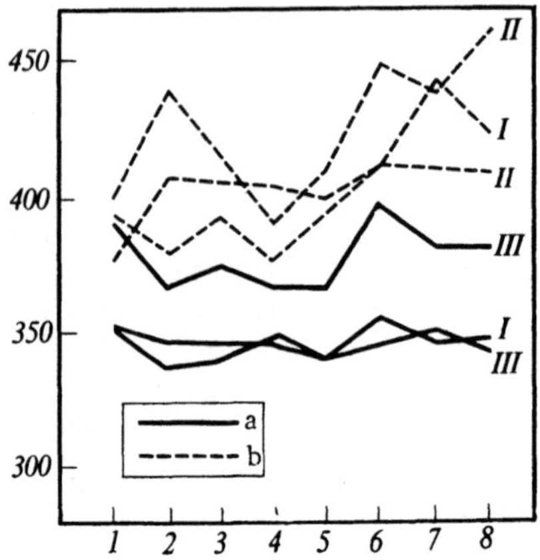

Fig. 32. Frequency of heart contractions (beats/min) in the control (a) and hippocampectomized rats (b) in experiments I, II, and III on switching. 1) Beginning of the experiment; 2) bell; 3) alimentary reaction; 4) turning off the bell; 5) flickering light; 6) bell against a background of light; 7) 2 sec after current is turned on; 8) 10 sec after current is turned on (after Weinstein and Pigareva).

The frequency of heart contractions changed insignificantly in hippocampectomized rats during the first trial in developing switching (Fig. 32). In an alimentary situation, as in intact rats, the sound signal elicited a decrease in frequency of heart contractions. Turning on the sound returned the frequency of heart contractions to the original level. Heartbeat frequency of the hippocampectomized rats also decreased when the flickering light was turned on, but when the current was turned on, and for the first 10 sec after, the frequency of heart contractions remained practically unchanged. Thus, on the first day of developing switching, the frequency of heart contractions in hippocampectomized rats did not differ from the base rate.

On the second day, in the intact rats, presentation of the conditioned sound stimulus elicited not a decrease, as in the preceding experiment, but a sharp increase in the fre-

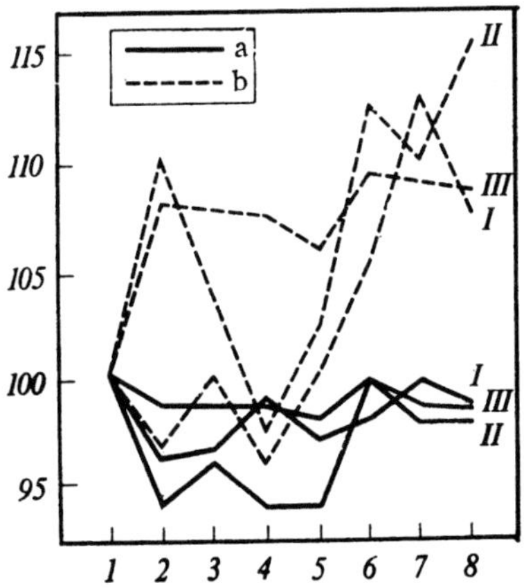

Fig. 33. Frequency of heart contractions in percent of the base, assumed to be 100% in experiments with switching. Notation as in Fig. 32 (after Weinstein and Pigareva).

quency of heart contractions (see Fig. 32). After the sound was turned off, the rate dropped rapidly to the original level. Increase in frequency of heart contractions was also observed when the sound was presented against a background of flickering light. An even greater increase in frequency occurred 2 and 10 sec after the painful stimulus was turned off.

In hippocampectomized rats, during the second trial, frequency of heart contractions also increased, particularly with the presentation of the sound stimulus against a background of flickering light, but the sharp rises and drops in the curve, characteristic for intact rats, were absent (see Fig. 32). It is interesting that, in response to the sound signal in a food situation, the hippocampectomized rats, as distinct from the intact rats, responded with a decrease in frequency of heart contractions and not a sharp increase in comparison with the base.

During the whole third experiment with the development of switching, in both the alimentary and defensive situations, tachycardia was observed in the intact animals, expressed in a greater or lesser degree depending on the stimuli used.

Other autonomic components of defensive reaction were also clearly apparent, but appropriate motor defensive reaction was absent in these rats as a rule. The frequency of heart contractions in hippocampectomized rats did not deviate appreciably from the base level (Fig. 33). During the third experiment, four of the hippocampectomized rats already recorded 100% and one recorded 90% adequate alimentary and defensive conditioned reflexes.

Now we can answer the question as to whether the hippocampus belongs to the system of brain structures that form emotional stress. The hippocampus *illegitimately belongs* to the array of emotiogenic structures if we consider it as a system of "centers" of fear, rage, and satisfaction, resembling the hypothalamus. The hippocampus *clearly belongs* to the number of structures that realize an emotional state since it ensures reactions to signals with low probability of reinforcement, that is, a form of behavior extremely characteristic for the emotionally excited brain. An animal deprived of the hippocampus simultaneously loses the marks of emotional stress and the ability to react to signals of low-probability events.

Evidently the hippocampus plays a role not only of an entry filter of information subject or not subject to registration in long-term memory (Vinogradova, 1975), but it also participates in extracting traces from memory to be used in ongoing behavior (Hirsh, 1974). If an animal without a hippocampus depends completely on present stimuli, and reacts according to the "stimulus—reaction" principle (remember the hippocampectomized rats in experiments with conditioned reflex switching), then, in the intact brain traces may be extracted from memory regardless of external stimuli and may provide for expectation of these stimuli by the mechanism of tonic conditioned feedback (Asratyan, 1974). In the latter case, excitation of the brain substrate of needs, hunger, thirst, etc., serves as a factor that activates engrams of previously perceived stimuli. The increase in number of reactions to signals of events with a low probability depends on the activity of two mechanisms: on expanding the scope of actualized traces and on decreasing the criteria for "reaching a decision" when present stimuli entering from the external environment are compared with these traces.

An electrophysiological correlate of the mechanism that quantifies the flow of engrams extracted from the memory is the theta rhythm so characteristic for electrical activity of the hippocampus. All the situations in which we observed an increase in theta rhythm, whether it was the orienting reflex, seeking behavior, organization of complex nonautomatic movements, display of traits of emotional stress, etc., had one characteristic in common: counting of cases requires active mobilization of conditioned connections developed earlier, extracting engrams preserved earlier in the memory for comparison with signals coming from outside or for "review," and recombination of traces for the purpose of constructing new adaptive actions. Preobrazhenskaya (1978) demonstrated that, in dogs, an increase in the frequency and regularity of the theta rhythm was observed in experiments with switching when: 1) the animal did not differentiate the defensive and alimentary situation with sufficient precision; 2) no mature instrumental defensive reflex was completely developed.

As a result of his systematic experiments, Oniani came to the conclusion that the theta rhythm in the hippocampus is evidence for the presence of motivational excitation that appears with the seeking of objects capable of satisfying a present need. Both of these symptoms (theta rhythm and motivated behavior) can be observed with stimulation of the lateral hypothalamus. If the stimulation of the hypothalamus does not elicit motivated behavior (for example, with stimulation of the dorsomedial nucleus), desynchronization of electrical activity is recorded in the hippocampus. Inhibition of motivated behavior (for example, with stimulation of the ventromedial nucleus) is also accompanied by desynchronization in the hippocampus (Oniani et al., 1970). The amplitude and frequency of the hippocampus theta rhythm in rats starved for 22 h rise appreciably more in comparison with the theta rhythm of rats that are subjected to a 3 h deprivation. Hungry rats actively search the environment as opposed to sated animals that move little (Ford et al., 1970).

Species characteristics of the theta rhythm by no means indicate that the theta rhythm has completely different functional significance in different species since species characteristics of the theta rhythm correlate with features of orienting-investigative behavior in representatives of any given species (Bennett et al., 1978). Several years ago, Frolov and I wrote: "The theta rhythm is especially characteristic for situations of active seeking of ways to satisfy a present need" (Simonov and Frolov, 1970, p. 154). The connection of the theta rhythm with external seeking behavior, just as with review of engrams preserved in the memory (including in the state of paradoxical sleep), is attracting the attention of more and more investigators (Arshavsky and Rotenberg, 1978).

The connection of the hippocampus theta rhythm with processes of fixation of traces in the memory and with processes of extracting these traces was disclosed in experiments of various types. At early stages of the development of a conditioned reflex (fixation of traces), the theta waves in the hippocampus anticipate the theta waves in the temporal cortex. When the conditioned connection is fixed, the theta waves of the entorhinal cortex anticipate the waves in the hippocampus, and production of traces occurs (Adey et al., 1960). In experiments with recognition of specific objects, a high degree of coherence within a narrow band of frequencies of approximately 6 Hz between the electrical activity of the hippocampus and the visual and sensorimotor cortex accompanied only correct responses (Adey, 1969). In one-time training of rats with electric shock, the degree of preservation of the conditioned reflex correlates well with the degree of expression of the hippocampus theta rhythm during the period after training (Landfield et al., 1972). Stimulation of the septum in rabbits and rats with parameters of stimulation that strengthen the theta rhythm in the hippocampus facilitated the development of the conditioned reflex and promoted its preservation (Wetzel et al., 1977; Korinevskaya, 1978). These and other similar facts serve as additional evidence in favor of the hypothesis of a connection between the theta rhythm and the mechanisms of extracting traces from the memory and comparing them with present stimuli.

There was one interesting difference in the processes of developing conditioned reflexes in intact and hippocampectomized animals (see Fig. 31). When the probability of reinforcement is on the order of 100-50%, the intact animal begins comparatively quickly to give a high percentage of conditioned reactions. In the hippocampectomized rats, during the first days of the combinations, conditioned reactions are practically absent, and then, during the next two or three experimental days, they rapidly reach the criterion of being fixed. The impression is created that, in the absence of the hippocampus, work of some kind of "reinforcement calculator" continues (evidently, the neocortex), and realizes the conditioned reactions only after accumulating statistics that reliably predict reinforcement. As far as the brain with an intact hippocampus is concerned, a comparatively small number of combinations is needed for it to "develop a hypothesis" on the sequence pattern of reinforcement after each presentation of the conditioned signal. Pribram and Douglas believe that one of the important functions of the limbic structures is the ability to "preserve a hypothesis" regardless of distraction and lack of reinforcement (Pribram et al., 1969).

All of this brings us to the important role of the hippocampus in the creative activity of the brain, the generation of hypotheses; all the more so since, in man, the hippocampus of the dominant hemisphere is involved in the analysis of verbal signals, and the hippocampus of the right hemisphere in the analysis of nonverbal signals. A similar functional asymmetry contradicts the idea of the hippocampus as being an old and, therefore, primitive formation capable only of accomplishing elementary functions.

On the other hand, being the "organ of fluctuations and doubts," the hippocampus is undoubtedly involved in the pathogenesis of neurotic illnesses. If we had the ability to temporarily and reversibly turn off the hippocampus, we would most probably have in our hands one of the most effective means of prophylaxis and treatment of neuroses.

THE HIERARCHICAL ORGANIZATION OF COEXISTING MOTIVATIONS: AN IMPORTANT FUNCTION OF THE AMYGDALA COMPLEX

If disruption of the hippocampus turns an animal into an automaton that reacts only to signals of high-probability events and ignores all other alternatives, then damage to the amygdala unequivocally orients behavior toward satisfying dominant needs without considering other motivations. According to data of Pigareva (1978), after bilateral damage to the amygdala complex, development of conditioned reflex switching in rats was possible only by combining a weak, painful stimulus with a high alimentary stimulus or by using a strong current after brief food deprivation (Table 4). These data agree well with the results of our experiments on the development of a conditioned reaction of flight from a cry of pain in rats.

TABLE 4. The Effect of Damage to the Amygdala on the Development of Conditioned Reflex Switching in Rats

Strength of current, mA	Duration of food deprivation			
	one day		three days	
	groups of rats			
	intact	operated	intact	operated
0.4	4 (0)	5 (0)	8 (2)	8 (5)
0.6	5 (2)	5 (0)	8 (4)	8 (4)
0.8	5 (3)	5 (0)	5 (5)	5 (0)
1.0	5 (4)	5 (0)	5 (3)	5 (0)
1.2	7 (5)	7 (4)	6 (4)	6 (1)
1.4	8 (3)	8 (5)	6 (3)	6 (0)

Note: The numbers indicate the number of rats in each group. Numbers in parentheses indicate number of rats that developed switching (three experiments in a row with 100% performance in both the alimentary and defensive reflexes) over a period of 60 experimental days.

After bilateral electrocoagulation of the nuclei of the amygdala complex in eleven rats, in which a conditioned flight reaction to painful stimulation of another individual had been developed earlier, the following occurred. In the first experiment after the operation, in six rats there was a decrease in the time the animal remained on the pedal that automatically turned on the painful stimulation of the paws of another rat, that is, there was an improvement in the reaction of flight. In two rats, the time they remained on the pedal increased, and in three it remained reliably unchanged.

The results of morphological studies do not allow ascribing these differences to the extent and location of damage. Much more important is the following fact: the rats in which the reaction of flight was improved after bilateral damage to the amygdala remained on the pedal a comparatively short time even before the operation, on the average from 1.40 to 2.66 min. The rats that exhibited no change in flight reaction, or deteriorated in this capacity, were on the pedal an average of 2.41 to 4.01 min. In other words, the results of the operation depended on which of the two competing motives was relatively dominant before the operation in the given animal: sensitivity to the signals

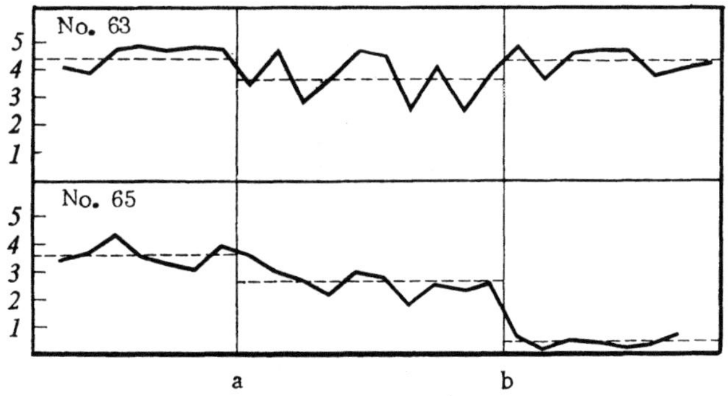

Fig. 34. Change in the flight reaction in rat No. 63 after damage to the amygdala. Ordinate: time the rat remained in the "house" (min); abscissa: subsequent trials: a) beginning of combination; b) after the operation. Dotted line, average time spent in the "house."

of defensive stimulation of the other rat or preferring the "house" with the pedal to open space (Fig. 34). Dependence of the results of amygdalectomy on individual differences of the animals was noted by Maeda Hisao. After bilateral disruption of the amygdala, the threshold of aggressive reaction with stimulation of the ventromedial nucleus of the hypothalamus increased in 12 cats, decreased in 1, and remained unchanged in 7 (Maeda Hisao, 1976).

White and Weingarten (1976) obtained similar results. Sated amygdalectomized rats exhibited greater investigative activity than the control, but feeding activity of both groups was the same. Investigative behavior of hungry amygdalectomized rats was less than that of the control, while their feeding activity exceeded that of the control. Thus, in the experiments of White and Weingarten, amygdalectomy increased behavior that was initiated by a dominant need.

It has been demonstrated many times that disruption of the amygdala weakens emotional reactions by affecting the development of conditioned reflexes only in those cases where the emotional component is particularly essential, for example in the development of the defensive reaction after a single combination (Vinnitsky and Il'yuchenok, 1973). Bilateral disruption of the basal nuclei of the amygdala depresses emotional reactions of rage in rats but does not prevent the development of conditioned defensive reflexes (Allikmets and Ditrikh, 1965). In monkeys, if the amygdala is disrupted on one side and the brain is split by cutting apart the chiasma and the commissures, the animals will exhibit aggressive behavior only if provoking stimuli are presented to the undamaged side of the brain (Mosidze and Akbardiya, 1973). Coagulation of the dorsomedial part of the amygdala eliminates aggressiveness in epilepsy patients (Saradzhishvili et al., 1977).

However, the function of the amygdala must not be reduced to a simple "modulation" of motivation and emotions in the sense of their being strengthened or inhibited. Most investigators are coming to the conclusion that the amygdala participates in the organization of behavior on the basis of past experience and takes into account the changed conditions of reinforcement. Gloor wrote: "The main defect that results from damage to the amydala can be defined as a derangement of the motivational mechanism that normally makes it possible to select behavior appropriate to a given situation" (Gloor, 1960, p. 1416). Since normal rats prefer familiar food, and amygdalectomized rats prefer new food, we might conclude that the amygdala is connected with the selection of food on the basis of experience acquired earlier. Similar views are held by Douglas and Pribram (1966), Richardson (1973), and Karli and his colleagues (Karli et al., 1972).

The conclusion that the amygdala belongs to the system of structures that determines selection of behavior may be accepted if we add that the amygdala participates in this selection by means of "weighing" competing emotions generated by competing needs. The amygdala is involved in the process of organizing behavior at comparatively late stages of this process when the actualized needs are already compared with the prospects of their being satisfied and transformed into corresponding emotional states.

The following facts are evidence that it is the emotions that are competing and not the needs (motivations) themselves. It has been demonstrated that the basolateral part of the amygdala is connected with the influence of past experience of satisfying thirst, and not with a "tissue thirst," not with the detection of water—salt balance (Rolls and Rolls, 1973). Damage to the amygdala affects reactions evoked in animals by fear, and not pain (Ursin, 1965; Reeves et al., 1977). That is why damage to the amygdala in dogs disrupts the classical conditioned defensive reflexes and does not affect the instrumental reflexes where signs of fear disappear only to the degree that the defensive conditioned reaction is fixed (Fonberg, 1965). The participation of the amygdala in emotional, and not strictly informational, evaluation of the external situation is confirmed by the fact that the transition to 50% reinforcement continues to have an effect on the process of extinction of the conditioned reflexes in amygdalectomized rats although the signs of emotional stress disappear (Henke and Maxwell, 1973; Henke, 1977). Disruption of the medial part of the amygdala in rats does not substantially affect the need for food and water, but disturbs feeding and drinking conditioned reflexes, particularly the competition between them in the case of deprivation, hunger, or thirst (Korczynski and Fonberg, 1976). All that has been said supports the view that the amygdala is a part of that brain substrate where "switching" functions of emotions are realized that orient behavior toward immediate satisfaction of overriding needs. Specialized structures of the amygdala, connected with states of hunger, thirst, fear, aggressiveness, etc., do not duplicate similar functions of the hypothalamus, but provide a hierarchical organization of these functions according to the current situation and past experience of the subject.

A view of the amygdala as a structure that organizes balance and the dynamic coexistence of motivations makes it possible to understand many experimental facts. Cherkes (1967) explained the preservation of conditioned motor reflexes reinforced by the presentation of the feeding trough and simultaneous elimination of hunting for live mice after bilateral disruption of the amygdala in cats by the differences between conditioned reflex behavior and instinctive behavior. Zagrodzka and Fonberg (1977) obtained similar results in disrupting the ventromedial section of the amygdala. But disruption of the dorsal and dorsolateral section has the opposite effect: the need for food diminishes (hypophagy), but hunting behavior is preserved (Zagrodzka and Fonberg (1978). The fact is that hunting behavior is motivated not only by hunger, but includes playful and aggressive components. This is why, depending on the location of the damage to the amygdala, we can obtain a dissociation of food-getting or aggressive, playful motives in the organization of the hunting behavior of predators.

Amygdalectomy does not simply disrupt the zoosocial behavior of the hamster, "weakening" or "disorienting" it; its effect depends on the rank of the amygdalectomized animal; aggressive reactions change in dominant individuals, and manifestations of subordination in low-rank individuals (Bunnell et al., 1970). In addition to amygdalectomy, removal of the orbital sections of the frontal cortex also has a definite effect on the zoosocial behavior of hamsters. Disruption of the hippocampus and medial frontal cortex does not have such effects (Shipley and Kolb, 1977). After the amygdalae are damaged, monkeys do not lose the ability for emotional reaction, but their threshold for these reactions is higher. As a result, the leader animals lose their rank in the colony because their aggressiveness decreases, and the subordinates change their rank because their fear of other members of the group decreases (Kling, 1972). So, once again, we see the selective effect of amygdalectomy on emotions and motives that are dominant in the given individual.

Thus, the most important function of the amygdala consists of organizing balance and hierarchy of coexisting or competing needs. Here both the present need and past experience of its being satisfied and the current situation and typological characteristics of the animal are considered. Anatomical connections between the amygdala (especially the nuclei of the basolateral group) and the orbital cortex, hypothalamus, and hippocampus correspond well with its functional purpose (Mukhina, 1973).

BEHAVIORAL FUNCTIONS OF THE HYPOTHALAMUS

Many experiments demonstrate the close connection between the functions of the hypothalamus and the amygdala. According to the data of Oniani, the effects of stimulating the amygdala must be mediated by the hypothalamus and other structures of the mesodiencephalon (Oniani et al., 1978). The amygdala has a regulating effect on the functions of the hypothalamus, and if these functions fail it compensates for the resulting defect. The structures of the neocortex participate in this compensation. Thus, in rats, after compensation for aphagy elicited by damage to the lateral hypothalamus, cortically propagating depression again elicits aphagy, which is maintained for many days after decortication. Damaging the nuclei of the amygdala itself or complete neural isolation of the amygdala complex is accompanied by less well-expressed behavioral changes than similar operations on the hypothalamus.

At present there is a sufficient basis for considering the hypothalamus as having a comparatively high level of integrative activity of the brain. It is very difficult to find structures in the hypothalamus whose stimulation does not elicit involuntary shifts with emotional reactions. Evidently there are no purely "autonomic centers" in the hypothalamus; the hypothalamus is connected with the organization of entire behavioral acts, including their autonomic components (Polyakov et al., 1978). The neurons of the hypothalamus are involved very quickly in the conditioned reflex response: activity of the neurons of the lateral hypothalamus changed in 150-200 msec after the curtain was opened for presenting food. A similar response of globus pallidus neurons was observed only after 300 msec with the appearance of the motor component, electromyogram changes connected with licking (Rolls et al., 1977). The reactions of the neurons of the lateral hypothalamus to the sight and smell of food were recorded only in hungry monkeys, and injection of glucose eliminated this effect (Burton et al., 1976). Burstlike activity of neurons of the ventromedial nucleus of the hypothalamus that appeared in hungry animals was strengthened when food entered the mouth and disappeared as the stomach was filled (Sudakov and Zhuravlev, 1979). Moreover, there are neurons in the hypothalamus that are activated by hunger and inhibited immediately after eating begins (Olds, 1977b). In experimental morphine addiction in rats, the neurons of the lateral hypothalamus were activated by a state of abstinence (need) and inhibited by morphine (reinforcement). Neurons of the medial hypothalamus, on the other hand, were activated by reinforcement and inhibited as the need was actualized. Similar data were obtained for thirst and drinking.

Many authors note the comparatively narrow specialization of the hypothalamic structures. According to the data of B. Olivier, the frontal section of the medial hypothalamus in rats controls passive-defensive reactions (Olivier, 1977). In rats, damage to the medial hypothalamus increases aggressiveness that is elicited by painful stimulation of the paws and has no effect on territorial aggressiveness, which is disturbed only when the lateral hypothalamus is disrupted (Adams, 1971). However, a few facts indicate the dependence of the results of stimulation and damage of the hypothalamus on the dominant state of the animal and on stimuli coming from the environment (Isaacson, 1978).

The effect of stimulating the hypothalamus with identical parameters of current with the same placement of the tip of the electrode depends on whether the stimulation is carried out in a feeding or defensive experimental situation, and on whether the animal is hungry or sated (Belenkov and Shalkovskaya, 1978). Stimulation in the area of the lateral hypothalamus elicits an attack reaction in a subordinate rat, but does not elicit aggressiveness with respect to a high-rank animal or a female (Koolhaas, 1978). When affected by stimulation of the hypothalamus, macaque rhesus monkeys attack predominantly subordinate males (Alexander and Perachio, 1973).

Of special interest to us are those cases where damage to the hypothalamus has an effect opposite to that of amygdalectomy. Thus, after disruption in the hypothalamus, animals stop reacting to "tissue thirst" and decrease of glucose in the blood, but continue to respond to conditioned signals of water and food (Olds, 1977a). Their previous experience acquires a recognized independence, being isolated from the present needs of the organism. Let us remember that when the amygdala was damaged, a directly opposite phenomenon was observed: for example, in rats, after disruption of the ventral section of the medial nucleus, conditioned reflexes were disrupted although the need for water and food did not undergo any particular change (Korczynski and Fonberg, 1976). We also observed this kind of result, opposite consequences of amygdalectomy, in rats in experiments with the flight reaction when another individual was painfully stimulated (Fig. 35). If amygdalectomy disrupts the balance between competing motivations and discloses the dominant motivation, then bilateral damage to the lateral hypothalamus, on the other hand, equalizes the strength of the motivations. "Getting stuck" between the pedal that turned on the current and the open space of the chamber was also characteristic for these rats.

Thus, at the level of the hypothalamus, conflict between competing motivations is unequivocally decided in favor of one of them because of the preponderance of the dominant motivation at the given moment of need. Participation of the amygdala makes this process more flexible, since emotions

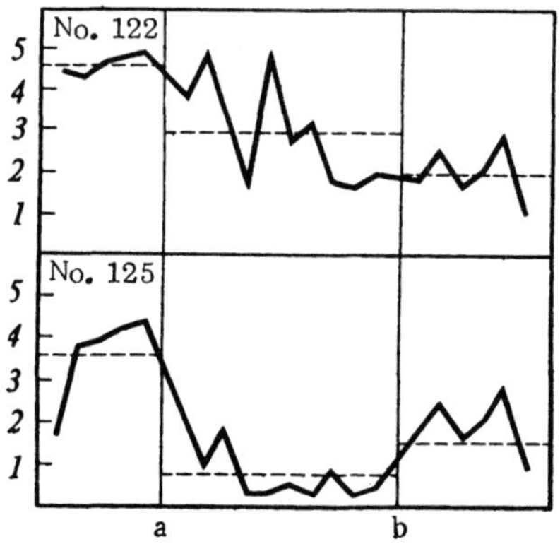

Fig. 35. Change in flight reaction in rats Nos. 122 and 125 after bilateral damage to the lateral hypothalamus. Explanation as in Fig. 34.

are involved in the conflict that depend not only on the strength of the needs, but also on the probability of their being satisfied and a consideration of past experience and the present situation. Due to the amygdala, the possibility arises of a coexistence of motives and their dynamic hierarchy. This possibility has an enormous adaptive significance: let us imagine a hungry animal that, in seeking food, suspends looking for signals of potential danger. In addition, the functioning of the amygdala is capable of complicating behavior by making the choice between competing stimuli more difficult. Like the hippocampus, the amygdala may also be called the "organ of fluctuations and doubts," not in the informational, but in the motivational sense. The hippocampus is involved in fluctuations connected with the attainability of goals, the amygdala with "weighing" their value.

INTERACTION OF BRAIN STRUCTURES ACCORDING TO THE SPATIAL ORGANIZATION OF THEIR BIOELECTRICAL POTENTIALS

Spectral correlation analysis of electrical activity of various brain formations added significantly to information on the functional organization of some forms of higher nervous activity of man and the higher animals. A very detailed study was made of the spatial relations of processes that occur in various brain structures during oriented reaction, during the development and extinction of conditioned reflexes, under natural and drug-induced sleep, and during certain mental operations carried out by healthy and ill persons (Livanov, 1972). Significantly less is known about the spatial organization of bioelectrical processes during the development of states of hunger, thirst, sexual arousal, and during behavior directed toward satisfying these biological needs.

A good model for studying motivated behavior and its electrophysiological correlates is the phenomenon of self-stimulation. However, traditional methods of self-stimulation with a rhythmic current exclude the possibility of studying the electrical activity of the stimulated structures, although stimulation of precisely these structures initiates all subsequent actions of the animal. This is why the use of a constant current for self-stimulation in animals made available for the first time essentially new possibilities for electrophysiological study of this form of motivated behavior (Pavlygina et al., 1975).

The systematic work of Rusinov (1967) and his colleagues demonstrated the advantage of constant current for producing stable dominant centers in the central nervous system. By polarizing the hypothalamic area of the brain of a rabbit, Pavlygina (1956, 1958) produced a dominant center that exhibited a definite effect on defensive conditioned reflexes and on the electrical activity of various brain formations and blood pressure. Proceeding to experiments, we found work in the literature on the polarization of emotional "centers" and the phenomenon of self-stimulation with constant current as well as data on the spatial organization of electrical activity of certain brain formations during motivated behavior of animals. Together with Pavlygina, Trush, and Mikhailova, we set up experiments on 16 white male rats. Total electrical activity of motor and visual areas of the cortex, hippocampus, olfactory bulbs, and emotionally positive and negative zones of the hypothalamus of six of the animals was recorded on a six-channel tape recorder (rats Nos. 13, 14, 15, 197, 221, and 222).

For monopolar stimulation, we used electrodes with a tip diameter of 60 μm clear of lacquer for 0.3-0.5 mm. A neutral electrode was inserted in the neck muscles. To obtain the phenomenon of self-stimulation, we stimulated structures of the medial bundle of the forebrain in the preoptical area and in the lateral hypothalamus. Emotionally negative reactions resulted when the dorsomedial area of the tegmentum was stimulated. Before positive zones were polarized, these points were tested for effectiveness with respect to self-stimulation with rhythmic current. For this purpose we used single, right-angle electrical impulses with a frequency of 1000 cps; duration of stimuli, 0.1 msec; duration of pulse burst, 0.3-0.5 sec; intensity, 240-560 μA. Polarization with small currents of 2-6 μA, which is usually used for producing dominant centers with an exposure of approximately an hour, was not practical in our experiments. We used a current of 20-100 μA and the animals were not on the pedal more than 3 min.

Ten days after the electrodes were activated, the rats were placed in a 21 × 25 × 40 cm Plexiglas box with a pedal at one wall. As a rule, during the first two or three days, a number of pedal pressings were recorded as a result of the rat's orienting—exploratory activity. Then the circuit was closed and each pressing of the pedal was accompanied by anode or cathode action of a constant current. Only those points were polarized whose reinforcement properties were preliminarily established by stimulation with a rhythmic current. If the rat did not approach the pedal for a long time, it was placed on the pedal and held there for several seconds. The effectiveness of polarization of emotionally positive zones of the hypothalamus can be judged according to the number of pressings and length of time spent on the pedal as well as by the dynamics of extinction of the self-stimulation reaction after the current is turned off. In some cases, the effect of a constant current was monitored according to avoidance of pedal pressing after polarization of emotionally negative points of "punishment."

Four-second intervals of recordings of the electrical activity of brain formations were processed on a computer. In this way, autospectra of potentials of each formation that was studied were evaluated as were cross-correlated coefficients and coherent functions between the potentials of each pair of structures studied. All spectral characteristics were evaluated in a range of 1 to 20 Hz. The methods of determining the frequency spectrum and computing the coherence function were described earlier (Trush and Korinevsky, 1978). Morphological inspection of the rat brain confirmed the location of pickup and stimulation electrodes.

The electrical activity of the motor and visual areas of the neocortex and the emotionally positive and negative zones of the hypothalamus was recorded in rats Nos. 197 and 221; according to autospectral evaluations, the frequencies of the theta and alpha ranges were, as a rule, dominant in base potentials of these structures (approximately 80% of the observations). When the rats were on the pedal and reinforcing constant current was on, in 40% of the recordings, delta waves were dominant. In approximately 50% of the cases when fluctuations of the theta and alpha ranges were most clearly expressed, the frequency of the dominant rhythm decreased by 1.5-3 Hz in comparison with the base. When the rat left the pedal, the frequency of the dominant rhythm increased by 60%, by 0.3-2 Hz, in all cases without exception.

In analyzing the evaluations of coherent functions of hypothalamic and cortical structures, it is most evident that each of the stages of behavior studied in the experiment corresponds to a specific "picture" of distribution of correlative connections (Fig. 36). This confirms the opinion of Livanov (1972) that it is precisely in the spatial organization of the biopotentials that various functional states of the brain find their reflection, as was convincingly demonstrated, for example, for the orienting reflex, for various stages of developing a conditioned reflex, and for certain inhibiting states.

The following notations are used in Table 5, which presents the results of an analysis of the evaluations of coherent functions of potentials in the brains of rats Nos. 221 and 222. Numbers indicate the percentage of cases recording a significant coherence (significance level $P < 0.05$) for frequencies of theta and alpha ranges when appropriate rhythmic components are present in the potentials of formations being compared.

Looking at Table 5, we can see that immediately before the pressing of the pedal the coherence of electrical activity of the emotionally positive point of the hypothalamus on the EEG from the motor and visual cortex and the coherence of potentials from the two cortical areas increase markedly (more than three times). Meanwhile, the correlations between the potentials of these structures and the emotionally negative zone of the hypothalamus remain substantially unchanged.

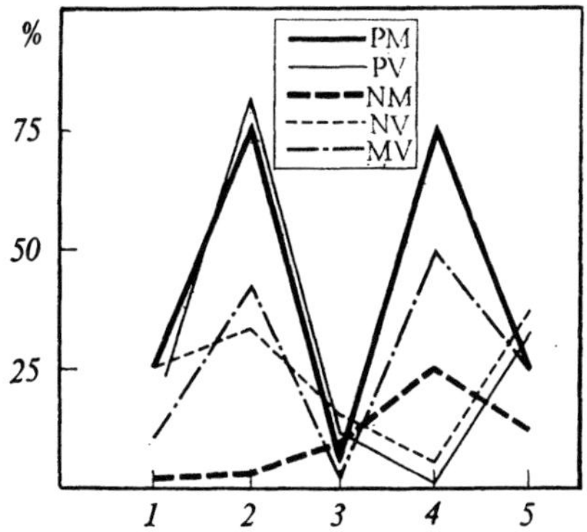

Fig. 36. Evaluations of probability of the existence of significant coherence between potentials of brain structures at various stages of behavior in carrying out the self-stimulation reaction. Ordinate: percentage of cases recording significant coherence at theta and alpha frequencies; abscissa: stages of behavior of the rats: 1) base; 2) before pressing the pedal; 3) during time on the pedal; 4) before leaving the pedal; 5) after leaving the pedal. The curves indicate behavior of coherence for potentials of various structures; P) emotionally positive point of the hypothalamus; N) emotionally negative point; M, V) motor and visual areas of the cortex, respectively (after Pavlygina et al).

We will recall that, according to Livanov (1972, p. 169): "...in the synchronicity of fluctuations of biopotentials of any cortical points, we see not the direct expression of connections between them, but only conditions that make their realization possible." In our case, the coherence evidently indicates the *readiness* to conduct stimulation along two channels: from the emotionally positive point stimulated earlier to the motor cortex and the visual analyzer that is receiving the conditioned signal of future reinforcement (the sight of the pedal, its location in the chamber, etc.). The coherence of the EEG of the motor and visual cortex also

TABLE 5. Presence of Significant Coherence between Potentials of Hypothalamic and Cortical Brain Structures at Various Stages of Behavior in the Production and Extinction of the Self-stimulation Reaction, in percent

Stages of behavior	Values recorded					
	P-N	P-M	N-M	P-V	N-V	M-V
Production of developed self-stimulation reaction						
Calm state	37	25	0	25	25	12
Immediately before pressing the pedal	45	76	0	82	37	45
During time on the pedal	62	3	3	6	12	0
Before leaving the pedal	50	75	25	0	0	50
After leaving the pedal	50	25	9	36	37	25
Extinction of self-stimulation reaction						
During time on the pedal	75	0	10	50	25	10
After leaving the pedal	87	50	0	75	42	25

Note: P) emotionally positive point of the hypothalamus; N) emotionally negative point; M, V) respectively, the motor and visual areas of the cortex.

increases by a factor of three since it is precisely the sight of the pedal that directs the movement of the animal, initiated by trace stimulation of the emotionally positive zone.

While the rat remains on the pedal, the coherence between the potentials of practically all the structures studied drops: the animal receives reinforcement through the constant current and remains completely passive. Such a drop in coherence together with the slowing of the rhythm of the potentials and strengthening of the delta activity observed at this stage make the state of the animal during self-stimulation with a constant current very similar in electrographic indices to such inhibition states as natural, narcotic, or electrosleep. An increase in coherence of emotionally positive and negative structures is characteristic for a self-stimulation situation; this may be a reflection of the gradual replacement of an emotionally positive state by an emotionally negative stimulation that makes the animal interrupt self-stimulation and leave the pedal.

Immediately before the rat leaves the pedal, the coherence of potentials of the negative point and the motor area increase first. The coherence of potentials of the motor and visual cortex increase simultaneously, as do those of the motor cortex and the positive point together with zero coherence of the electrical activity of the visual cortex and the hypothalamus. Certain features of the formation of a new program of action are reflected in this picture of the spatial organization of the bioelectrical activity. In this case, characteristic differences between the new motor task, the reaction of flight, and the task that was activated before the pedal pressing are primarily a different final goal and the stimulation of a different motivational center for initiating the motor activity. It is possible that the totality of electrographic characteristics recorded at the given stage also reflects such a feature of the state of the brain as the special struggle of two tendencies: to remain on the pedal in order to prolong the reinforcement or to leave it because the action of the constant current is becoming more and more aversive. The activation not of just the negative point of the hypothalamus (in approximately 30% of the observations there was a speeding up of the rhythm of the potentials and in not one case was there a slowing down) and the increase in the correlative dependence between the electrical activity of the negative and positive zones of the hypothalamus on the one hand and the EEG of the motor cortex on the other may be connected precisely with this.

After the rat leaves the pedal, the coherence of the potentials of practically all these structures returns to the level characteristic for the situation that preceded the beginning of the development of the self-stimulation reaction. In this case the coherence of the potentials of the negative point and the motor area of the cortex, somewhat higher than the base, may be connected with the presence of traces of an emotionally negative state.

A quite characteristic picture was observed at the first stages of extinction when the rat, pressing the pedal, did not receive reinforcement with the constant current. In this case, the coherence of the potentials of the positive point and the visual cortex increases, indicating the necessity for continuing to seek the absent reinforcement. After the rat leaves the pedal, its brain remains in a state of increased readiness for new action: the spatial organization of the bioelectrical activity is practically identical with that which was observed in the situation before the animal began to move toward the pedal. The coherence of the positive and negative points, increasing while the rat remains on the pedal and reflecting the "struggle" between the state of lack of satisfaction and the quest for future reinforcement, reaches its highest values.

Thus far we have analyzed the data that pertain to electrical activity of emotionally positive and negative zones of the hypothalamus and the motor and visual areas of the cortex. What part in motivated behavior do the structures of the hippocampus and olfactory bulbs play in carrying out motivated behavior? In rats, these structures belong to the brain substrate of investigative actions not necessarily connected with the analysis of smell stimuli. Appropriate factual material was obtained by analyzing the electrical activity recorded simultaneously from the hippocampus, emotionally positive point of the hypothalamus, olfactory bulb, and the visual area of the cortex in rats Nos. 13, 14, and 15.

Changes in the evaluations of the autospectral functions of potentials of these formations were, to a significant degree, similar at all stages to those described earlier for the electrical activity of the hypothalamus and the cortical structures in rats Nos. 197, 221, and 222. Some differences were noted only in the potentials of the olfactory bulb where the delta wave was almost always dominant. However, even here, certain speeding up and slowing down of the dominant rhythm parallel to corresponding changes in potentials of the hippocampus, hypothalamus, and cortex were noted.

The results of an analysis of evaluations of coherent functions are presented in Table 6 in the same form as data obtained in the experiments with rat No. 13. Similar results were obtained with rats Nos. 14 and 15. Table 6 is constructed on the same principle as Table 5.

Comparing the distribution of correlations between the potentials of these structures during self-stimulation and during the process of its extinction, we find the greatest difference during the period when the rat is on the pedal. During reinforcement, coherence between the potentials of all formations drops. But if the rat does not receive reinforcement with constant current while it is on the pedal,

TABLE 6. Presence of Significant Coherence between Potentials of the Hippocampus, Hypothalamus, Olfactory Bulb, and Cortex at Different Stages of Behavior in The Production and Extinction of the Self-Stimulation Reaction

Stages of behavior	Values recorded					
	H-P	H-V	H-O	O-N	O-V	P-V
Production of developed self-stimulation reaction						
Directly before pressing the pedal	80	75	88	42	80	75
During the time on the pedal	0	0	0	0	32	20
After leaving the pedal	0	20	50	60	80	90
Extinction of the self-stimulation reaction						
Directly before pressing the pedal	37	40	72	42	80	67
During the time on the pedal	0	60	50	75	88	75
After leaving the pedal	17	34	66	42	67	82

Note: H) hippocampus; P) emotionally positive point; O) olfactory bulb; V) visual area of the cortex; N) emotionally negative point.

the coherence increases, particularly between the potentials of the positive point and the olfactory bulb (almost doubling) and the hippocampus and the visual cortex (by 20%). When we analyze these data, we must consider that the observed organization of electrical activity must reflect specifically such a feature of the state of the central nervous system as the unsatisfied animal's seeking the missing reinforcement. When the rat leaves the pedal, a new system of correlations of electrical activity of these brain structures is organized. Characteristic here is the circumstance that the synchronicity of potentials of the hippocampus with the potentials of all the structures studied is higher than that observed in an animal that had obtained reinforcement with a constant current. Thus, in this situation, the hippocampus becomes one of the central formations in the system of structures whose electrical activity is connected by significant correlative dependence. Changes in the percentage of cases of significant coherence at the theta and alpha frequencies in rat No. 13 are presented in Fig. 37.

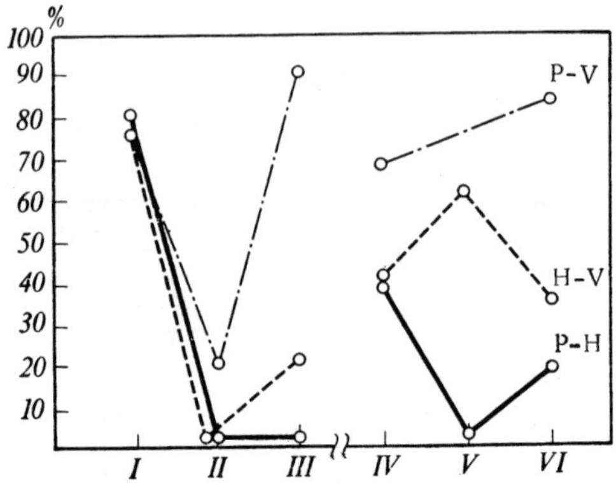

Fig. 37. Probability of the presence of a significant coherence between potentials of brain structure at various stages of behavior during the self-stimulation reaction. Ordinate: percentage of cases recording a significant coherence in the theta and alpha frequencies; abscissa: stages of behavior of the rat: I) before pressing the pedal; II) during the time on the pedal; III) after leaving the pedal; IV) before pressing the pedal in the extinction experiment; V) during the time on the pedal in the extinction experiment; VI) after leaving the pedal. Curves indicate changes in coherence for potentials of various structures: P) emotionally positive point in the hypothalamus; V) visual area of the cortex; H) hippocampus (after Pavlygina et al.).

The results of the experiment can be more easily considered if we use the diagram in Fig. 38. In this diagram, solid lines indicate a high (more than 50%) percentage of cases of significant coherence, and dotted lines represent an average (from 20-50%) percentage. A low percentage (less than 20%) is indicated by no lines. If we assume the basic postulate of Livanov's concept that "...in the interrelations of cortical-subcortical connections that form as the conditioned connection is established, we see not the ways the reflex closes, but the ways that the influences that deter-

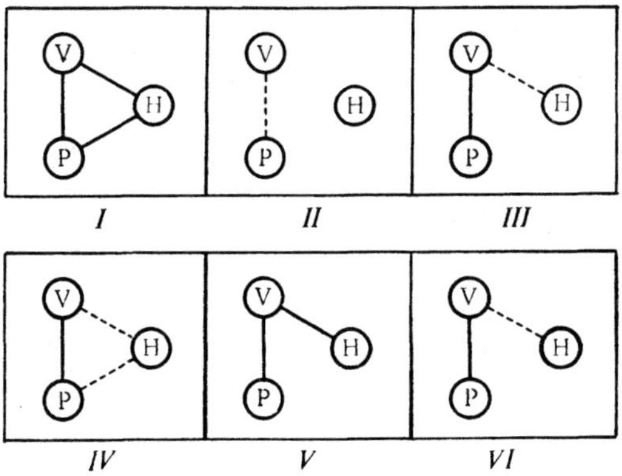

Fig. 38. Diagram of the interrelation of electrical activity of brain structures. Solid lines: percentage of cases of significant coherence, more than 50%; dotted lines: from 50 to 20%; no lines: less than 20%. Other designations as in Fig. 37.

mine the possibility of transmission of a stimulus in the cortex of the brain operate" (Livanov, 1972, p. 88), then the dynamics of the functional interrelations of the three structures we are studying becomes most interesting.

We see that at all stages of behavior the connection of emotionally positive structures of the hypothalamus with the visual cortex of the cerebral hemispheres is most stable. In this functional dependence we see the manifestation of a bilateral conditioned connection between the structures that receive the conditioned signal and the structures to which the reinforcing action is addressed. The very important significance of this kind of conditioned connections in the reflector mechanisms of motivated behavior has been studied intensively by Asratyan. Quite stable also is the interaction between the visual cortex and the hippocampus. Most interesting is the functional dependence between the hypothalamus and the hippocampus: here a high percentage of cases of significant coherence was recorded only at a single stage of behavior: directly before the rat mounts the pedal, closing the circuit. At all the other stages this percentage is below 20%.

We have not worked out the conditioned motor reflex of self-stimulation in hippocampectomized rats. As we have said above, the natural alimentary and defensive conditioned reflexes can be developed quite well after the hippocampus is disrupted. The experiment with self-polarization is important for us at this time in only one respect: it demonstrates once again the presence of behaviorally significant interactions between the motivational—emotional structures of the hypothalamus and the hippocampus. Anatomical connections between these formations were traced very well: the basic ascending path of activation of the hippocampus passes through the posterior and anterolateral hypothalamus.

THE NEED-INFORMATIONAL ORGANIZATION OF THE INTEGRATIVE ACTIVITY OF THE BRAIN

We have attempted to generalize in a diagram, presented in Fig. 39, the whole aggregate of experimental data on the role of the anterior sections of the neocortex, hippocampus, amygdala, and hypothalamus in the genesis of emotional states and, correspondingly, in the organization of goal-directed behavior. It is understood that the diagram coarsens and oversimplifies the real complexity of the interaction of brain formations. At the same time we are convinced of the productivity of just such simple plans because only simple plans can be tested experimentally.

It is difficult to find any other formation in the brain that could, with respect to its significance, be placed in the same rank as the frontal cortex, hippocampus, amygdala, and hypothalamus. Moreover, there is no room for yet another structure in the system of coordinates, "needs—probability of their being satisfied." All the other formations of the brain play an executive or auxiliary "service" role whether they are sensory systems, mechanisms for developing movement (pyramidal and extrapyramidal), or systems for regulating the level of vigilance and autonomic functions. With respect to certain sections of the brain that could have "pretensions" of participating in the organization of behavior, their functions, as a rule, have a partial character. Thus, the septum is so closely connected with the hippocampus that most investigators prefer to speak of a single septo—hippocampal system. The central gray matter is connected with the evaluation of aversive stimuli. The nonspecific thalamus serves as a place of convergence of sensory

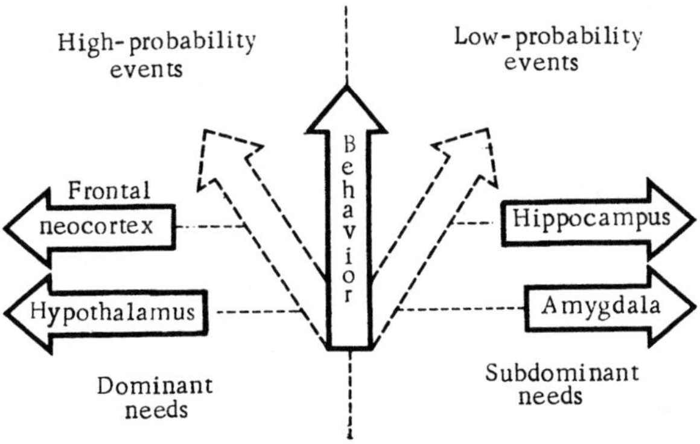

Fig. 39. Basic diagram of the participation of brain structures in the genesis of emotional states and in the organization of goal-directed behavior.

and motivational impulses (Casey and Keene, 1973), but its significance does not go beyond the limits of relay-transmission functions. In a word, we have not been able thus far to find the "fifth structure."

As far as the four sections of the brain enumerated above are concerned, analysis of individual differences in their interaction, like the variants of their damaged functioning, seems to be very alluring and worthy of further experimental development. The studies of Rusalov (1978) of the behavior of man in a reliably organized environment disclosed three basic groups of people. The representatives of the first group subjectively underestimate the frequency of recurrence of an objectively quite frequent event (strategy of probability indifference). Representatives of the second group reflect the environment adequately (strategy of probability conformity), and representatives of the third group overestimate the frequency of quite frequent events (strategy of maximizing). We may hypothesize that the basis for these types of behavior is a relative strengthening (or weakening) of the activity of the frontal sections of the cortex and hippocampus that feel the individually varying influence of the amygdala and hypothalamus. From the developmental point of view, the strong type of nervous system (according to Pavlov's classification) is characterized by a relative predominance of the "hypothalamus—frontal cortex" system while in the weak type the "amygdala—hippocampus" predominates with its symptoms of diffidence, indecisiveness, and inclination to overestimate insignificant events. Individual dominance of the "hypothalamus—amygdala" system is characteristic for introverts; in extroverts, conversely, the "frontal cortex—hippocampus" system is predominantly developed and is turned toward the external environment.

No less plausible is the disruption of the interaction of these systems in neuroses. Thus, abnormal functioning of the "hypothalamus—amygdala" system leads to the impossibility of deciding a motivational conflict in favor of one of the competing motivations. As a result, the subject cannot find an escape from the situation he is in. In a different variant of the dysfunction of the motivational system with traits of relative dominance of the hypothalamus, the dominant need is no longer adjusted to motivations coexisting with it. Involvement in this process of the frontal sections of the right (nonverbal) hemisphere, together with the dominance of social needs "for the self," gives behavior definite hysterical characteristics. The state of chronic anxiety is evidently connected with dysfunction of the hippocampus and, because of this, a very broad circle of external stimuli acquires the significance of signals of indefinite misfortune and of objectively nonexistent danger threatening the subject. Depressing the function of the "amygdala—hypothalamus" system leads to a type of depression-like melancholy and loss of desires and interest. A defect in the mechanisms of the frontal neocortex may play a large role in the genesis of persistent actions and persistent thoughts, and this may make inhibition of reactions to signals and to traces of these signals that have lost their true sense more difficult.

The phenomenology of the action of a number of narcotics and, most of all, alcohol suggests a functional involvement of the "system of doubts" (the hippocampus and amygdala). As a result, the behavior of the subject seems to be oriented toward satisfying the most immediate needs, including simplified and coarsened needs. Having lost the capacity for considering competing motives and signals pertaining to these motives, the subject disregards both: he is knee-deep in the sea. As paradoxical as it may seem, the fearlessness, intrepidity, and stupid stubbornness of an intoxicated person is a distorted model of the functioning of a will that has, in the given case, lost its individual and social values.

Thus far we have analyzed the plan of interaction of four structures, so to speak vertically and horizontally. But we must consider it diagonally as well. In light of the concept of "psychic mutagenesis" or the "theory hypothesis" of Popper, the role of generator of hypotheses should most naturally be ascribed to the "hypothalamus—hippocampus" system. A strong need stimulation, having arisen in the hypothalamus and coming to the hippocampus, can generate an improbable combination of traces and present stimuli. To the system "frontal cortex—amygdala" is left the function of selection, and here the amygdala is concerned with the selection of stimuli, taking into account past experience of their satisfaction and the actual present situation, and the frontal cortex is concerned with selection of associations that confirm validity or contradict it.

Functioning as the only integrative complex, the four structures are necessary and sufficient for organizing behavior in the system of coordinates "needs—probability of their being satisfied," for in the living organism there is nothing more important than its needs, and the external world is essential (meaningful) for the organism to the extent that it is able to satisfy those needs.

The Psychology of Emotions

The significance of the information theory of emotions for psychology is not limited to an answer to the question, "What is emotion?" or to an analysis of the reflective—evaluative and regulatory functions of emotions at the individual and populational levels. Disclosing the complex internal structure of emotions now presents a series of problems that in essence touches on almost all the basic manifestations of the higher nervous (psychic) activity of man.

Observing the infinite diversity and richness of human emotions, we cannot avoid establishing more precisely the quantity and quality of needs which give rise to one set of emotional reactions or another. Of course, besides need, emotion depends on evaluation of the probability (possibility) of its being satisfied, and this evaluation occurs consciously as well as subconsciously. This means that we cannot bypass the problem of consciousness, including subconscious forms of higher nervous activity. Further, the probability of achieving a goal (satisfying a need) depends in a decisive measure on the actions of the subject, on their effectiveness. Consequently, we cannot ignore the question of activity since it is in the process of activity that the more complex dynamics of transformation of the need arise, and new needs develop when the means of achieving the goal are converted into a relatively autonomic goal. Finally, we come unavoidably to the problem of will, so closely connected with emotions that some authors prefer to speak of a single affective-volitional sphere of the psyche and behavior. Thus, Rubinstein (1952) replaced the traditional division of psychic phenomena into intellectual, emotional, and volitional (mind, feeling, will) with two groups of intellectual and affective phenomena, considering will to be the "apical layer" of affective processes (desires, strivings).

By "splitting" emotion into separate components consisting of its genesis (need, state of preinformation, information coming at a given moment, etc.), we discovered an approach to these components and were confronted by the necessity of analyzing a series of phenomena interlinked with emotions. Essentially, emotions themselves, being secondary and derivative psychic formations, are less important and interesting than the factors that give rise to them. Very frequently emotions are only *indicators* of events that are being played out at a deeper level than emotions. In this sense, the information theory of emotions is not so much an elucidating principle as a *method* of studying the higher forms of the activity of the brain, and recording the emotional reactions, a technology of this methodological approach. We are deeply convinced that it is not speech and not action, but precisely emotions, because they are involuntary, that are the most promising and objective index of motivation of higher nervous activity in man, the "salivary gland" of the processes that are being played out in his brain.

The internal logic of the study, its "self-movement," turns the chapter on the psychology of emotions into a statement of the key problems of the total psychology of man.

CLASSIFICATION OF EMOTIONS

The variety of needs that coexist, as a rule, and comprise the complex, hierarchically organized systems, makes constructing any "complete," "detailed" classification a matter that is absolutely unthinkable and hopeless. This is why most authors try to determine a limited number of basal emotions, not being satisfied with dividing them only into positive and negative. Since the probability of satisfying needs depends to a very large measure on the subject's actions, we suggested that it is precisely the character of the actions that can serve as a classifying principle for disclosing the fundamental emotions that occupy the central position in the sphere of the emotional states of man (Simonov, 1966a). The interaction with the object that satisfies a need, in its turn, is either of the contact type, which

TABLE 7. Classification of Emotions Depending on Extent of Need, Probability of Its Being Satisfied, and Type of Action

Extent of need	Evaluation of probability of its being satisfied	Contact interaction with object	Remote action		
			Mastery, possession of object	Protection, preservation of object	Winning the struggle for object
Increasing	Exceeding prediction	Delight, satisfaction	Rapture, happiness, joy	Lack of fear, boldness, confidence	Triumph, inspiration, courage
Slight	High	Indifference	Tranquility	Weakening	Imperturbability
Increasing	Dropping	Dissatisfaction, aversion, suffering	Agitation, sadness, grief, despair	Caution, anxiety, fear, terror	Impatience, indignation, anger, rage, fury

TABLE 8. Examples of Situations and Mixed Emotional States Arising on a Base of Two Coexisting Needs

Second need	First need					
	satisfaction	aversion	joy	grief	fear	anger
Satisfaction	Summation	—	—	—	—	—
Aversion	Threshold states, satiation	Summation	—	—	—	—
Joy	Often combined	Seeing a scoundrel laid low	Summation	—	—	—
Grief	Religious "acceptance of suffering"	Need to do something in grief	A meeting before parting	Summation	—	—
Fear	Attraction, risk	The sight of a snake	A desired meeting with unknown outcome	New danger against background of recent loss	Summation	—
Anger	Vengeance	Contempt	Delight in others' misfortune, celebration	Indignation	A variety of hatred	Summation

the subject may interrupt or continue, but not avert, or of the remote type. As far as remote actions are concerned, according to military science, they exist in three basic variants: attack (surmounting), defense (protection, preservation), and retreat (loss of positions occupied earlier). Emotions corresponding to these types of interactions are presented in Table 7. In the case of simultaneous actualization of two or more needs, they may engender more complex emotional outcomes (Table 8). We must emphasize that the states and situations enumerated in Table 8 are no more than examples, quite approximate and conditional, and by no means a detailed classification of mixed emotions.

Indications of the basic significance of the emotions enumerated in Table 7 are found more and more often in current literature. For example, Strasser, the Dutch philosopher we have already mentioned, writes: "We differentiate three basic emotional tendencies: an innate desire for satisfaction and animosity toward all that may prevent satisfaction of this desire; an innate need for safety and aversion toward the causes of fear; a desire for strength and a tendency toward avoiding personal helplessness. In behavior these are characterized by the following contrasting pairs: love and hatred, an elated state and fear, and triumph and despair" (Strasser, 1970, p. 303). In their study of individual (typological) features of the emotional sphere of man, Ol'shannikova and her colleagues consider the emotions of joy, fear, and anger as basic (Borisova et al., 1976).

Besides the character of actions, the origin of basal emotions may be connected with three basic groups of needs (see below). Then fear will correspond to the biological needs of self-preservation (in the broad sense). Anger arises in a sphere of intraspecific interaction, and secondarily spreads to inanimate objects. A person may become enraged trying to overcome an obstacle of stone or trying to start a broken motor, although it is absurd to be enraged at stones or a machine. As far as positive emotions such as joy are concerned, they first arise in a child in the process of his getting to know the surrounding world (the formation of mechanisms of seeing clearly and the convergence of visual axes) and his first association with others. Satisfaction of biological needs (hunger, temperature discomfort) does not elicit any external manifestations of positive emotions in a child: he simply quiets down and goes to sleep. Emotions of satisfaction and aversion arise in contact interaction in connection with satisfying any need: we may delight in tasty food and in contemplation of a work of art, although it is understood that these delights are of very different types. Thus far it is difficult to answer the question of which factor plays a decisive role in the origin of the three fundamental emotions: the type of action or the three basic classes of needs. It is quite possible that in the process of evolution both factors played their roles: actions and the needs engendering them. We will now move on to analyzing these.

NEEDS AS A BASIS AND MOVING FORCE IN HUMAN BEHAVIOR

A refusal to consider human thought as a primary source and moving force of man's activity and recognizing needs as a determining cause of human actions represents a major conquest of Marxist philosophical thought that serves as the beginning of a genuinely scientific explanation of goal-directed behavior of people. In the words of Engels: "People have become accustomed to explaining their actions on the basis of what they thought instead of explaining them on the basis of their own needs (which are, of course, reflected in the head, recognized), and in this way as time passed, this idealistic world view arose and governed the minds, particularly since the time of the passing of the ancient world" (Marx and Engels, *Works*, 2nd edn., Vol. 20, p. 493). Later we will consider the question of how, specifically, and to what extent people recognize the needs that move them, but now it is important that we remember that "no one can do anything without doing it at the same time for the sake of some need of his and for the sake of an organ of this need" (Marx and Engels, *Works*, 2nd edn., Vol. 3, p. 245).

Although the idea of the central position of needs in the structure of human personality has long been generally accepted, the role of needs frequently seems to descend to a secondary level when we move to a concrete analysis of behavior. We still find ourselves prisoners of the traditional concept of consciousness as the superior regulator of behavior: man directed by socially valuable motives we call "intelligent," and infractions of community norms, egoism, and antisocial acts we ascribe to "lack of intelligence." There is nothing surprising in this unique "cult of intelligence." Engels, in a letter to Mering, wrote "The true moving forces that move him (the thinker, P. S.) to action remain unknown to him. He is concerned exclusively with the material of thought; to put it plainly, he believes that this material is originated by thinking and he does not, on the whole, concern himself with seeking any other source more removed and independent of thought...for him all action seems to be based, in the last analysis, on thinking because it is brought to a conclusion through the mediation of thought" (Marx and Engels, *Works*, 2nd edn., Vol. 39, p. 83). Dubinin writes: "Human behavior is determined by thinking, will, feelings, level of recognition of the laws of nature and society, and by the degree of development of self-knowledge" (Dubinin, 1972, p. 57). If for Dubinin needs were "skimmed," "assimilated" by the will, feelings, knowledge, etc., then Kudryavtsev admits the presence of determinants of behavior that coexist with needs on equal footing: "Both problem situations and life plans are, for the most part, closely connected with actual or potential needs of man, including striving to ensure their unimpeded satisfaction at a given moment or in the future...On the other hand, many plans are not connected with a specific situation. They may be independent of direct aspects of the external environment and of actual needs. Such a plan is the product of creative thinking, imagination, fantasy, etc." (Kudryavtsev, 1978, pp. 19-20).

In our opinion, there are two reasons why other sources of motivation that exist together with needs and are independent of them are recognized. First, we sometimes forget that the circumstances, values, interests, and goals of the subject are *derivatives* of needs and are generated by them (Diligensky, 1977, p. 115). Second, we still continue to undervalue the riches and diversity of needs, stubbornly reducing them to a limited number of material-biological needs for food, clothing, housing, etc. Thus, R. Eisenberger specifically considers activities "not connected with needs," for example striving to vary external stimuli (Eisenberger, 1972). Moreover, it has now been convincingly demonstrated that a need for information (for novelty, variability of the external environment) is one of the oldest independent needs of living systems. Experiments with so-called sensory deprivation in animals and man and study of the phenomena of information starvation and boredom serve as convincing confirmation of this (Berlyne, 1974). Lomov is completely correct in introducing the need for information into the very definition of a living being: "The human needs for material, energy, and information appear to be an objective necessity that, in the final analysis, determine his behavior" (Lomov, 1977, p. 53).

All the stranger is the impression made by concepts where the question of the role of needs is completely absent. "Man is activated by plans, prospects, and programs that are formed in the process of the conscious life of people; they are social in their origin and are accomplished with the very close participation at first of external and then internal speech. Every thought formulated in speech elicits a whole program of action directed toward achieving this goal" (Luria, 1978, p. 125). Assessing the genesis of active, voluntary human behavior, Luria writes: "At early stages a child submits to his mother's commands; at later stages, when the child himself is able to speak, he begins to use his own speech as a means of determining his behavior...The child begins to reproduce spoken instructions that adults gave him and, giving them to himself, submits to them and begins to carry them out" (Luria, 1977, p. 74). In this brief presentation of the essence of the "activity approach," the main point is completely incomprehensible: Why does a child "submit to an adult's commands?" *Why* does the child "begin to reproduce spoken instructions" (of course, he can also not reproduce them)? *In the name of what*, giving himself instructions, does the child "submit to them and begin to carry them out?" Of course he cannot submit and not carry them out. Moreover, from the point of view of theory, where activity *precedes* need and creates it, such questions do not arise. The impression is created that, in the study of activity and its "convoluted" interiorized form, thinking, the perspicacious warning of Vygotsky is sometimes forgotten: "Thought is not the last stage. Thought itself originates not from another thought, but from a motivating sphere of our consciousness that encompasses our inclinations and needs, our interests and incentives, our affects and emotions. Behind thought stands the affective and volitional tendency. Only it can give an answer to the last 'why' in the analysis of thought" (Vygotsky, 1956, p. 379).

Need is the selective dependence of living organisms on factors of the external environment essential for self-preservation and self-development, a source of activity of living systems, a stimulation and goal of their behavior in the surrounding world. Rubinstein wrote: "The concept of need, as opposed to the concept of instinct, will have to occupy an important place in Marxist—Leninist psychology, entering into the inventory of its basic concepts. On the basis of the concept of need, all teaching on motivation of human behavior assumes a principally different status from that which is usually ascribed to it on the basis of teaching on instincts and inclinations" (Rubinstein, 1976, p. 40). The fact is that "instinct" always assumes something innate and common to animals, while need may be as complex and socially determined as one pleases.

Sechenov, the founder of materialistic psychology, also shared the view that need was the point of origin of the organization of behavior. He wrote: "Vital needs engender desires, and these entail actions; desire will then be a motive or goal, and movement an action or means of attaining a goal...Without desire as a motive or impulse, movement would be totally senseless" (Sechenov, 1952, p. 516).

The key position of needs among any manifestations of the human psyche (thinking, volition, feelings) indisputably follows from the information theory of emotions. That is why we are convinced that the "problem of needs and motives is the central problem of psychophysiology, and perhaps even of all of the psychology of our day...Progress in the general neurophysiology of the brain ever more clearly indicates that neither physiology of the sensory system nor effector formulation of reactions can be understood without taking into account the motivational component...This problem takes on even greater subtlety and actuality in the sphere of psychophysiology and human psychology. It has become completely obvious that between the socioeconomic factors and the personality there is a layer of patterns that determine many elements in education and in the social behavior of man" (Simonov, 1970b, p. 25). It is natural that it was with great satisfaction that we came to the same conclusion that Lomov reached in analyzing the correlation of the social and biological as a methodological problem of psychology: "If we trace the developmental trends of modern psychology, then it is not difficult to see that the problem of motivation increasingly becomes its logical center... Needs belong to the category of the integral properties of man; they as if 'permeate' the whole psychic system, all levels of the psyche, encompassing its biological, its psychological, and its social characteristics...The monistic principle in understanding man must be successively realized in the study of the whole system of human needs, both material and spiritual" (Lomov, 1976, p. 93).

Admitting the key role of needs in human behavior, we still have no well-founded and generally accepted classification of them. On the other hand, discussion still continues on what is common and primordial that is realized in the diversity of personal needs. Most authors, as before, consider survival and preservation, in the broadest sense, to be the general principle, whether it be preservation of the individual, progeny, species, group, civilization, its cultural accumulations, etc. This principle has acquired a truly global significance in the system presented by Skinner (1971). He maintains that survival is the only value according to which judgment will be made, in the last analysis, of civilization and any practice that promotes survival has this value by its own definition.

Shvyrkov (1978, p. 6) wrote: "A necessary goal of *any* behavior of the organism, that is, preservation of the integrity and organization of metabolic processes" (author's italics). Of course it would be stupid and naive to reject the most important significance of the tendency toward preservation of the whole: only that which survives can develop and progress. But preservation is only a necessary condition for development, but not the essence of self-movement of a living nature that gave birth to and includes man, not the dominant tendency of this self-movement.

It is difficult for us to agree with the opinion of Lomov and Shvyrkov concerning survival as the final goal of any behavior, even that of beings living at the prehuman stages of evolution. These authors write: "The theory of a functional system is directly connected with evolutionary teaching. In the final analysis, the principal result that biological systems attain is survival. For this reason, behavior of biological systems is goal-directed, and any behavior is carried out to achieve some positive adaptive result that, in the last analysis, makes survival possible" (Lomov and Shvyrkov, 1978, p. 4). According to Sudakov, "higher motivations arise on the basis of mechanisms of lower biological motivations...in man, essentially all (?!) forms of goal-directed activities are based specifically on the need for food and satisfaction of this need" (Sudakov, 1971, pp. 272-276). How much more penetrating was Dostoevsky in his affirmation that "without a firm understanding of why he is alive, man will not consent to live and will sooner destroy himself than remain on Earth even if he has all the things he needs." Psychoneurologists know that it is precisely the loss of the sense of one's life ("why live?") that is sometimes the reason for suicide in a state of depression when all material needs are completely satisfied.

Although the ability to preserve the individual, progeny, and species represents a necessary condition of the very existence of life on our planet, it serves only as a background for the realization of the tendency toward growth, development, improving living systems, the tendency to occupy and to master the surrounding space in the sense of Vernadsky's idea. He wrote: "in the course of geological time there was evidently a process of uninterrupted expansion of the boundaries of the biosphere, its settlement by living substance...The living substance is plastic, changes, adapts to changing environment, but possibly has its own process of evolution that is manifested in the course of geological time in a change independent of the changed environment...Man met a great number of species, mostly now extinct, large and small mammals...Mammals gave him his basic food, which enabled him to reproduce rapidly and occupy large spaces. The beginning of the noosphere is connected with this struggle of man with mammals for territory" (Vernadsky, 1977, pp. 15-46). After the appearance of that which Vernadsky called the "noosphere," occupying the surrounding space took on not only a physical, but also an intellectual character: thus, science masters depths of a universe physically inaccessible to people.

Very close to the ideas of Vernadsky is the view of Ukhtomsky, according to which "the basic tendency in the development of motives is expansion in the sense of mastery of the environment in ever expanding spatial—temporal scales ("chronotope"), and not reduction as in striving to "protect" oneself from the environment, toward equilibrium with it, or discharge of internal stress" (Yaroshevsky, 1975, p. 15). We see that in Soviet science of the 20th century a theoretical direction has been formed that differs substantially from the ideas of equilibrium with the environment, a direction that reduces the attraction to and structural formulation of this equilibrium in the form of a closed "reflector circle." There are similar theoretical concepts in foreign science. Among these, in the first place, we will cite the "two-phase theory of motivation" of Schneirla, according to which strengthening of motivation (needs, strivings, inclinations) can serve as a "reward" for living beings just as weakening of an exceptionally strong need does (Schneirla, 1959). The information theory of emotions made it possible to demonstrate that the rewarding properties of increasing need are realized through the brain apparatus of positive emotions. Allport's concept of the personality as an open system is similar in the area of the psychology of the "two-phase theory of motivation" (Allport, 1955).

The complex of sciences of man, to which physiology, psychology, and sociology all belong, does not have a generally accepted classification of needs at present. Maslow (1943) differentiates seven groups of motivations: 1) physiological needs for survival (food, thirst, sleep, territory, activity, and influx of stimuli); 2) the need for safety and preservation from damage; 3) the needs for love and belonging to a group; 4) the needs of prestige (of respect, domination); 5) needs of self-realization of the personality (success, self-knowledge, self-esteem, development of creative potentials); 6) cognitive, and 7) esthetic needs.

Obukhovsky (1972) reduced this classification to four groups: 1) needs for preservation: physiological (individuals) and sexual (species); 2) cognitive need; 3) a need for emotional contact, to which all group motivations belong; 4) the need to know the meaning of life. Ackoff and Emery (1972), having made a systematic analysis of human behavior, came to the conclusion that people strive for four basic ideals, that is, toward goals that are not attainable, but contribute to progress and bring satisfaction in the process of moving toward those goals. These goals are as follows: 1) abundance (complete satisfaction of biological needs); 2) good (social need for justice); 3) truth (the need to know); 4) beauty (esthetic need). Diligensky (1976) limits himself to dividing needs into two groups: needs for the physical and social existence of people, which result from the dual nature of man as an autonomic personality and member of society. Chkhartishvili (1971) simply assumed that all human needs are derived from the universal need for activities, for exercises, for using the functional systems of the organism. For example, the need for an influx of sensory information, for novelty, is a need for perceptive activity of the organs of feeling.

Among the needs of the higher socially determined order, different authors isolate extremely various motivations. According to Erich Fromm (1960), there are five needs of this kind: 1) the need for human ties; 2) the need to extend being to infinity; 3) the need to strive toward a stable social organization; 4) the need to identify with a class, nation, religion, fashion; 5) the need for cognition. L. Garai (1966) distinguishes three needs that are mainly inseparable from biological needs for food, sex, etc.: 1) the need for personal contact, for connections with other people; 2) the need to strive for absolute truth; 3) the need for actions that have their own ends, like games.

Looking at all of these classifications, one after the other, one is struck not only by their diversity, but also by their optional character, arbitrariness, and absence of precisely stated principles of classification. One can only wonder that every author names his own number of needs: Maslow has 15, MacDougall, 18, and Murray and Peron, 20.

The theater art of "producing as practical psychology" served as an experimental model for our own analysis of the problem of needs (Ershov, 1972). Stage action represents a unique *model* of human behavior in a social setting, that "magnifying glass" of which Mayakovsky spoke. Developing our classification of needs jointly with Ershov,* we proceeded from the following basic criteria.

First, we based our thinking on Vernadsky's idea about mastering the surrounding world, which includes: 1) the physical settlement by growth and reproduction (place in the geosphere); 2) the necessity to occupy a certain position among other living beings of one's own and other species (place in the biosphere, which at the human level is a place in the sociosphere); 3) intellectual mastery of the world by acquisition of already existing cultural values and of knowledge that was not available to preceding generations (place in the noosphere). It seems entirely natural that man in his ontogenetic development repeats the evolution described by Vernadsky. A newborn has needs that provide for his physical growth and preservation. He has neither social nor ideal (cognitive) needs. Only contact with other people actualizes the innate, primary (in the sense of independent) need that promotes belonging and fear of being alone, and this social need is not derived from either the need for food or from early sexuality (Masson, 1976). The need for knowing the surrounding world is formed even later.

Second, the presence of positive and negative emotions pointed to the two basic groups of needs that underlie them: those in the first group provide for preservation of the living systems and the results of their activity, and those in the second make possible the development and perfecting of these systems as well as the increased complexity of their internal organization. Following the example of Allport and Maslow, we may call these two groups of motivations the "needs of necessity" and the "needs of growth."

Third, the dual nature of social animals and, even more so, of man as autonomic individuals and elements of organization of a higher order (family, flock, species, group, community) unavoidably assumes the presence of such motives

---

*Ershov's views are presented in greater detail in his book, *Producing as an Art of Interpretation* (in press).

of behavior as would favor the preservation and development not of individuals, but also of populations. Such motivations we will arbitrarily designate as needs "for self" and "for others."

On the basis of the principles listed, we can propose a classification of human needs that, from our point of view, is well-founded and consistent.

1. *Biological* needs and the material needs dictated by them: the need for food, clothing, housing, and technology necessary for producing material goods, for means of defense against harmful actions, for ensuring individual and species existence.

2. *Social* needs in the narrow and proper sense of the word (since all human drives are socially determined). In this case we are speaking of the need to belong to a social group (community), to occupy a specific place in the group, and enjoy attachments to and attention of other members of the group, and to be an object of their attention and love. Attempts to reduce all the diverse social needs of man to a "thirst for power" are hopelessly antiquated. The need for leadership is only one of the many varieties in this group of motivations. The need to be a "follower" sometimes hides a desire to be a leader in strength and wit.

3. *Ideal* (spiritual, cultural) needs for knowledge in the broadest sense: knowing the surrounding world and one's place in it, knowing the sense and purpose of one's existence on earth. Without a doubt, the so-called esthetic need belongs to this group.

The parameter of "eliminating goals," according to Ershov ("personal prospects" according to Makarenko) serves as an important objective index of the belonging of a need to one of the three groups. Satisfaction of material—biological needs (hunger, for example) cannot be postponed for any very long period. Satisfaction of social needs is limited by the duration of human life. Achieving ideal goals may be relegated even to the more distant future.

We find a very similar (if not identical) division of needs in Hegel.

In his *Esthetics*, Hegel writes: "Surveying the whole content of our human existence, even in our everyday consciousness we find a great diversity of interests and their satisfaction. We find an extensive system of physical needs, and for satisfying them a very large and ramified network of industrial undertakings, commerce, navigation, and technical crafts. Above this system of needs we find the world of law, rules, life in the family, separation of the estates, the all-encompassing area of government; then we have the religious need that we find in every soul, and this finds its satisfaction in the life of the church. Finally, we come to the infinitely specialized and complex activity that consists of science, the accumulation of knowledge and cognition that encompasses everything that exists" (Hegel, 1968, pp. 102-103).

Besides the biological, social, and ideal (cognitive) needs, Hegel also names the "religious" need. From our point of view this need cannot be given the same ranks as the first three. Religion represents a clear case of *setting standards* for the satisfaction of all other needs: the biological (for example, regulation of family—marriage relations, ritual fasting, prohibition of alcohol for peoples especially sensitive to its effects, as the latest biochemical discoveries have shown, etc.), social ("to God what is God's, to Caesar what is Caesar's"), and cognitive. The norm for satisfying cognitive needs is regulated by religion especially strictly since all science is constructed on a consciousness of justice and all of the knowledge of the world and man that is available at a given moment. From this is derived the thousand-year conflict between religion, which preserves the historically passing norms, and science (and art to the same extent) which supersedes these norms.

Dostoevsky, who is, according to Stefan Tsveig, a "psychologist among psychologists," not only noted three basic groups of human needs, but he based this on a recognition of their great plurality, independence, and irreducibility to any single ultimate source.

In *Brothers Karamazov*, Dostoevsky indicates three fundamental needs (or three groups of needs) that people have and that determine their behavior in the natural and social environment. He begins with "bread" as a collective concept that includes the aggregate of material goods necessary for maintaining life. Dostoevsky fully recognizes the role that "bread" plays and clearly describes how much people are forced to give up to satisfy their material needs. He recognizes the force and persuasiveness of that point of view that with a voice of "wisdom and knowledge," proclaims that "there is no crime, and therefore, there is no sin either, there are only the hungry." "Feed them, and then ask them to be virtuous."

But granting the due power of hunger not only over the body, but also over the spirits of people, Dostoevsky denies that the two other basic human drives are secondary to or derived from the need for bread. And the first of these drives is the need to know, "for the secret of human existence is not only to live, but to live for something."

"To live in worldwide union is the third and last torment of man. Humanity as a whole has always without fail tried to settle worldwide." Even knowledge, most of all knowing the sense and purposes of life, does not satisfy a man if he is the only bearer of the discovered truth. Man needs a community of ideals and he is more ready to accept "a miracle, secret, and authority" that is completely unsupported than to remain in a state of tormenting dissatisfaction and to bring on himself "the terrible time of freedom of choice."

The "triad of needs" can be found in the statements of many thinkers, social activists, and poets.

In the *Declaration of Independence*, Thomas Jefferson wrote: "We hold these truths to be self-evident, that all men are created equal, that they are endowed by their Creator with certain unalienable Rights, that among these are Life, Liberty and the Pursuit of Happiness." The right to life is ensured by satisfying biological needs, freedom is a concentrated symbol of the social ideal, and pursuit of happiness assumes the seeking of the fullest self-realization of the personality.

The three motifs of the "triad" with which we are already familiar, modified by the dominance of the tendency toward "growth" and "for others," also come through in Bertrand Russell's statement that three passions, simple, but exceptionally strong, directed his life: a thirst for love and knowledge and an unbearable pity for the sufferings of mankind.

The fact is that all three groups of needs named above (biological, social, and ideal) in their turn form two variants, one of which may be called the "needs of necessities" and the second the "needs for growth." These two variants of needs depend on the dialectics of preservation and development that is part of the process of self-movement of living nature, including man and society. Satisfying the need of necessities means preserving and maintaining the constants genetically given or achieved earlier in ontogenesis. Hunger may serve as an example of need in the sphere of biological needs. In the area of satisfying social needs, the need is to preserve an occupied position; growth is improving that position. Mastering already available information satisfies the need to know. The need for growth relative to cognitive activity stimulated a seeking of the wholly new that is not yet a part of modern science.

The presence of the needs for necessities, for growth, preservation, and development explains the fact, observed daily, that satisfaction of needs in some cases reduces or weakens the need and, in other cases, induces or strengthens it (Magun, 1978). Earlier (Simonov, 1970a) we presented a system of proofs to support the statement that, in the process of evolution, the tendency for preservation and development led to the formation of two basic variants of emotion, the negative and the positive.

In a letter to Lavrov, Engels noted the relationship of positive emotions and tendencies toward development; he wrote that, owing to industry, "it became possible, as you properly note, for 'man to struggle not only for existence, but for joy; and *for an increase in his joy*, he would be ready to renounce lesser joys for a greater joy...' If we accept this category for the present, the struggle for existence then turns into a struggle for joy, into a struggle not for only one means of existence, but also for the means of *development*, for *socially* produced means of development, and categories from the animal kingdom cannot be admitted to this rank" (Marx and Engels, *Works*, 2d edn., Vol. 34, p. 137).

The principal difference between positive and negative emotions is apparent in the satisfaction of even comparatively elementary needs, for example the need for food. Dire hunger, endured by the subject as a negative emotion, stimulates the subject to satisfy it with any edible substances if only to save himself from an agonizing state. Satisfaction obtained from food necessarily requires variety, a seeking of new edible substances, new combinations and methods of preparation. In other words, even at the level of need for food, positive emotions play a creative-seeking role and assist in the mastery of new spheres of the surrounding reality.

In the area of sexual behavior, the significance of positive emotions is even greater, and the significance of negative emotions decreases. No matter how distressing sexual abstinence might be, as distinct from hunger, as they say, "nobody has died of it." An analysis of suicide in cases of unrequited love shows that man is driven to this desperate step not by sexual deprivation, but by social dissatisfaction, and specifically of his ideal needs. The source of the tragedy of unfortunate love lies in higher human motivations: betrayed trust, crushing of vital ideals, loss of the sense of life. A study of depressed states of psychogenic (not organic) origin shows that it is not the difficulties of life or social lack of success that lead to depression. Whatever would appear to be the direct cause of depression, betrayal by a loved person, loss of a job, etc., it is not the parting in itself, not the loss of a career in itself, that forms the depressed state, but the injustice of what has happened, the outrage over vital ideals of the given personality and their loss of value. Negative emotions arising on a base of unsatisfied social needs are, as a rule, sthenic and aggressive. In his social lack of success, a man is inclined to blame others, the intrigues of those who wish him ill, the circumstances that prevail. Depression does not threaten him.

Finally, at the apex of the hierarchic pyramid of needs, we find motivations that are fostered almost exclusively by positive emotions. Such is the need to know and its diversity; it is difficult to formulate in words the need to create and to perceive works of art, the so-called esthetic need. As distinct from hunger and thirst, sex, the need to occupy a definite place in a group, etc., neither scientific theoretical cognition nor art has any intrabrain apparatus of punishment. Their fascination is ensured only by the joy that comprehension of the truth carries, only by that high enjoyment that man seeks in coming in contact with beauty.

Creation is always colored with positive emotions at the stage of the appearance of a hypothesis. The mechanism of this pattern can be explained very well by the information theory of emotions. Of course, a new conjecture, hypothesis, or project subjectively increases the probability of attaining a goal right up to the moment when logical or experimental confirmation determines their true value. "The pain of creation" is characteristic of the stage of seeking and selecting that is so often concluded with complete disappointment.

The folk perspicacity in the well-known saying that "wanting to is better than needing to" has always recognized the greater driving force of the need to grow in comparison to the need of necessities. Like all other needs, necessity and growth differ in different individuals. Evidently, it is precisely the relative predominance of one of these needs that leads to the fact that in a study of the so-called level of claims, subjects can be divided into two groups: those who strive for success and those who mainly avoid failure.

The *pre-eminent* connection of the need for growth with positive emotions, and the need for necessities with negative emotions does not negate the secondary spreading of these emotions to contiguous groups of motives. Both positive and negative emotions take on specific traits, depending on the character of the need. Chronic negative emotion that arises when the need for necessities is not satisfied has the quality of anxiety, and when the needs for growth are not satisfied, it has the quality of frustration. Anxiety combined with a refusal to act is typical of neurosis (Rotenberg, 1975). Two forms of depression occur: melancholy or anxiety, depending on whether it is the need for growth or for necessities that is not satisfied.

The third and last parameter for classifying needs is their division into groups "for the self" and "for others." An example of biological need for others may be the parental instinct that inspires the saving of progeny at the risk of one's own life. The need for others is particularly characteristic of social motivations. In essence, conscience is nothing other than the socially determined norm for satisfying the need "for others" that is innate in any person. Ideal (cognitive) needs cannot be divided in this way since no subjective truths "for self" and "for others" exist. It is a different matter that the process of exploiting the results of cognition involves the material and social needs in all their diversity and contradiction. The dominance of ideal (cognitively creative) needs in the structure of a given personality is qualified by certain investigators as its predominant orientation "for the work" as distinct from for self and for others (Bozhovich, 1970; Gershuni, 1971). Moreover, orientation "for the work" may be dictated by a need for equipment (facts, habits, etc.) about which we will speak later.

For a proper understanding of the patterns of human behavior, it is important to remember that, although all of the enumerated needs are closely connected with each other and seldom appear in an isolated, pure form, they are not, in essence, derived from each other and do not replace each other. Any degree of satisfaction of one type of need does not save a person from having to satisfy a need of a different type: this is the source, specifically, for the so-called amoral quality of the association of need.

There is no person who would be indifferent to the opinion others have of him. Levi, in one of his books, quotes the words of Pascal: "No matter what a man possesses in the world, excellent health, any good things of life, he is, nevertheless, not satisfied if he is not respected by people...Having all possible riches, he does not feel satisfied if he does not occupy an advantageous place in their minds...Nothing can divert him from this goal...Even those that are despised by humanity, that treat people like cattle, even they want people to admire them and to believe them..." (Levi, 1973, p. 250).

The same is true of the need "for others," ineradicable even in those with a nature that would seem to be completely closed in egoistic solitude. Thus, in Bulgakov's novel, *The Master and Margarita*, Pilot feels an attachment to his dog. In the same way, the deaf and constantly solitary Gerasim worries about Mumu (the dog, in "Mumu," a short story by Ivan Turgenev; translator's note).

It is important to consider the original independence of needs and the fact that they are not interchangeable, in developing scientific bases for education and measures for combatting antisocial behavior. According to Kudryavtsev (1974), only 3.7% of thefts committed by youth were connected with material want in the family. In many cases, aggression in youth is completely free of profitable goals and represents the result of a deformed need for self-affirmation in a group hierarchy. Spiritual hunger, the lack of satisfaction of the need of a diverse, intelligent life, rich in impressions, draws a youth to vodka, which swiftly simplifies the sphere of needs of the subject: any co-drinker is a friend, any woman is desirable, any stranger is an object of aggression. As a result, 80% of homicides and 90% of incidents of vandalism are committed by youths who are intoxicated.

Kapitsa was completely justified in thinking that the growth of moral and intellectual qualities of the population may be qualitatively determined according to the decrease in the number of crimes, neural disorders, and cases of drug addiction just as improvement in a healthful form of living may be evaluated according to longevity, and improvement in the material state according to gross national product per inhabitant. It is specifically the first evaluation that we must consider as the most important, since it determines the fate of a given social structure (Kapitsa, 1977).

A concrete complement of needs, their hierarchy, the dominant position of some drives, and the auxiliary role of others, forms the "nucleus" of a personality, its most essential characteristics. Although any person has all the groups of needs, although people belonging to the same epoch, the same socioeconomic formation, class, nationality, have a similar historically determined structure of needs, their individual composition is unique and, to a major extent, determines the unique personality. Their other traits, specific abilities, temperament, belonging to the so-called "intellectual" or "artistic" type, have an important, but secondary significance. Tolstoy said, "The best person is the one who lives predominantly by his own thoughts and by the feelings of others; the poorest kind of person is the one who lives by the thoughts of others and by his own feelings...All the different people are made up of various combinations of these four bases, the motives for action" (cited by Markusha, 1979, p. 66). If we translate this classification into the language of needs, then the best person would be the one with a dominance of the tendency "for others," in the sphere of biological and social needs in combination with a need to know that is free of extraneous influences. The poorest would be one who is egoistically oriented toward himself, whose judgments are not subjected to objective truth, but are borrowed and are useful and convenient for his own views.

The development of personality is most of all and mainly the enrichment and "exaltation" (Lenin) of the needs of a given person, the readiness "for a higher satisfaction having renounced lower satisfactions," in keeping with Lenin's "law of elevating needs" (Lenin, *Complete Works*, Vol. 1, pp. 101-102). A clear illustration of this law may be the admission of Aleksei Stakhanov, quoted in a paper by Stoletov: "'What was I trying to achieve in life?' is the question posed by Stakhanov, the founder of the Stakhanov movement, and the answer: a) in the initial phases, to be sated; b) later, to earn a good income; c) to get 'human respect'; d) with the development of class consciousness, a desire to prove that without you, the mine, the whole collective, could not get along; e) finally, an understanding of the 'necessity to be better and greater than myself'" (Stoletov, 1976, p. 3). As distinct from the preservation criteria of "survival" about which Skinner wrote, for Marxism "...the higher cultural and moral values are those that promote the development of society and the development of all aspects of the personality to the greatest degree" (Fedoseev, 1973, p. 36).

Of all the human needs, cognition and creativity most harmoniously unite the personal and the social, "skimming off" dialectically the dilemma of "for onself" and "for others," since for them no such division exists. Any human activity is all the more free of the necessity of "combining the personal and the social," the more it expresses its creative—cognitive source. It is absurd to foster the "need for work" without relating it to its motives: even a money grubber works at his own trade. Only work as a creative activity, as an expression of the essential human strengths, brings joy and satisfaction before it is finished. But creativity is possible only when the subject attains a certain level of *skill*.

Only skilled activity is capable of becoming action for others (remember what Tolstoy and Dostoevsky said about active love and contemplative love). An experienced physician who is an egoist is more useful to those around him than a flaming altruist who, by reason of his professional incompetence, sends a patient off to the next world. That is why skill in any area most reliably leads to a harmonious satisfying of the whole complex of needs, ensuring material recompense, social prestige, love of neighbor, and satisfaction with the process itself of realizing one's own capabilities and skills.

It is this difficulty in detecting the underlying motives of behavior that gave rise to the belief in the presence of some kind of super-regulators that control needs, although they do not always cope with them. The need for such regulators is dictated also by the switching function of emotions. Since emotions depend not only on needs, but also on the probability of their being satisfied, there is always the threat of chronic reorientation of behavior to less significant, but more easily attained, goals. This is all the more reason for the existence of a regulator for controlling behavior and determining the sequence and permissibility of satisfying one need or another.

Traditionally, the will and consciousness have been regarded as such regulators. Later we will try to demonstrate that the will does not control needs, but joining any one of them, cooperates in their being satisfied. As far as consciousness is concerned, it is occupied by providing the means and methods for the satisfaction of the needs. Thus, both will and consciousness are the result of a transformation of needs, a stage in their further development. In the case of antisocial behavior of a subject, an underestimation of this circumstance leads to persistent attempts to appeal to his "intelligence," which has not succeeded for any reformer—utopian and, in everyday life, vitiates the effectiveness of pedagogical practice. At any level of higher nervous activity of man, a need can be opposed only by another need.

THE PSYCHOLOGY OF THE WILL

The concept of the will as a phenomenon opposed to needs and acting on them with greatest arbitrariness was put forward by Chkhartishvili: "Voluntary behavior owes its name to the circumstance that it is not any kind of need, but the personality itself, as a subject of will, that gives it primacy and controls it over its entire extent...These two phenomena, need and will, therefore occupy completely different places in the psychological structure of the personality" (Chkhartishvili, 1967, pp. 72-81). Bakanov (1977) holds similar views, believing that will is the subject's subordinating his drives to the logic of objective necessity as he perceives it, and making the drives and objective necessity coincide (within limits). Consciousness, evidently, reflects the logic of objective necessity. This means that the es-

The human being is marked by the "limitlessness of his needs and their potential for expansion" (Marx, *Archives of Marx and Engels*, Vol. 2(7), Moscow, 1935, p. 235). The insatiability of needs is a condition of development, of mastering new spheres of activity, seeking new, earlier unknown means and methods of satisfaction. Insatiability of needs indisputably requires *norms* of satisfaction that are social and historically variable by nature. "The dimension of so-called indispensable needs as well as the means of their satisfaction are in themselves a product of history" (Marx and Engels, *Works*, 2nd edn., Vol. 23, p. 182). Not only biological and social needs, but also cognitive needs, are regulated. Each historical epoch, each social formation or class is characterized by its own code of norms: customs, laws, morals, ideologies. The development and formulation of norms is a most important function of individual and social consciousness.

The totality of norms of a given social community or epoch forms its *culture*. We consider a person cultured if his behavior corresponds closely to these norms. Since norms differ, ideas of culture also differ: for example, a highly cultured European who is poorly acquainted with the behavior accepted among the Japanese may be seen by them as a person of little culture.

Direct motives for crimes are, as a rule, obvious. The primary, original drives are difficult to discover; for the most part, they are deeply hidden from both the outsider and from the subject himself. For example, a woman goes to buy a coat. It is perfectly clear that she needs the coat. She will be happy if she buys it, and disappointed if she does not find a coat that suits her (a good illustration of the "objectivization of emotions"). But the "need of a coat" is the result of a whole complex of needs: biological, social—prestige, esthetic. In the given case, which of these played the deciding role, decided the time of purchase and selection of the object? Even the woman buying the coat cannot always answer this question.

Many examples might be given of a person who, while believing sincerely that he is acting for others, is satisfying his own exclusively egoistic need. It happens conversely that one who firmly believes in following his personal goals is actually moved by a need for others.

Marx emphasized: "Various internal needs are connected with each other into a single natural system..." (Marx and Engels, *Works*, 2nd edn., Vol. 23, p. 368). The close connection between needs results especially in the fact that the same means may serve to satisfy many needs. Means (knowledge, skills, equipment, material resources) obtained for satisfying one need can, as a rule, be useful for satisfying other needs also. From this follows the universal *need to be equipped.* A clear example of the existence of such a need and its relative independence is game behavior in its broadest sense.

The autonomy of game motivation is borne out, for example, by the fact that the playful struggle of young animals does not contain competitive elements and is free of symptoms of aggressive behavior (Lorenz, 1967). Like other needs, it is reinforced under conditions of deprivation: golden hamsters isolated from each other on alternate days double the duration of their playful behavior when they meet (Slonim, 1976). The goal and, therefore, also the determining mark of any game is to improve the player and not to achieve a goal that is external with respect to the subject. Thus, because of games, children acquire habits which they will need only in the future.

The need for being equipped reaches its highest and most complex transformations in an adult. Accumulation of knowledge and skills or, let us say, money, as the universal means of satisfying biological and social needs may acquire an independent meaning as happened, for example, in the case of the miserly knight in Pushkin's tragedy.

The need for equipment is supplemented and adjusted by the *need for economy of forces.* If one and the same goal can be achieved by different actions, those actions that require the least expenditure of energy resources are preferred. The transformations of this need are exceptionally diverse: from ordinary laziness to the complete professionalism of the virtuoso. It is no joke that most inventions are produced by laziness, the desire to simplify work and make it easier. We must only recall that the striving for economy of energy must in no case be made absolute since it is only one homeostatic side of human activity that coexists with the insatiability and expansion of other human needs.

sence of will, according to Bakanov, lies in subordinating the drives of the subject to his consciousness. Consciousness, needs (drives), and will function as independent and sometimes conflicting forces.

Sechenov holds other views. Rejecting "free will" not determined by innate endowments and rearing conditions, Sechenov did not deny, however, either the activity of human behavior nor the presence of will as a real and specific mechanism of brain activity. Moreover, he emphasized that the "teaching on the lack of freedom of the will" that he developed has a most important practical significance: it provides a theoretical basis for the possibility of a controlling effect on the process of forming the human personality in a direction desirable for society. "The external side of actions with which society defends itself against depraved members," wrote Sechenov, "consequently remains unchanged, whether a man is admitted to have free will or not. Only the sense of these actions is changed in the respect that, instead of retribution, it becomes correction" (Sechenov, 1952, p. 443).

According to Sechenov, "...neither everyday life nor the history of nations present even one case where one cold, impersonal will could accomplish any kind of moral feat. Together with it, *there is always, determining it,* some moral motive in the form of either a passionate thought or feeling...(Will) alone, in itself, cannot act, but it acts only in the name of reason or feeling..." (Sechenov, 1952, p. 260). Stanislavsky maintained: "Will is powerless until it is inspired by passionate desires" (1957, p. 290).

Admitting the dependence of the will on the motive that determines it at once poses the question: which of the coexisting needs, or competing needs, will the mechanism of the will cooperate to satisfy? Sechenov responded to this question in the following way: "...the role of free will is transferred as a whole to a drive that overpowers all else" (Sechenov, 1952, p. 436). Such a formulation, however, requires further refinement of the idea included in the concept of the "drive that overpowers all else." It is impossible to consider the will as dominant at any given moment of need. A smoker who has decided to give up smoking, who nevertheless goes out to buy cigarettes, or a gambler, in defiance of all arguments of reason, making his way to the card table, are obeying needs that are stronger than anything else. Nevertheless, these examples can serve to illustrate the extreme lack of will, regardless of the fact that both subjects are completely aware of both the reason for their actions and their possible consequences. Consequently, will is not simply a controlling need, but a certain special mechanism complementary to one of the competing motivations that cooperates in transforming it into actuality, into an action.

We assume that the phylogenetic prerequisite for voluntary behavior is the "reflex of freedom" described by Pavlov. In the resistance of a dog to attempts to limit its motor activity, Pavlov saw incomparably more than diversity of defensive reaction. The "reflex of freedom" is an independent form of behavior for which an obstacle serves as no less adequate a stimulus than food for food-getting actions or pain for defensive reactions, and a new and unexpected stimulus for orienting reaction. "But for it (the reflex of freedom)," wrote Pavlov, "any smallest obstacle which the animal might meet on its way would completely interrupt the course of its life" (Pavlov, 1951, p. 343).

This idea of Pavlov's was developed in the concept of a "stimulus—barrier situation" worked out by V. P. Protopopov (1935, 1950). He demonstrated experimentally that the "reaction of surmounting" that arises in the presence of a barrier and is complementary to a need that primarily initiates behavior (food, sex, etc.), plays a most important role in the formation of adaptive actions. Meeting with an obstacle on the way to food, an animal begins to use not those variants of action that led earlier to food reinforcement, but methods of surmounting similar obstacles that were preserved in the memory. It is precisely the character of the barrier, and not the primary motive, that determines the composition of the action selected in the process of organizing behavior capable of ensuring the attainment of a goal.

At the human level, interrelations between the reaction to a barrier and the primary motive become exceptionally complex. The activity elicited by the barrier in certain cases may force the initial stimulus back to second place, and then we will meet with obstinacy, with behavior where surmounting has become a goal in itself and the original motive has lost its significance or has even been forgotten.

For man, an obstacle need not necessarily be an external barrier. The barrier may be a competing need. Then the dominance of one of the competing motives will be determined not only by their relative strength, but also by the development of activity with respect to which the subdominant motive is the barrier, the "internal interference." We see similar situations in almost all cases where we speak of "voluntary suppression" of emotions or, more precisely, of the needs that cause the emotions. We must remember that the qualities of the will of a subject have no positive significance in themselves, and like other psychological properties depend to a decisive degree on the social value of the primary drive.

Thus, the will is the need to overcome obstacles. Like all other needs, it may be a source of positive or negative emotions caused by the very fact of overcoming (or not overcoming) the barrier to attaining the end goal. Sports can serve as a clear confirmation of the relative independence of this need. If the goal of sports competitions were only victory over an opponent, the athletes would have to prefer the weakest opponents. It is well known, however, that victory over a weak opponent does not bring them joy or satisfaction.

On the other hand (and Sechenov has already noted this), a complete autonomy of the will loses its adaptive significance and becomes senseless obstinacy. This is why the central question of the psychophysiology of the will remains a question of the mechanism through which the will begins "to serve" precisely one need and not another.

Here we must note that competition between needs occurs at the level of their transformation into corresponding emotions. For example, in a dangerous situation, the struggle between the instinct for self-preservation and the need to respond to certain ethical standards is experienced by the subject as a struggle between fear and a feeling of obligation, a feeling of shame at the thought of possibly running away from the fight.

Now we will return to our example with the smoker. It is taken for granted that the instinct for self-preservation in man is stronger than the need for nicotine. But, from the point of view of the subject, the probability of a mortally dangerous illness is small in the first place, and is referred to some indeterminate distant future in the second place. According to the information theory of emotions, in this situation the need for self-preservation does not engender the negative emotion of fear for one's health or even fear of dying. At the same time, the need for nicotine generates an adequately strong negative emotion of abstention together with a memory of the positive emotion of the satisfaction of inhaling tobacco smoke. Thus, the forces of the emotions are clearly not equal and behavior is oriented toward satisfying the potentially weaker (in comparison with self-preservation) need for tobacco.

A person who has a developed will and decides to give up smoking opposes the inclination for nicotine not because (more precisely not only because) he fears cancer of the lungs, but because he perceives the inclination as a barrier, as a lack of freedom, which engenders a secondary need to overcome the barrier. We note that intervention of the will does not reverse the universal regulatory function of emotions since the will intervenes in the competition of motives and again at the level of emotions, negative in the case of inability to overcome the "internal interference" and positive in the case of "victory over oneself."

In essence, defining will as a "drive that is stronger than all else" (Sechenov) is correct, with the reservation that what we have in mind is a need that is persistently dominant in the structure of the given personality. If the satisfaction of this dominant need takes place under conditions in which it engenders the strongest emotion, organization of behavior will not involve the brain mechanisms of the will. Will is not needed by the mother who goes to the aid of her child, and it is not needed by the person who is wholly engrossed in an extremely interesting matter that then becomes irresistably attractive for him. If, however, a subdominant competition of motives generates emotions that are stronger than the emotion dictated by the dominant motive, the mechanism of will is turned on, ensuring the attainment of the strategically important goals.

The disclosure of a persistently dominant need takes placed in a situation of selection; that is why, in the most critical situations, we turn to the principle of voluntarism instead of appealing to the system of social incentive or resorting to command. The principle of voluntarism by no means contradicts determinism, if only for the reason that persistent domination of one of the needs in itself is the result of a whole preceding history of the formation of the given personality, the merging of its natural endowments, and the conditions of rearing. Here it is fitting to recall the penetrating idea that man "...is capable of escaping one thing or another not because of a negative force, but because of the positive force of disclosing his true individuality..." (Marx and Engels, *Works*, 2nd edn., Vol. 2, p. 145). At the moment of selection the "true individuality" of the subject is revealed, that is, the transformation of the dominant motive into an action. John Locke said that a person is free to the extent that his actions correspond to his wishes.

A characteristic opposite of the will is suggestibility, including a predisposition to hypnosis. This conclusion has been confirmed by so many investigators that it has been included in encyclopedic definitions of suggestibility. "Suggestibility is the susceptibility to suggestion; in a broader sense, it is one of the manifestations of a weakly developed will...Suggestion is a method of psychic action of one person on another, carried out in a waking and hypnotic state...Suggestion is accompanied by the weakening of the will of the person who is subjected to suggestion and by subordination of his will to that of the person making the suggestion" (Great Soviet Encyclopedia, 2nd edn., 1951, Vol. 8, p. 306). A similar definition may be found in the last edition, the third, of this encyclopedia, "Suggestion in the broad sense of the word is the action on a personality that leads either to the manifestation by the person, in spite of (and sometimes against) his will and consciousness, of a definite state (for example boldness, confidence), feelings (for example fear), relations (toward an object, toward himself, toward his state), or to the person's committing an act not following directly from the norms and principles of activity that he has adopted..." (Great Soviet Encyclopedia, 1971, Vol. 5, p. 169). The weakness of the type of nervous system is an important condition of heightened suggestibility of a personality (Chasov, 1959).

Evidently, at the present time, most soundly based is the concept of hypnosis as a special case of imitative behavior. A person under hypnosis (follower) renounces his independence and transfers responsibility for the situation to the hypnotist (leader), maintaining responsibility before him for carrying out the suggestion (Hunt, 1979).

According to the data of V. A. Bakeev (1971a, b; 1974), anxiety is positively correlated with suggestibility in 83.5% of persons studied. Submitting to hypnosis, the subject goes from a situation of information deficit to a completeness of information about what and how he must act since the source of such information becomes not contradictory reality, but an "all-knowing" leader, the hypnotist. It is natural that such transition is accompanied by the development of a very positive emotional state. The close connection of the primary apparatus of positive emotions with the mechanisms of inhibiting (deactivating) influences on the higher divisions of the brain facilitates the development of a hypnotic state significantly in cases where the hypnotist makes appropriate suggestions. Sleep is a secondary result of the hypnotic state, and not a primary mechanism that makes suggestion possible and effective. The correlation observed between deep hypnotic sleep and the effectiveness of suggestion is evidence only of the presence of a common mechanism as a basis of both of these symptoms, and by no means of the reason for the dependence of suggestibility on deep sleep.

Unfortunately, objective data on the brain mechanisms of the will remain extremely limited. For behaviorism, the will simply does not exist, there is no place for it in the system of "stimulus—reinforcement" (reward or punishment). The attitude of neurophysiologists is less decisive although they do not reject the very fact of the presence of the will, but dissolve its role in extremely indistinct definitions. For example, what real physiological and psychological sense is conveyed by Delgado's definition? He believes that "the role of the will devolves to bringing into action already assembled mechanisms of motor acts (Delgado, 1971, p. 186). We do not find a place for the will or even a mention of it in any of the physiological diagrams of integrative activity of the brain, whether it be the T-O-T-E principle of Pribram or the functional system of Anokhin. It is not surprising that for those investigators who seem to be following Skinner and simply delete will from the system of concepts on brain activity, it is necessary only to establish the inability of modern physiology to say something credible about the connection of the will with brain mechanisms.

In light of concepts about the decisive role of four brain structures, the functions of the "emotional" subsystem hippocampus—amygdala correspond to the role of emotions in the organization of behavior: its orientation toward satisfying actual need, taking into account the current situation (amygdala), and extending the range of significant external stimuli (hippocampus). The subsystem frontal cortex—hypothalamus may be considered as a cerebral substrate of the will, since this subsystem facilitates the stabilization of behavior directing it toward satisfying the dominant need, regardless of unfavorable prediction and competing motives. Damage to precisely these two formations makes behavior definitely "weak-willed" since there is an impairment of the ability to choose between competing motivations, between highly significant signals, and those of very low significance.

Thus, following Sechenov and Pavlov, we define will as a specific *need to overcome* a barrier ("the reflex of freedom") that differs from other needs in that it is always "attached" to some other need that initiates behavior and is generated by the need to overcome. According to Sechenov, the will is a "drive that is stronger than all others," but it is by no means a synonym for a motive that, for some reason, rules over all the others at a given moment; it is not a "label for inhibition of a stronger stimulus" (Harriman). Will cooperates in the transformation of need that is persistently dominant in the structure of a given personality into externally realized behavior, into an activity, an action. It is precisely the persistence of the dominant need that frequently moves a person to act in a way that is incongruous with the circumstances, regardless of the circumstances, that engenders in a bystander (and even in the subject himself) an illusion of "free will," as if it were independent of the conditions of the environment. Actually, the behavior remains determined not by the prevailing situation, but by a dominant need formed most of all and mainly by conditions of training of the person over the course of his whole preceding life. It is understood that the innate endowment of the personality, including the distinctness of the "reflex of freedom," plays a decisive role here. Depending on the individual traits of the mechanisms of the will, on the volitional qualities of the personality, the dominating need may or may not be transformed into an act. A weak-willed person may be satisfied with a "titmouse in the hand," while he continues to recognize the incomparably greater worth of a "crane." A need that is not realized externally, but continues to exist, influences the activity of a number of other brain mechanisms, specifically the generation of "psychic mutations" (see below), the seeking of methods of resolving the motivational conflict. Knowing the means of achieving goals (or guessing them intuitively) and the ability to use these means do not always coincide, nor do they coincide for all people. "In man, talent is a happy combination of many creative abilities combined with creative will" (Stanislavsky, 1957, p. 30).

The function of the will that stabilizes behavior has its "Achilles' heel" that becomes particularly obvious in the case of the need of a creative approach to resolving problems that confront the subject. One of the notable paradoxes of human higher nervous (psychic) activity is that the "reflex of freedom" (we will use this Pavlovian term once again) makes the subject remarkably not free in the sphere of creativity, compelling him to move persistently in one and the same direction designated earlier. This is why, in the process of evolution, a special mechanism was formed that preserved certain stages of creative activity from interference by the will (see below).

Three key stages can be identified in developing concepts on the psychophysiology of the will.

First is the position stated by Sechenov that, together with will, "there is always some determining moral motive," that the "role of free will is transferred as a whole to a drive that overcomes all else." This remarkable idea explains why a person very often acts not in correspondence with, but contrary to prevailing circumstances, why he displays a relative independence from immediate external influences.

A second critical instance is connected with Pavlov's discovery of the "reflex of freedom," for which the presence of a barrier serves as an adequate stimulus. Because of this discovery it became clear that the will represents not the most dominant need, but the brain mechanism that complements the motive that is the primary initiator of behavior and makes up the stimulus—barrier situation. In other words, the will is an independent "need to overcome," not identical with the motive that it "serves" and strengthens, being a complementary source of activity of higher living beings. The discovery of a special mechanism that Pavlov called the "reflex of freedom" enriched science with a concept of the phylogenetic prerequisites of volitional human behavior. Of course, as distinct from other phenomena of higher nervous activity, i.e., emotions and rudiments of mental capacity (extrapolating, generalizing, basically rational), for a long time will did not have its analogs at prehuman levels of evolution, and this substantially impeded its neurophysiological study.

With all the significance of the theoretical contribution of Sechenov and Pavlov to the problem of will, this contribution was not given its deserved evaluation by psychologists because under the term "need," psychologists continued to understand only comparatively elementary biological and material human needs, and will was traditionally connected with consciousness, with intellect, with the capability of taking into account distant consequences of one's actions. This is why a third critical step was necessary: the recognition and experimental verification of the diversity and complexity of human needs, including such varieties of these needs as the need to know, to create, to produce works of art, etc. Marx, Engels, and Lenin, proposing to explain the behavior of man not by his thinking but by his needs, contributed precisely this universal sense to the concept "need." A natural science affirmation of the diversity of needs (including will itself as one of them) is the information theory of emotions, which disclosed the presence of need as a basis of any human emotions.

Simultaneously, the information theory of emotions demonstrated the complementarity of will with respect to emotions since the dependence of emotion not only on dimension (strength) of the need, but also on probability (possibility) of its being satisfied poses the threat of reorientation of behavior to more easily attained goals. As a counterbalance to emotions, will stabilizes behavior and facilitates the maintenance of important, but difficult to attain, goals.

Having made the internal nature of will and its relation to needs, emotions, and thought more precise, the information theory of emotions made it possible to indicate ways to study the brain mechanisms of will.

DETERMINISM AND PERSONAL RESPONSIBILITY

For more than 100 years the materialistic teaching on the activity of the brain has been based on the position formulated with complete precision for the first time by Ivan Mikhailovich Sechenov in 1863: "A selection among many possible ends of a single psychic reflex, consequently, is decidedly impossible, and the seeming possibility is only an illusion of consciousness...the first cause of all man's activity lies outside him" (Sechenov, 1961, p. 92). However, ethics, of which the personal responsibility of the subject is a cornerstone, of necessity requires freedom of choice for the actions he takes. Otherwise the categories of conscience, personal guilt, and responsibility would lose their meaning. This circumstance was emphasized by Hegel in his time: "Ethics...a concept of oneself as an absolutely free being is naturally the first idea" (Hegel, 1970, p. 270).

Classics of Marxism indicate the principal possibility of avoiding this contradiction. Lenin wrote: "The idea of determinism, establishing the necessity of human actions, rejecting a foolish tale about freedom of the will, does not by any means abolish human reason or conscience, or evaluation of man's actions..." (Lenin, *Complete Collected Works*, Vol. 1, p. 159). Insisting on personal responsibility of the subject, society requires him to observe the norms and laws of the given society. Even if a person committed an act as a result of poor upbringing, not to punish him (that is, to proceed "justly" with respect to the deed committed) would mean to proceed unjustly with respect to other members of the society. Responsibility before society arises as an unavoidable consequence of the social nature of man. The teaching, "immoral" from the point of view of Sechenov's critics, on the "lack of freedom" of the will is more humane and more moral than lofty phrases about its "freedom." The dependence of human actions on the environment and on conditions of training stimulates a striving to improve the environment and to improve training. Society can counter a free, evil will only with severity.

The philosophical resolution of the problem of the relation between determinism and free choice does not exclude, but rather assumes, the necessity to study, to specify how and with the aid of what psychophysiological mechanisms of human social behavior both fundamental principles, determinism and personal responsibility, are realized. It would seem that the problem can be resolved comparatively simply: conscience and the feelings of guilt and responsibility are only the social norms of behavior "transferred" into the head of the subject. It is precisely in this way that Feierbakh resolves this problem: "...as one who belongs to this community, as a member of this breed, this nation, this epoch, I have in my conscience no special and criminal codes...I reproach myself only with what another reproaches me" (Feierbakh, 1955, p. 630). With all the seeming plausibility of such an explanation, it generates a multitude of questions. Of course, there are very many of these "others" around me, and one of these "others" may reproach me precisely for something that, from the point of view of a second "other," deserves every encouragement. The norms of my group, my immediate social circle, may differ substantially from the norms of society as a whole, and Feierbakh's "son of the epoch" is quite capable of being confused in the face of the diametrically opposed requirements of en epoch swirling with contradictions.

Skinner, evidently, would willingly subscribe to the statements of Feierbakh. In his widely known book, *Beyond Freedom and Dignity* (1971), he brings the idea of mechanistic determinism to a logical conclusion. According to Skinner, the personality is not responsible for actions since they are wholly predetermined by external circumstances and conditions of training. In classifying anything as a flaw or virtue, society simply determines what it will punish and what it will encourage. The concepts of "freedom of will" and "moral responsibility" must also be eliminated from the science of behavior as in its time physics parted with "thermogen," astronomy with its concept of the Earth as the center of the Universe, biology with the "life force," and psychology with the myth of the immortal soul.

We will note that criticisms of Skinner sometimes clearly yield to the logical elegance of Skinnerian arguments. Which explains, by the way, the following argument: Man is not fatalistically determined in his thoughts and actions: as an organism, he can react differently to the same actions ...all people have, in one way or another, to a greater or lesser degree, a recognized independence in the selection of the goals of their activity, in the preference of some means for attaining a goal, others for exercising control over the circumstances of their lives, etc....people's conscious activity is not dictated only by external circumstances. Many reasons for human drives and actions are based in man himself and are by no means confined to heredity" (Arab-Ogly, 1972, p. 15). Is it permissible to ask: What is this secret "third" that is neither innate, imitative, nor acquired in the process of personal experience as influenced by the social environment?

The Skinnerian concept of conscience, the feeling of guilt and morals, like the concept of the conditioned-reflex fear of possible punishment, cannot withstand criticism. The striking unanimity of great artists of the past and contemporary scholars stands as a protest against such a primitive notion. Dostoevsky wrote: "All of these banishments to labor camps and, in the past, with flogging, reformed no one, and the main thing: they prevented almost no crime at all; crimes not only did not decline in number, but the farther away (the exiles) went, the more crime increased" (Dostoevsky, 1958, p. 83). J. P. Scott, in his accurate observations of children and experiments with animals, demonstrated that punishment in itself not only does not eliminate aggressiveness, but encourages and reinforces it (Scott, 1973).

The inadequacy of a formal knowledge of rules, norms, and laws of social life for forming a socially valued personality was obvious even for Socrates who set himself the goal of understanding why it happens that man knows what is good, and but does what is bad. The power of conscience as an internal regulator of socially acceptable behavior is determined precisely by its relative independence from immediate social reward or punishment. "It is not difficult to hold the judgment of others in contempt; it is impossible to hold one's own judgment in contempt" (Pushkin). "When no one sees and no one knows, I still will not do it: that is what conscience is!" (Korolenko). Subjective disinterestedness of a socially valuable action, as V. Dneprov noted correctly, is the essence of moral dielectics (Dneprov, 1968). Sukhomlinsky wrote: "It is most important that positive social evaluation of personal accomplishment be expressed not in prizes, awards, etc., and not by comparing the accomplishments of one with the deficiences of another. Such an evaluation, instead of training in collectivism, trains children in careerism; it is dangerous because it hides in itself a moral charge for the rest of life: a small careerist grows into a great scoundrel" (Sukhomlinsky, 1979, p. 58).

In the subjective perception of the disinterestedness of an action "according to conscience," there is a removal of the imagined contradiction between a truly existing determinism and seeming freedom of choice. Spinoza wrote: "People consider themselves free only because they recognize their actions, but they do not know the causes on which the actions are based" (Spinoza, 1932, p. 86). But why do people not fully appreciate the causes of the actions they take? Because these causes are complex, contradictory, not easily accessible to objective analysis? Or is it that not knowing, or incomplete or partial consciousness of motives, represents an objective necessity for the organization of behavior?

Before we attempt to answer these questions, we must define more precisely the concept of consciousness and unconscious manifestations of brain activity.

We assume that the key to explaining the nature of consciousness as a special form of the activity of the human brain is contained in its name: "consciousness." First of all, this is knowledge about something whose validity can be confirmed in practice. Marx noted: "The way consciousness exists and how nothing exists for it, that is "knowledge" (Marx and Engels, *From Early Works*, 1957, p. 633). The very term "knowledge" requires more precise definition. Knowledge is not a trace of an event (object) passively recorded by brain structures. Knowledge is knowing only to the extent to which it can serve as a means for satisfying a need, as a means for attaining a goal. Let us say that in a brief (tachistoscopic) presentation of visual images, my brain memorized a stimulus that I could recognize among other stimuli when they were presented again. Before the presentation, the trace of this stimulus was passively preserved in my memory, not being knowledge, since I could not use it in my goal-directed behavior for satisfying needs that existed for me.

We will emphasize that the quality of knowledge as a means is only one, important, but single characteristic of consciousness. Consciousness presupposes specifically "co-knowing" (compare "sym-pathy," "com-passion," "co-experience," "col-laboration"), that is, such knowledge as can be transmitted, be made available to other members of society. Consciousness is thinking together with someone else. To be conscious means to acquire a potential possibility to teach, to transmit one's knowledge to another. According to current representations, to be conscious of external stimuli, one must have a connection between the gnostic zones of the neocortex of the cerebrum and the motor speech area in the left hemisphere (in right-handed people) (Sperry, 1966; Kostandov, 1978).

Individual, and particularly social consciousness plays a decisive role *in determining norms* for satisfying needs.

These norms reflect the level of development of a civilization, the means available to the society for satisfying needs, and the degree of knowledge of the nature of man and the world surrounding him. At the same time, consciousness, as a rule, lags behind the process of development of needs and means of satisfying them, a fact that the founders of Marxism repeatedly pointed out. This is why there is a chronic preservation of "experiences" among people.

Thus, consciousness is that reflection by the brain of means and norms for attaining goals (satisfying needs) by which information about these means and norms can be transmitted to other members of society. Consciousness carries a basically social character because knowledge which I cannot share is not experience recognized by the subject.

Together with consciousness there exists an enormous sphere of forms of brain activity of which the subject is not usually conscious. These include involuntary memorization, unconscious automatized actions, perception of weak (subthreshold) external stimuli, and certain stages of creativity. We must consider especially the last variety of the psychic unconscious. Kubie, an American psychologist, maintains: "The creative personality is one that in some way, which is still considered to be random today, preserves the capability to use its subconscious functions more freely than other people who are, perhaps, potentially gifted to an equal degree" (cited by Yaroshevsky, 1967, p. 79). Vernadsky wrote: Intuition and inspiration — the basis of great discoveries, subsequently based and proceeding in a strictly logical way — are not elicited by either scientific or logical thought, are not connected with words or with concepts of their genesis" (Vernadsky, 1977, p. 111). According to Baroyan, "scientific intuition is a feeling (and most of all, a feeling!) for the prospects in the development of a problem. Intuition begins where logical means of analysis of a problem end, where knowledge alone is helpless. The psychological roots of intuition lie in the emotional force and color of abstract thinking. This force that approaches passion, in the words of Pavlov, 'is the main thing in the work of a scientist.' It is precisely his own emotional relation to a problem that lets a scientist see that which others pass by, to be at odds with logic and common sense, to wonder at what no one else wonders at, to pass by the universally accepted 'golden veins.' This is the quality that is one of the main factors determining the growth of science" (Baroyan, 1967, p. 11).

Manifestations of brain activity of which we are not aware are usually called "the subconscious." As a result, phenomena that are extremely different from each other appear to be of equal rank, for example, hormonal effects on the human psyche and creative inspirations of a great artist. Uniting such different processes under one aegis carries the threat of a "short circuit" between the representations of the nature of these processes. Then we have the illusion of cause and effect connections that do not exist objectively. More complex manifestations of the human psyche, generated by social and ideal (cognitive-creative) needs, are forcibly reduced to a single biological source, be it sex or the need for food.

An attempt to separate, order, or differentiate the manifestations of the unconscious psychical is perceived at present as an urgent necessity. This attempt was remarkably apparent in the creative quest of Stanislavsky.

THE CONSCIOUS AND THE SUBCONSCIOUS IN ARTISTIC CREATIVITY

Perhaps there is no other area in human activity where the basic positions of the information theory of emotions are confirmed so convincingly and constantly as in the area of art.

Responding to the question, "What is art?", Tolstoy wrote: "To evoke in oneself a feeling experienced once, and having evoked it in oneself, to transmit this feeling through movements, lines, sounds, images, verbal expressions in such a way that others experience that same feeling — this comprises the activity of art. Art is a human activity that consists of one person consciously, by means of recognized external signs, transmitting what he feels to others, and others becoming infected with those feelings and experiencing them" (Tolstoy, 1955b, p. 357). This classical definition requires essential refinement: Of what kind of feelings are we speaking? It is completely obvious that "emotional resonance" of the reader is not a goal in itself, otherwise naturalistic reproduction of pictures that freeze the blood would be the apex of literary skill. The view of art as "a transmission of feelings" was subjected to critical analysis by Vygotsky, who made a detailed study of the main differences between emotions elicited by literary work and emotions experienced by a reader in his everyday life (Vygotsky, 1965, pp. 316-317). As in all other cases in life, emotions of a reader, viewer, or listener depend on *what his needs are and to what extent they are satisfied by the information* contained in the work of art (Ershov and Simonov, 1965). The feelings of the author have significance only as being an important factor in his creative activity, which we will consider later. The statement that "true musicians do not express feelings through music, but convert music into feeling" holds for any artistic work. For a reader, it is not the emotions of an author that are important, but "information" about the world and man, about good and evil, about truth and justice that a literary work carries (or does not carry) in itself, although the content of this "information" is completely untranslatable from the language of images to the language of logic even in poetry, let alone in painting or music. Tolstoy wrote to his son: "I think you possess that which is called talent, and this is very ordinary and not of great value, that is, a capacity to see, note, and transmit, but thus far in your tales the internal, sincere need to express yourself is not yet apparent..." Many years later, William Golding continues the thought of Tolstoy: "In part art includes information, but only in part. The rest is discovery...Nevertheless, I...firmly believe that art which does not contain information is useless" (Golding, 1973, p. 216).

The more significant the information of the artist, the greater the extent to which it possesses the traits of a discovery of a great truth about the world and man, and, on the other hand, the greater the need of the viewer (reader, listener) to grasp this truth, the stronger will be the emotional response of the viewers, the more obvious the desired effect of co-experiencing. Such coincidence we call the autocracy of art. Like all other activity, artistic creativity can simultaneously serve as a means of satisfying other coexisting needs of the artist, material or social, but at the moment when "disinterested" and self-fulfilling striving for knowledge is eliminated from the complex of motivations, art stops being art. Since intuition always works on the need that is dominant in the structure of a given personality, the dominance of the artistic need to know represents an obligatory component of giftedness and potential suitability for professional involvement in art.

The goal of science is fact. The goal of art is truth. In the "Foreword to the Works of Guy de Maupassant," Tolstoy wrote: "An artist is an artist only because he sees things not as he wants to see them, but as they are. One who has talent, man, may make a mistake, but talent...will open and expose the subject and make us love him if he is worthy of love, and hate him, if he is worthy of hatred." Fact and Truth. From this fundamental difference between two forms of cognitive human activity, as secondary and derivative, come all their other specific traits: operating with concepts or with sensibly immediate images; the significance of measurement in science and the basic "immeasurability" of works of art; satisfying the needs for relative or absolute truth; reflecting the world as it is or the world as it is in relation to man, etc.

The content of a work of art cannot be exhausted by critical analysis or presented in a system of concepts. Kozintsev, the director, wrote about Shakespeare's *Hamlet*: "There is no more fruitless task than to form conceptions about this play. That which remains beyond the limits of each of them is what is most valuable" (Kozintsev, 1965, p. 59). Great works of art are interpreted, commented on, explained over centuries, but still remain unexhausted, giving food for contemplating and experiencing to each new generation. As distinct from relatively objective truths of science, works of art carry fragments of absolute truth about the world and man, and this is the reason for their inexhaustibility. The lifespan of great works from which each generation draws its own impressions once again indicates that art is not just a means of coding emotions the artist builds into his work. The emotions of the present-day viewer are similar to or different from the emotions of a viewer of past ages to the extent that the needs of these viewers that are satisfied by the information contained in the given work are similar or different.

Since art is a cognitive activity, a key instance in this activity is discovery, where the role of hypothesis is played by a phenomenon that Stanislavsky called the superpurpose. He wrote: "Just as a plant grows from a seed, exactly so must a work grow from a discrete thought and feeling of a writer...Let us agree...to call this basic, principal, all-encompassing purpose that includes in itself all the purposes without exception...the superpurpose of the work of a writer" (Stanislavsky, 1954, Vol. 2, p. 332).

A superpurpose is characterized by the following traits:

1. While closely tied to the worldview of the artist, with his civic position, a superpurpose is not identical with them since it is an esthetic category, a specific phenomenon of artistic activity.

2. A superpurpose can be defined only approximately in words because, on the whole, it cannot be translated from the language of images to the language of concepts. Because of this, there is a multitude of interpretations of the supergoal of one and the same work.

3. The process of discovering the superpurpose takes place in the sphere of unconscious psychic activity, although the way to this discovery, like the subsequent evaluation of its esthetic, philosophic, and social significance, is characterized by the active participation of consciousness. Just as the hypothesis of a scientist becomes knowledge that objectively reflects the actual activity only after it has been confirmed in practice, the propriety and scale of an artistic superpurpose is confirmed by the public practice of perceiving a work of art. As a result of this confirmation, some of these works enter into the treasure house of artistic culture and serve people over the course of centuries and others are rejected and sentenced to oblivion.

Stanislavsky persistently cautioned against attempts at direct volitional interference in those aspects of the creative process that are not conscious and are not usually subject to any kind of formalization. "One must not squeeze a feeling out, to be jealous, love, suffer just for the sake of jealousy, love, or suffering. Feeling must not be forced since this ends in the most repulsive actor's play...It appears of itself from whatever went before that evoked jealousy, love, suffering. Think diligently of that which went before and perceive it around you. Do not worry about the result" (Stanislavsky, 1954, Vol. 2, p. 51). In this statement, Stanislavsky is strikingly close to the advice Tolstoy gave in a letter to Strakhov, "...everything is as if ready for writing — fulfilling my earthly obligation — what is lacking is a push, faith in myself, in the importance of the work, there is no energy for wandering, earthly, elemental energy which cannot be fabricated. Yet I cannot begin. If you begin to insist, you will not be natural, you will not be true..."

Rejecting the possibility of direct arbitrary action on the unconscious mechanisms of creativity, Stanislavsky insisted on the existence of indirect ways of consciously affecting these mechanisms. An instrument of such influence is the professional psychotechnique of the artist that is summoned to resolve two problems: to prepare the soil for the activity of the subconscious and not to interfere with it. "Let us leave all that is subconscious to nature, the enchantress, and let us turn to what is accessible to us, to the conscious approaches to creativity and to a conscious application of psychotechnique. These, more than anything, teach us that when the subconscious enters the work, we must know enough not to interfere with it" (Stanislavsky, 1954, Vol. 2, p. 24).

Shalyapin maintained that "The appearance and formation of a stage image in an actor can be noted only approximately. This will be one half of a complex process, the half that lies on this side of the fence. I will say, however, that the conscious part of the work of an actor has an unusually great, perhaps even decisive significance — it awakens and feeds intuition, fertilizes it...Whatever inspirations strike the actor with the further development of the role, is a later matter. He cannot know this and he must not think about it, it will come as if despite his consciousness; by no zeal and no volition will he be able to prevent it. But he must know very well, he must know precisely what he must reject in his creative zeal. That is, with a conscious effort of the mind and will, he must develop for himself a view of the work that he is undertaking" (Shalyapin, 1957, pp. 287-288).

For us, particularly interesting is the fact that, speaking of the unconscious stages of artistic creativity, Stanislavsky constantly uses two terms: "the subconscious" and "the superconscious." According to Stanislavsky's idea, "...true art must reach how to consciously awaken in oneself the unconscious, creative nature for the superconscious organic creativity" (Stanislavsky, 1954, Vol. 1, p. 298). In his works we can find a direct definition of the concepts of the sub- and superconscious. Nevertheless, we must try to show that introducing the category of the superconscious is not a random freedom of expression, but the true need to isolate two forms of the unconscious psychic, which is of basic significance for both the system of Stanislavsky and for modern concepts of higher nervous activity in man.

TWO SPHERES OF THE UNCONSCIOUS PSYCHIC: THE SUBCONSCIOUS AND THE SUPERCONSCIOUS

In our time, the mathematician Schreider wrote: "I am in complete agreement with the opinion that it is more reasonable to identify the intuitive side of creativity not with the subconscious, but with the 'superconscious'...We are speaking not of something that stands 'below' everyday consciousness, but of something that stands 'above' the simple rational approach" (Schreider, 1976, p. 115).

The need to distinguish two kinds of unconscious psyche was studied by Yaroshevsky (1973) in his work on the "superconscious" as a most important category of scientific creativity. Yaroshevsky explains the difference between the subconscious and the superconscious with the following example. I forgot someone's name and could in no way remember it until a chance association or another occurrence of this name led to its reconstruction, that is, its being known. This means that the forgotten name continued to exist, was preserved in my memory, but outside the sphere of knowing, "under it." It is a different matter when a scientist seeks a solution to some problem, and the appropriate hypothesis develops as a result of the activity of the superconscious. How does the investigator "recognize" this hypothesis, how does he recognize the correctness of the concept that develops even before it is logically or experimentally confirmed? He does not have a ready gauge in his memory for such recognition! Evidently, a unique "anti-engram" or "minus-engram," a gap in the logical chain of earlier known fact, serves as such a gauge. Superconsciousness is oriented toward the end elements of a break that already exists in the memory, filling it in with "psychic mutations" (see below). Thus, a hypothesis on the corpuscular-wave nature of light filled in the break between facts, some of which pointed to the corpuscular theory and others to the wave theory.

Unconsciousness of the phenomena of the first, "subconscious" group emerged in the process of evolution as a very economical adaptation, as a method of "relieving" consciousness from petty custody of processes that could be automated. But how can we understand unconsciousness of the most complex and responsible manifestations of the higher (psychic) activity of man?

We assume that unconsciousness of certain stages of creative activity of the brain emerged in the process of evolution as a necessity to counteract the conservatism of consciousness. The dialectics of the development of the psyche is such that the collective experience of humanity is concentrated in consciousness and must be protected from what is random, dubious, not approved in practice. Nature defends the fund of knowledge just as it guards the genetic fund from the vicissitudes of external influences. This virtue of consciousness dialectically turns into its defect, an obstacle to the formation of essentially new hypotheses. Briefly, a complete consciousness of creating, the possibility of its formalization, would make creating impossible! This is why the process of forming a hypothesis was saved by evolution from interference of consciousness for which is reserved the more important function of selecting hypotheses that adequately reflect actual reality. "Intuition is the capacity for comprehending the truth by discerning it directly without basing it on evidence...Intuition is adequate for discerning truth, but it is not adequate for convincing others or oneself of it. For this, evidence is needed" (Spirkin, 1972, pp. 343-344).

Let us note that the basic laws of nature are expressed in the form of prohibitions: it is impossible to build a perpetual motion machine (thermodynamics), transmit a signal with a speed that exceeds the speed of light in a vacuum (theory of relativity), simultaneously measure the coordinates and speed of an electron (quantum mechanics). We are convinced that unconsciousness of critical creative moments, the essential absurdity of compounding its "formulas," its algorithms, represents one of these fundamental prohibitions. We will repeat, the programming of all stages of creating without exception (were it theoretically attainable) would make creating impossible. What we are concerned with here is not the limitation of our knowledge of the higher manifestations of the activity of the brain, but with the main limitations imposed by nature itself.

In the neurophysiological plan, the mechanisms of creativity must not be understood as a process of direct reflection by the brain of connections between objects in the surrounding world. This activity takes place more likely according to the principle of "psychic mutagenesis" (Fig. 40), according to the principle of selection of new neural connections, essentially already developed in the brain (Simonov,

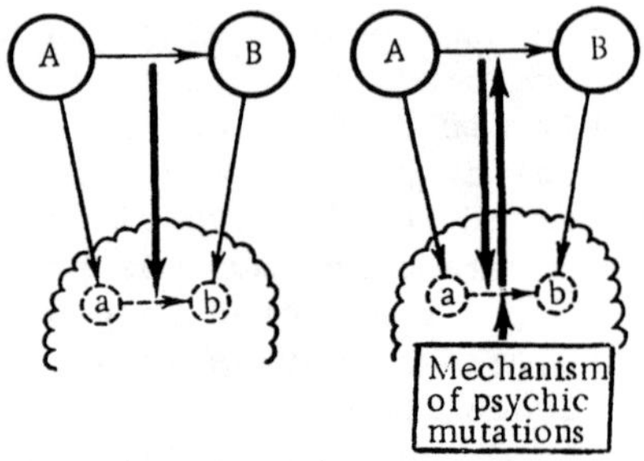

Fig. 40. Diagram of two types of reflection of the connection between events A and B.

1966b). What has been said above in no way represents any kind of diminution of the role of consciousness in human creative activity. Consciousness not only makes a selection of hypotheses, but actively sets the *question* before the knowing mind, determining at the same time the *direction* of psychic mutagenesis.

Timiryazev (1939) was one of the first to express the idea that individual creativity is similar to the "creativity" of nature, to the mechanism that generates new species in the process of the evolution of living beings. This analog is attractive in that both processes are better understood and studied at the stage of selection than at the stage of formation of variants. Darwin's theory explains very well the functioning of selection but provides little for the understanding of the growing complexity of living beings, since "...natural selection, as if carrying out a protective function, is by its nature extremely conservative" (Ohno, 1973, p. 11). "The combination of the capability to make nonpredictable selections with the capability to learn from experience (and particularly, to learn by using the results of preceding selections) is as close to the capability to create new information as a result of an act of free will as this is possible at all (if we are to judge by objective criteria)," concludes Quastler (1964, p. 31).

The difficulties experienced by evolutionary teaching also spread to attempts to apply the principles of biological development to the evolution of culture. They appear in their fullest extent in the conception of Popper, whose ideas we referred to earlier. Metlov writes: "Of the two-stage process of evolution, the origins of variability and assorting of variants by natural selection, Popper considers only one stage, the assorting of variants. He analyzes the process of the origin of variability, the process of the development of that which is sorted, as an instance, a stage of the evolutionary process" (Metlov, 1979, p. 84). All of the ideas of similarity between organic and cultural evolution continue to enlist new partisans. According to Dawkins (1977), in the evolution of culture, the "meme," a stable unit of motives, ideas, technology, etc., corresponds to the biological gene. Being long-lived, having the capability to reproduce, and precision of copying, memes are subject to mutations and selection. Danin (1976) expressed a curious idea: just as the mechanisms of immunity protect the individuality of the organism by tissue incompatibility in biology, in the sphere of culture, art helps people to protect the uniqueness of their personality.

It is understood that "psychic mutagenesis" does not imply purely random combining of neural traces. Earlier experience not only presents material for "mutation," but predetermines, to a significant degree, the direction of mutation. It is evident that laws are acting here that resemble the laws of populational genetics, particularly the need for isolation for accumulating mutations and the excess of engrams that are preserved in the memory. It is not by chance that the surplus of intellect resembles the surplus of biological immunity. The greater the number of variants the subject has for solving a problem, the broader is the range of possible selection. Unconsciousness ("superconsciousness") of the initial stages of creative activity of the brain provides the activity that is necessary for defense against premature interference by consciousness, from suppressing what is already recognized, what is already known. But this subjectively perceived freedom of the creative imagination does not hinge on freedom from fact, from objective reality, from truth with which the hypothesis of the scientist or the "message" of the artist is compared.

Because of the extreme limitation of our knowledge of the neurophysiological bases for activity of the superconscious, we can point only to isolated facts that are worthy of attention and further development.

Here, an important role undoubtedly belongs to the right, nonverbal hemisphere of the brain, involved in operating with images not mediated sensually, with musical and combinatorial capabilities (in right-handed persons). Some authors, uniting the functioning of consciousness exclusively with the left hemisphere, the hemisphere of speech and comprehension, are inclined to minimize the role of the right hemisphere in higher manifestations of brain activity. This circumstance once again stresses the need to introduce concepts of the superconscious in place of the erroneous reference of processes of creativity to the subconscious as to something that clearly is inferior to the conscious, and is not comparable to it.

The physiological reality of "psychic mutations" confirms the mechanism of the dominant described by Ukhtomsky, and the ability of the dominant stimulation focus in the brain to respond to external stimuli that can only hypothetically appear to be adequate for the given reaction (for example, defensive reaction). The dominants give the phenomena of reality a signal significance that they do not possess objectively. A long-term, stable stimulation focus may result in an increased content of noradrenalin in the brain tissues, and this in its turn is capable of increasing sensitivity of the synaptic membranes of nerve cells to acetylcholine. As a result there is a closure of temporary neural connections not because of the action of external stimuli combined in time, but primarily "from within." Another possible mechanism of primary closure was suggested by Roitbak (1978). A powerful stimulation focus will be accompanied by an accumulation of intercellular potassium, which promotes the activation of myelinization of the axon endings and makes synapses effective that were not effective earlier. Thus, the hypothesis of the possibility of a primary closure of temporary neural connections does not, in principle, contradict the data of current neurophysiology.

Exceptionally important is the function of the hippocampus, that section of the brain that regulates the flow of information drawn from the memory. The structures of the hippocampus have a high sensitivity to the action of chemical substances, hallucinogens with the fantastic combinations of visual and aural images that are characteristic for them. There are bases for assuming the direct participation of the hippocampus in the genesis of "psychic mutations," of combinations of traces of impressions preserved in the memory that are not predicted (but are not random!). In a state of sleep, this mechanism participates in the formation of dreams, and in a waking state in the mechanisms of creativity at the stage of intuitive guesses, hypotheses, and assumptions.

The selective deprivation of REM sleep affects people's ability to carry out creative tasks such as the Rorschach test. On the other hand, the proportion of REM sleep increases in a situation that requires a creative approach (Greenberg and Pearlman, 1974; Glaubman et al., 1978). According to Rotenberg (1978), REM sleep is a continuation in sleep of the attempt to solve problems and settle motivational conflicts on the basis of image thinking. Being aware of dreams is an indication that the reconciliation was successful.

Let us try to determine the criteria for differentiating the two forms of the unconscious psychic: the sub- and the superconscious.

These two spheres of the human psyche emerged as a result of two basic tendencies of the self-movement of living nature: preservation and development. The subconscious is connected with the needs of "necessities," the superconscious, with satisfying the needs of "growth." Since the same dialectically contradictory existence of needs for preservation and development resulted in the formation of negative and positive emotions, it is not surprising that we recognize the activity of the subconscious by predominantly negative emotions, and the activity of the superconscious by positive emotions.

Up to the moment of consciousness, the subconscious makes itself felt mainly through negative emotions. Whatever the concrete manifestations of the subconscious we might touch on, from the most elementary to the most complex, the subconscious either remains silent or makes itself felt through the language of negative emotions. Only an interruption of well-automated actions draws to it the "spotlight" of consciousness. Our brain obligingly increases the thresholds of perception of signals that remind us of events that are unpleasant or painful (the mechanism of so-called psychological defense). We will illustrate the subconscious function of preservation with an example borrowed from Kon. I envy another, knowing that the feeling of envy is degrading and shameful. Then I unconsciously begin to find faults and inadequacies in this person which would justify my unfriendliness. The subconscious helps me eliminate the resulting contrariness and to preserve the status of complete responsibility toward the ethical norms of my social sphere. The subconscious is always defensive; it is the instrument of mental equilibrium and compromise.

The superconscious is another matter. Inspiration and creative enthusiasm are experienced as a state of joyous freedom, liberation, and ability to do anything. Even when accomplishing mortally dangerous acts of self-sacrifice, the subject perceives them not as a burdensome duty, not with a melancholy feeling of inescapable doom, but with a feeling of greater freedom of personality that would overcome death itself and rise above it. This deep kinship of negative emotions with the subconscious and positive emotions with the superconscious must not be taken to be absolute: both types of emotions can participate in phenomena that can be related to both the sub- and superconscious. We are speaking only of tendencies, or preferential interconnections.

The subconscious operates with what was realized earlier (automatization of habits) or may be realized under certain conditions: material involuntarily fixed in the memory, the cause of a pathogenic state disclosed independently or with the help of a psychiatrist, etc. Processes in the sphere of the superconscious are not subject to being realized, as we learned from the example of scientific and artistic creativity. The subconscious deals with what is already preserved in the structures of the brain. Because of the superconscious, something new emerges that did not exist before.

In the process of the activity of the subconscious, a person is oriented "toward self": automatized habits, which have, therefore, stopped recognizing motor habits, engrams of involuntary memory, egoistic drives that conflict with the social norms; all of these belong exclusively to the given personality as a unique, individual being. The superconscious, on the other hand, works "for others" since both knowledge and creativity are converted into disinterestedness if the knowing subject is the only possessor of truth.

Thus, we have determined the minimum five criteria of the definition of sub- and superconsciousness that make it possible to differentiate these varieties of unconscious manifestations of the reflective activity of the brain: 1) the subconscious may become conscious, the superconscious cannot; 2) the subconscious serves tendencies for preservation, the superconscious for development; 3) the subconscious is predominantly connected with negative emotions, the superconscious with positive; 4) the subconscious operates with what is already preserved in the memory; in the process of superconscious activity, a new combination of engrams is generated; 5) the subconscious is oriented "toward self," the superconscious "for others."

Are the functions of the superconscious as a special variety of brain activity limited only to its participation in the processes of artistic and scientific creativity? Or does the mechanism of the superconscious have a more universal significance for the human psyche, for human behavior in the environment of man's social sphere?

"SUPERPURPOSE" OF HUMAN BEHAVIOR AS A FUNCTION OF MAN'S SUPERCONSCIOUS

The subconscious—conscious—superconscious...Is this not reminiscent of that other triad of another three-member structure of human personality postulated by Sigmund Freud: the id, the ego, and the superego? We do not want to minimize the achievements of Freud, not of his discovery of the important role of the unconscious psyche nor of his formulation of the inner need that is present in the interaction of the conscious ego with both variants of the unconscious. Nevertheless, our definitions of the sub- and superconscious are based on completely different objective characteristics of the human psyche.

According to Freud, the basis for a number of psychic disturbances in human activity is a conflict between the sphere of biological inclinations (id) and the requirements of society, represented in the psyche of the individual by the superego complex. With respect to the sovereign personality, the superego (and its derivatives: conscience, a feeling of guilt, etc.) act as a source of repression, as a weapon for subordinating the individual to society and its prohibitions, norms, and commands. This is why the pressure of the superego is no less strange and dangerous for the rational ego than the dark impulses of the id. As far as the creative source in the psychic activity of the brain is concerned, it emerges only as a means of reconciling the contrary struggling forces of the id and the superego between which the conscious ego wanders in search of a compromise.

The superconscious does not reconcile conflicts, but discloses them and places them before the conscious as something requiring analysis, confirmation, or refutation. If the functions of the subconscious are connected with "displacement," that is, the transition from the conscious to the unconscious, then the superconscious is a breaking through of the results of the activity of intuition into the sphere of the conscious, an appeal to it.

In a system of need—motivation coordinates, the subconscious is at the juncture of the biological and social needs, and the superconscious in the "overlap zone" of social and ideal needs. We must stress at once that in the first case we have in mind not a conflict of socially unacceptable drives with norms and prohibitions stipulated by society, but conflict with the need of the subject to follow those norms and respond to them. Socially determined norms are subject to pressure not only from the material—biological needs, but also from the ideal needs. The results of the cognitive activity of the mind is far from always in agreement with what the person finds in the social reality around him. Drobnitsky rightfully noted that morality is not the norms alone (taboos, prohibitions, customs) that are a part of the society, but the attitude of the personality toward these norms, prohibitions, and regulations. The moral emerges only when what exists is confronted by what is required as the given personality perceives it (Drobnitsky, 1972, p. 109).

The sub- and superconscious are the children of need, derivatives of their complex and contradictory interactions. All the teachings of Freud are constructed on the conflict of the biological (id) and the social (superego); this is why the material of Freud's analysis was only the sphere of the subconscious. In the system of his concepts, there is no place for the category of the superconscious just as there is no independent group of ideal needs in that system. Since the area of the superconscious exists, nevertheless, and discloses itself quite clearly, let us say, in the sphere of artistic creativity, Freud has no recourse but to once again turn to the conflict between the biological and the social, to the "sublimation" of suppressed sexual inclinations, and similar mythology of orthodox Freudism.

We must not be surprised that in reconstructing the "life of the human spirit," Stanislavsky naturally came to the concept of the "superpurpose," the "super-superpurpose," and the "superconscious." As a great artist, he simply could not limit himself to the subconscious. The arbitrariness of interpreting human motives, acts, and dreams, ruling with such authority in the pages of psychoanalytic tracts, if it were transferred to the stage, would be the same falsehood which, without need for any logical evidence, is considered to be incompatible with true art. It is sufficient to recall the attempts to treat Shakespeare's *Hamlet* in the spirit of the Oedipus complex in order to understand how primitive such a plan seems compared to the riches of the great work.

Social needs growing out of the "social instincts" of animal forebears ("the social instinct was one of the important controls in the development of man from apes" [Engels, in: Marx and Engels, *Works*, 1964, Vol. 34, p. 138]) held a dominant position in the structure of the human personality. But this subordination to the norms of the social environment could lead (and did lead, if we remember the vitality of the "survivors") to excessive rigidity of historically passing norms, to a threat of the development of a subjective feeling of more complete irresponsibility predicated on the conviction that it is not I who am responsible, but my teachers and the "environment" that formed me.

Between the social and the ideal, meanwhile, there emerges a contradiction not less, but more deep and dynamic, than the Freudian conflict between the biological and the social. The essence of the conflict between an adopted social norm and a value of a higher order was brilliantly embodied by Dostoevsky in the remarkable dialogue of Ivan and Alesha Karamazov.

Telling Alesha about a child that was hunted down by dogs, Ivan Karamazov asks what Alesha believes should be done with the killer leader-dog.

"'Shoot it!' Alesha said quietly, and with a pale, distorted kind of smile, he looked up at his brother.

"'Bravo!' cried Ivan with some agitation, 'As soon as you said it, it means...Oh, yes, you monk! So that's the kind of little demon that lives in your heart, Aleshka Karamazov.

"'What I said was absurd, but...'

"'That's just it, but what...' Ivan shouted. 'You know, novice, that absurdities are quite necessary on earth. The world stands on absurdities, and without them, perhaps, nothing would happen'" (Dostoevsky, 1958, p. 305).

It is not difficult to see that the norms of Christian morals which seemed to be so deeply and organically adopted by Alesha as to become his true conviction, would have dictated an entirely different response in the spirit of forgiving all and not opposing evil. Surprising even himself, Alesha nevertheless enunciated that "Shoot it," that "absurdity," on which "the world stands." With hindsight, we see that the requirement "to shoot," not acceptable from the point of view of historically passing Christian norms, reflects a system of values, the loss of which would lead to deformation of the very essence of man as the carrier of the civilization that had emerged on earth.

Many years after Dostoevsky, the authors of fantasies, Arkadii and Boris Strugatsky, in their story, "The Distant Rainbow," turned to the "tear of the child" as a criterion of higher moral values.

...A small planet where a colony of earthlings is carrying out scientific experiments is struck by an inevitable catastrophe. There is only one starship at the disposal of the people. The question arises: Who is to be saved, the best scientists, the flower of earthly science, or the children? Of course, the people saved the children. Why? Because otherwise everything would have lost meaning: both the genius of the scientists and their great discoveries that would be needed by no one. "And if the suffering of children had to be included in the sum of suffering needed to purchase truth, then I would say in advance that all of truth is not worth that price" (Dostoevsky, 1958, p. 302).

But, of course, formal analysis might have led to a different conclusion: eminent scientists are more useful and valuable not for themselves, but for "others," for "humanity," than children from whom no one knows what will come.

The superconscious makes it possible for man to proceed "irrationally" and in this irrationality, at the same time, is concealed the mechanism of creating new moral norms that have only been dreamed of in the crisis of social relations that existed earlier, only guessed at in the dynamics of social development. For the contemporaries of ancient, slave-owning societies to comprehend the truth that a slave is a man was evidently no less difficult than for their descendents to reconcile themselves to the discovery of Copernicus or the theory of Darwin. This kind of illumination is needed as a defense against the conservatism of the conscious no less than the hypotheses of scientific discoveries.

DETERMINISM AND FREEDOM OF CHOICE: "REMOVING" THE PROBLEM

It is specifically the mechanism of the superconscious, using the objective determination of actions that we all make with the genetic endowments and conditions of training that we have, that generates the subjective feelings of personal responsibility for our actions, that is, the need again and again to ask oneself: was I right in acting this way?

The capacity to have doubts about the propriety of our actions, the capacity to analyze their possible consequences, the capacity to relate these consequences to a system of values that humanity has formed over the course of its whole history ("conscience is the memory of society assimilated by the individual," said Leo Tolstoy) represents an internal mechanism, the objective reality subjectively perceived of freedom of choice. Rejection of such self-evaluation, unthinking copying of models of behavior borrowed exclusively from one's closest circle is also a choice as long as we are speaking of a psychically healthy subject. The importance of training the capacity to analyze one's actions from all aspects has been dealt with very well in a paper by the husband-and-wife team, Nikitina and Nikitin: "We try to bring up a child so that in complex situations he would learn to act not from fear, but from some interest, not on the principle that 'they're beating us!' and not because 'I want it to be my way!' but because of justice. In order that the child might be able to evaluate every situation, to decide who is right, who is to blame, whose side to take" (Nikitina and Nikitin, 1979, p. 7).

In addition, the capacity for self-analysis may be the subject for reflection, an endless sorting of evidence "for" and "against."

"...When Levin was thinking about what he was and why he was living, he did not find an answer and came to despair; but when he stopped asking himself about it, he as if knew both what he was and why he was living because he steadfastly and definitely acted and lived; even during that last time, he lived more steadfastly and definitely than before.

"...Cogitations brought him to doubt and interfered with his seeing what should be done and what should not. But when he did not think, but lived, without stopping to feel in his soul the presence of an infallible judge deciding which of the actions was better and which worse: as soon as he did something he should not have done, he felt it immediately" (Tolstoy, 1955a, p. 856).

It is understood that the "infallible judge" was not assigned to Levin at his birth, but was formed by all the past life of the hero, beginning in early childhood. But it is far from always that the human brain, in choosing an action, analyzes all alternatives, recalls all evidence in favor or against a decision, all examples of similar situations experienced by the subject himself or by others known to him; as a rule, he is not in a position to weigh all possible consequences of proposed actions. There is usually not enough time for such a rational analysis. The need that is stably dominant in the structure of the given personality dictates its decision, and the subject accepts it as the "dictates of conscience," "the call of the heart," "the inner judge."

Evidently, an important role in the processes of transforming objective needs of developing society into the personal attitudes of the subject and into the motives of his behavior is played by the activity of the superconscious and the emotions that accompany this activity. The concept of the direct transition of the needs of society into motivation of individual behavior of its members by logical recognition of these needs does not correspond at all to reality. As Garai, the Hungarian philosopher, has properly stressed, "...the determinants that come from community life are mediated not by individual consciousness (or self-knowledge), but by phenomena, fundamental to psychology, that are independent of it, by needs, interests, etc." (Garai, 1968, p. 24). We have said before that the "dictates of conscience," the "inner judge," serve as a social norm, deeply assimilated by the subject, that has passed into the sphere of the subject's psychic unconscious. But such a transition can evidently be made only by norms that retain their meaning for humanity over a long period of time. These higher values must be provided with reliable protection against the vicissitudes and contradictoriness of current influences. Massive "brainwashing" demonstrated its effectiveness more than once in the course of history, very quickly bringing broad circles of a population to following reactionary slogans. A consciousness distorted in this way proceeded to a different course, driven by the inflamed instincts for total permissiveness. But there were always people who were capable of opposing the "liberation from the chimera called conscience" and who listened to its voice.

Immutably stressing that moral norms are class-dependent, Marxism will not accept moral relativism. Class (if we speak of classes that represent progressive trends in historical development) does not contradict what is common to man, nor does it coincide with it. It is characteristic that forces progressive for their time invariably came forward with ideals of equality, fraternity, dignity, and value for each separate person. Reactionaries of all colors, on the other hand, following their class interests, stubbornly appealed either to the subconscious (to the sphere of primitive instincts, tendencies toward self-preservation, fear, helplessness) or to egoistic rationalism, to calculating, to conclusions of the type "So what can I do?" "Force will break a straw," etc. An alternative to "zoological individualism" in such cases usually was not self-esteem and dignity of the person, but a cult of the "masses" that proposed blind following of the authoritarian leaders.

This is why the concept of the "societal" remains without content as long as we do not precisely define its historical value. "An act is considered moral if its motive corresponds to the requirements of duty...Duty requires subordinating personal will to the will of society" (Bandzeladze and Gaprindashvili, 1971, p. 136). Here it is necessary to specify: duty to whom, and what can we make of "the will of society?" "The common good comes before the personal," such was one of the twenty-five points of the Nazi program adopted in Munich in 1920 (Nuikin, 1971, p. 198). There is a difference between the common good and the common man.

"Should the Nazi judges who followed the laws of the Third Reich be judged?" asked Stanley Kramer in the film,

Judgment at Nuremberg. Not from the point of view of the victors (then why the court procedure?), but in the context of the patterns of the existence and development of human civilization. And, as we remember, artist's intuition suggested to Kramer the most convincing refutation of the formally indisputable evidence of the lawyer: the director left the decisive word not to the judge, but to one of the accused.

That which we find today as a desired exception (note that the response of the accused in *Judgment at Nuremberg* is more the "move" of the director than the real action of the former Nazi) must become the natural norm in people of the future. "...In *human* relations, the punishment will actually be nothing more than a sentence which the person acknowledging guilt will carry out on himself...In other people, on the other hand, he will find the natural saviors from this punishment which he has placed on himself" (Marx and Engels, *Works*, 1955, Vol. 2, p. 197).

The human psyche is a product of human history, its social existence. It is doubly determined by the system of social relations because man grows up in a social environment, and because he adopts the experience of preceding generations. But the receiver and carrier of these social influences is a material, bodily organism, the brain, which works according to its own laws, but is capable nonetheless of learning other laws of nature. The more completely and deeply we learn the laws of our own behavior, the more effective will be the means of forming and perfecting the personality and the methods of training, education, and reeducation. Just like other achievements of science, success in the study of man may be used for both progressive and reactionary purpses: for the harmonious development of the morally rich, creative, active personality or for mass production of living robots.

We will be optimists and will limit ourselves to the first variant. Does it not hide a potential threat to further development of civilization? What if psychologists of the future, with the best intentions, begin to form ideal people according to the historically limited concepts of the authors concerning this ideal? And then, what if it develops that their ideal was not perfect, that not everything was anticipated in their "model" of the harmonious man? The ideal people will then also go about the world without satisfying the requirements of the Future...

We will say it outright: such a danger does not threaten mankind. It does not threaten because nature has placed a prohibition, similar to the prohibition against the invention of a perpetual motion machine or against the simultaneous determination of the speed of an electron and its position in orbit. This prohibition is the presence of the superconscious, the impossibility *in principle* of arbitrary interference in the mechanisms of the creative activity of the brain. A man may be deprived of his life or his rationality, but his thinking and his behavior cannot be *completely* programmed. And in this materialistic sense, his psyche has freedom to develop, of which he can be deprived only if he is deprived of life itself.

Thus, the superconscious is a special mechanism of higher nervous (psychic) activity by means of which the biological and then the social evolution "removed" the contradiction between objective determinacy of the human psyche and the need of subjectively perceived freedom of choice as a necessary condition for the development of personality and the enrichment and ennobling of his needs. According to its functional purpose, this mechanism may be compared with the role of mutation in the progressive development of living nature from the simple to the complex, having in mind not the best adaptation to the environment, not an increase in stability (capacity for self-preservation), but the complication of internal organization that makes it possible for living beings to claim new spheres of the surrounding world that were previously inaccessible.

Even at this level, the emergence of living beings that are new in principle and possess increased and extended functional possibilities seems to us to be a synthesis of determinism and freedom. The process of biological evolution at one and the same time is "not free" with respect to natural selection and relatively "free" and independent of the environment in the sense of variation, variability, and novelty of the material subject to selection.

According to Timiryazev's valid statement, creative activity of the brain is like the "creativity of nature." This activity is not free with respect to reality, for it must be an adequate, objectively true reflection of reality, regardless of whether we are speaking of scientific theories or of works of art. Moreover, only the recognized freedom from the pressure of experience accumulated earlier that the process of forming scientific hypotheses and artistic ideas has makes the development and improvement of human culture possible.

Finally, at the level of the social behavior of man, we meet once again with the dialectically contradictory unity of determinacy and freedom. Human behavior, the decisions man makes, his actions, are determined to a decisive degree by conditions of his individual development, his education, including the whole complex totality of historical, economic, class, national, etc., factors. Social requirements placed on the subject are not only diverse, but are also contradictory: the family may require one thing, the close circle (informal review group) another, and the interests of society something else again. In the end, that behavior is productive which corresponds to the trends of social progress, and those trends do not always agree with norms that developed earlier and were adopted by the subject. This is why his relation to the norms must, from the very beginning, be creative to that degree of criticality that is necessary for any creative process.

Thus, an analysis of higher and more complex manifestations of psychic activity of man has led us not to resolving the problem of determinism and free choice, but to "removing" this problem as being improperly posed. Like human thought, human behavior, to the extent that it is creative, is determined by probability (not predictable to the end) at the stage of generating variants and, more precisely, at the stage of selection. The function of selection belongs to consciousness which reflects actual reality, taking into account the personal and, mainly historical, experience of humanity. The conscious makes the selection, guided by two criteria: 1) the presence of actual need (in which the needs of society are represented), and 2) the possibility of their being satisfied with the help of the whole totality of the means available to the given man in the given epoch (social group, class, etc.), and in conformity with the norms existing in the given social environment. An incomplete, only partial realization of needs leads to the state where consciousness is preoccupied with means, equipment, and norms of satisfying the needs.

This is why a direct appeal to consciousness represents an ineffective method of affecting behavior. Moreover, what has been said in no way detracts from the role of consciousness in forming the human personality if we consider that consciousness is a way into the sphere of needs and motives *through* the means of their satisfaction and with the cooperation of emotions in the process of satisfying the needs that arise. In essence, any education is a formation of the system of needs of the one being educated: their complement, hierarchy, and norms of their satisfaction. And what those complement, hierarchy, and norms will be depends on the educators.

Conclusion

The information theory of emotions, put forth and experimentally supported in the preceding chapters, belongs to the Pavlovian direction in the science on the activity of the brain. Founded by Ivan Petrovich Pavlov, the science of higher nervous (psychic) activity is neither traditional physiology of the brain nor psychology, since it represents a qualitatively new area of knowledge based on a *systemic* approach to the psyche and behavior. In essence, this approach consists of an attempt to encompass both sides of the psyche: its neurophysiological mechanisms and its reflective-regulatory functions, its interdependence with the needs of the organism (personality) and with the surrounding world. This is why the information theory of emotions was productive equally for the study of the physiology of the brain and for the analysis of a number of complex problems of general psychology.

The theory enriched the closely connected reflective—evaluative and regulatory functions of emotions at the individual and populational levels, and disclosed their organic interdependence and mutually cooperative condition.

In the area of the *physiology of emotions* we demonstrated that the autonomic symptoms of emotional stress are determined not by the volume of the passing or present motive load, but by the dimension (force) of the need and the probability (possibility) of its being satisfied. It developed that various involuntary shifts depend variously on these two factors. Thus, for example, the galvanic skin response is more closely connected with the information component of emotion, with the dimensions of the increment or decrease in probability of satisfying the need in comparison with earlier prediction.

Taking into account the complex and nonuniform internal structure of emotions made it possible to understand why changes in the electroencephalogram do not directly follow the fluctuations in the level of emotional excitation since the dynamics of the EEG are predominantly connected with the flow of information coming from the external environment (alpha rhythm) or with information drawn from memory (theta rhythm).

The significance of the quality of the need, on the basis of which the emotional state arises, was demonstrated in the study of the effect of emotions on activity. Of exceptional significance here is the question as to whether we are speaking of need that initiates a given activity or of an emotion that generates some secondary motive.

In the area of the *neuroanatomy of emotions*, the need-information approach, coming directly from the information theory of emotions, made it possible to propose an essentially new diagram of the interaction of brain structures. It was demonstrated that for the organization of behavior in a system of coordinates, "needs and probability of their being satisfied," four formations are necessary and adequate: 1) those isolating the dominant need (hypothalamus) and taking into account the competing or coexisting subdominant motivations (amygdala); 2) those that provide reaction to signals with high (frontal cortex) or low (hippocampus) probability of being reinforced (satisfaction of need). Our own experiments and data from the literature confirmed that the sections of the brain listed above actually have these functions.

In other words, the information theory of emotions made it possible to propose a diagram for the integrative activity of the brain comparable to its anatomical structure, that is, moving from hypothetical block diagrams to placing functional dynamics on a morphological substrate.

There is reason to assume that individual differences of functioning of the four brain structures mentioned above are the basis for types of higher nervous activity, but in the case of pathology, they determine the main varieties of neurotic states.

The information theory of emotions is no less, and in a certain sense is even more productive for the psychology of emotions, "the least productive and most boring of all the areas of this study" (Vygotsky, 1970, p. 127).

Developing the fundamental position of Marxist philosophy on needs as the basis and moving force in human behavior, information theory definitely indicated the diversity and complexity of needs that are by no means reducible to the needs for physical survival. On the basis of the Leninist definition of the self-movement of living nature as a dialectically contradictory unity of tendencies for preservation and development, and on the ideas of Vernadsky and Ukhtomsky, we, together with Ershov, isolated three basic groups of needs: material—biological, social, and ideal (cognitive). Each of these three groups, in its turn, can be divided into the needs of "necessities" (preservation) and of "growth" (development), and these first two groups have still another variant, "for self" and "for others." Further analysis disclosed at least three complementary needs: the need to overcome (will), the need to be equipped with means and methods of satisfying potential needs that have not been actualized at the given moment, and the need to conserve energy.

Needs have the capacity for unlimited growth and extension, which engenders the objective impossibility of historically determined norms for their being satisfied. The working out of these norms represents an important function of individual and social consciousness, a collective knowledge that is a knowledge of the means, methods, and norms of satisfying needs that may be transmitted to other members of society.

Outside the sphere of knowledge, there are two varieties of higher nervous (psychic) activity. First, there are secondarily automatized actions, engrams of involuntary memory, causes of conflicts between biological needs and social norms for their being satisfied. This variety of the unconscious psychic might well be called the subconscious, which is connected with needs for preservation, "necessity." Second, there are the unconscious stages of creativity (including the creation of new norms) and the mechanisms for generating "psychic mutations": hypotheses, intuitive guesses, and illuminations. This second variety of the unconscious we designate as the superconscious (Stanislavsky's term) or the hyperconscious (Yaroshevsky's term). The superconscious is connected with needs for development, "growth"; its activity is frequently apparent in a conflict between social and ideal (cognitive) needs of the subject.

In the area of higher nervous activity, the functioning of the superconscious and consciousness can be compared to mutation and subsequent selection in the process of the evolution of living nature. At the first stages of creativity, the unconscious protects it from premature interference by consciousness, from pressure from experience accumulated earlier, and from fixed norms. In this inaccessibility of the sources of creativity to consciousness are concealed the deposit and condition for further development and the essential impossibility of fully programming the activity of the human mind. The impossibility of formalizing creativity represents the same kind of "prohibition" as is enforced by the laws of nature, like the conservation of energy, the speed of light, or the principle of complementarity in physics.

Hypotheses on the decisive role of needs, the interaction of will, consciousness, and the superconscious brought us not to the resolution of the problem of determinism and free choice, but to removing this problem as being improperly set forth and therefore outdated. The objective determinacy of human actions according to man's inherited endowment and conditions of his being reared is combined with a subjective feeling of freedom of choice and a feeling of personal responsibility. This feeling moves the subject to analyze all aspects of a given situation as well as the consequences of his actions. The mechanism of the superconscious protects the need that is stably dominant in the structure of the given personality from vicissitudes of external influences and facilitates the overcoming of norms the subject had adopted if they contradict the results of recognizing a continuously developing social reality. Man is relatively "free," not at the stage of selection where he is determined by heredity, education, experience, and the influence of the given situation, but at the stage of generating variants underlying selection: if I have only variants A and B, I cannot objectively select variant C, which is best, because I am not aware of it. The richer the "psychic mutations" are that combine past experience into new combinations not predetermined by experience alone, the broader is the scope for possible selection in the transformation of its results into action or into a hypothesis to be subjected to further confirmation.

What conclusions for the theory and practice of psychology can be drawn from the concepts we have developed?

1. To the end, we must understand that emotions are only a secondary product of needs that hide behind them, only indicators of the degree to which the needs are being satisfied. For example, fear is the natural reaction of any man if the probability of the need for preservation (of himself, other people, equipment, etc.) becomes very low. Neil Armstrong, the first man to step on the moon, said that fear is a feeling that we all know. Cowardice is another matter; it is fear that is built on a base of a dominant need for self-preservation that dominates other social and ideal motivations that compete with it, it is "the worst of all human defects" (Bulgakov). "It is much more common to hear complaints about passions, but as Mably has validly said, the stronger passions are, the more useful they are in society; controlling them may only be harmful" (Lobachevsky, 1976, p. 41). Discussions of "bad and good" emotions, of "educating emotions," of "developing and enriching the emotional sphere of the personality," etc., belong to the yesterdays of science. Education is the formation of such complement, hierachy, and norms of satisfying needs as would be optimal for the development of the personality and society as a whole.

2. An appeal to knowledge and consciousness is the least productive way to form a sphere of motives. The real way is to equip the subject with those means and methods, the use of which would engender positive emotions on a base of socially valuable motivations. Of special significance here are needs of the cognitive—creative type that are capable of producing joy and satisfaction in the process of the activity itself, right up to the moment of achieving its required material and social result.

3. Instead of infinite theoretical explanations of why activity "for others" is more valuable and better than egoistic striving for goals "for self," it is necessary to focus maximum effort on increasing the qualifications of the subject in whatever area he might be working. Only highly qualified activity is objectively activity "for others," which, at the same time, satisfies a whole complex of needs that the subject has: material (compensation), social (respect, prestige), and ideal (realization of potentials and endowment).

4. Since will and the superconscious (intuition) are connected with the need that is stably dominant in the structure of a given personality, they may be indicators of this need in a diagnosis of the social and professional orientation of the subject. Different professions have different "tolerance" for the dominance of one set of motives or another. For example, a man may be very productive in carrying out technological tasks, being predominantly oriented toward material needs "for self." A teacher or doctor are professionally not suited if they do not have a dominant need "for others," and a future scientist or artist will never achieve great results if a need for knowledge as an end in itself is not predominant in the system of his needs. It is understood that the ideal still is a harmonious development of the personality, but since the world is not made up of ideal people, the recognition of needs that are actually dominant is infinitely more important for professional orientation than the total number of points received on an entrance examination at an institute.

We have mentioned only certain, and perhaps not the most important, conclusions emerging from the information theory of emotions. Its development is a matter for the future. "We need to go from theories that are logically consistent to man himself in all his living specificity and reality...Our time is alive with the birth pangs of this new method. It will enrich our life and thought a hundredfold more than its prototype, the method of Copernicus" (Ukhtomsky, 1973, p. 255).

References

Ackoff, R., and Emery, F. (1972), On Purposeful Systems, Aldine, Chicago.

Adams, D. B. (1971), "Defence and territorial behaviour dissociated by hypothalamic lesions in the rat," Nature, 232: No. 5312, 573.

Adey, W. R. (1969), "Cellular mechanisms and the characteristics of the neural system in processing information," in: Systemic Organization of Physiological Functions [Russian translation], Meditsina, Moscow, p. 219.

Adey, W. R., Dunlop, S. V., and Hendrix, C. E. (1960), "Hippocampal slow waves, distribution and phase relationships in the course of approach learning," AMA Arch. Neurol., 3: 74.

Adrianov, O. S., Molodkina, L. N., Shugalev, N. P., et al. (1978), "A comparative analysis of capacity for extrapolation in cats after disruption of the caudate nucleus and prefrontal lobectomy," Zh. Vyssh. Nervn. Deyat., 28: No. 5, 913.

Akutagawa Ryunosuke (1974), Short Stories [Russian translation], Khudozh. Lit., Moscow.

Alexander, B. K., and Roth, E. M. (1971), "The effects of acute crowding on the aggressive behaviour of Japanese monkeys," Behaviour, 39: No. 2-4, 73.

Alexander, B. K., and Perachio, A. (1973), "The influence of target sex and dominance on evoked attack on rhesus monkeys," Am. J. Phys. Anthropol., 38: No. 2, 543.

Allikmets, L. Kh., and Ditrikh, M. E. (1965), "Effect of disturbances in the limbic system on emotional reactions and conditioned reflexes in rats," Zh. Vyssh. Nervn. Deyat., 15: No. 1, 86.

Allport, G. W. (1955), Becoming. Basic Consideration for a Psychology of Personality, Yale University Press, New Haven.
Allport, G. W. (1961), Pattern and Growth in Personality, Holt, Rinehart and Winston, New York.
Anderson, P., and Eccles, J. (1962), "Inhibitory phasing of neuronal discharge," Nature, 196: No. 4855, 645.
Andreev, L. N. (1969), "The problem of the mechanism of hyperreactivity in lobectomized and caudatectomized animals," Zh. Vyssh. Nervn. Deyat., 19: No. 6, 1082.
Anokhin, P. K. (1964), Emotions [in Russian], Great Medical Encyclopedia, 2nd edn., Vol. 35, p. 339.
Anokhin, P. K. (1966), "Cybernetics and integrative activity of the brain," Vopr. Psikhol., No. 3, 10.
Anokhin, P. K. (1968), The Biology and Neurophysiology of the Conditioned Reflex [in Russian], Meditsina, Moscow.
Anokhin, P. K. (1969), The Systemic Organization of Physiological Function [in Russian], Meditsina, Moscow, p. 10.
Arab-Ogly, E. (1972), "Rejection of freedom and dignity," Lit. Gaz., No. 49, p. 15.
Arnold, M. B. (1960), Emotion and Personality, Vol. 2. Neurological and Physiological Aspects, Columbia University Press, New York.
Arshavsky, V. V., and Rotenberg, V. S. (1976), "Seeking activity and its effect on experimental and clinical pathology," Zh. Vyssh. Nervn. Deyat., 26: No. 2, 424.
Arshavsky, V. V., and Rotenberg, V. S. (1978), "Effect of different types of behavior reactions and emotional states on pathophysiological and clinical syndromes," Usp. Fiziol. Nauk, 9: No. 3, 49.
Asratyan, E. A. (1938), "Simultaneous development of different conditioned reflexes to one and the same stimulus," in: Third Conference on Physiological Problems [in Russian], Izd. Akad. Nauk SSSR, Moscow-Leningrad, p. 31.
Asratyan, E. A. (1959a), Physiology of the Central Nervous System [in Russian], Izd. Akad. Med. Nauk SSSR, Moscow.
Asratyan, E. A. (1959b), Lectures on Certain Problems of Neurophysiology [in Russian], Izd. Akad. Nauk SSSR, Moscow.
Asratyan, E. A. (1970), "Causal conditioned reflex," Vopr. Filosof., No. 10, 117.
Asratyan, E. A. (1971), "On the physiology of the reinforcement of the conditioned reflex," Zh. Vyssh. Nervn. Deyat., 21: No. 1, 3.
Asratyan, E. A. (1974), "The reflector theory and the problem of motivation," in: Basic Problems in the Electrophysiology of the Brain [in Russian], Nauka, Moscow, p. 5.

Bakanov, E. N. (1977), "Stages of development of volitional processes," Vestn. Mosk. Gos. Univ., Ser. Psikhol., No. 4, 12.

Bakeev, V. A. (1971a), "The relation of suggestibility and anxiety," in: Proceedings of the 4th All-Union Congress of Psychologists, Tbilisi, p. 57.

Bakeev, V. A. (1971b), "The relation of will and suggestibility," in: New Research in Psychology and Adult Physiology [in Russian], No. 1, Izd. MGU, Moscow.

Bakeev, V. A. (1974), "The anxious-suggestible personality type," in: New Research in Psychology [in Russian], No. 1, Izd. MGU, Moscow, p. 19.

Ball, G. (1969), "Separation of electrical self-stimulation and electrically elicited eating in the hypothalamus," Commun. Behav. Biol., A3: No. 1, 5.

Bandzeladze, G. D., and Gaprindashvili, G. G. (1971), "The problem of interrelations of need and duty," in: Proceedings of the 4th All-Union Congress of Psychologists, Tbilisi, p. 136.

Baroyan, O. (1967), "The talent of an investigator," Lit. Gaz., No. 10, p. 11.

Bassin, F. V., and Rozhnov, V. E. (1975), "The modern approach to the problem of unconscious psychic activity (of the nonconscious)," Vopr. Filosof., No. 10, 94.

Bazhin, E. F., Vanina, T. M., Malyukova, I. V., et al. (1970), "Studies on the features of probability prediction with local damage to the brain and in certain mental disorders," in: Principles of Probability Organization of Behavior, Recognition, and Medical Diagnosis [in Russian], Leningrad, p. 17.

Beatty, J., Greenberg, A., Deibler, W., and O'Hanlon, J. (1974), "Operant control of occipital theata rhythm affects performance in a radar monitoring task," Science, 183: No. 4127, 871.

Begleiter, H., and Platz, A. (1969), "Cortical evoked potentials to semantic stimuli," Psychophysiology, 6: No. 1, 91.

Bekhtel', E. E. (1968), "Some notes in connection with the point of P. V. Simonov on the biological existence of emotion," in: Problems of Psychiatry [in Russian], Vologda, p. 246.

Bekhtereva, N. P. (1971), Neurophysiological Aspects of Human Psychic Activity [in Russian], Meditsina, Leningrad.

Belenkov, N. Yu., and Shalkovskaya, L. N. (1978), "The significance of dominant motivation in the manifestation of effects of electrical stimulation of the hypothalamo-limbic structures," Zh. Vyssh. Nervn. Deyat., 28: No. 1, 62.

Belov, V. P. (1971), "Personality traits and psychosomatic interrelations in patients with ulcers of the stomach (duodenum) and ulcerative colitis," Zh. Nevropatol. Psikhiat., 71: No. 9, 1385.

Bennett, T., French, J., and Burnett, K. (1978), "Species differences in the behavior correlates of hippocampal RSA," Behav. Biol., 22: No. 2, 161.

Berlyne, D. E. (1974), "Information and motivation," in: Human Communication: Theoretical Exploration, Hillsdale, New York, p. 19.

Berlyne, D. E. (1978), "Curiosity and learning," Motiv. Emotion, 2: No. 2, 97.

Bespal'ko, I. G. (1976), "The features of perception of mimicry by schizophrenia patients in connection with disruption of their probability evaluations," Zh. Nevropatol. Psikhiatr., 76: No. 12, 1828.

Borisenko, S. A. (1977), "The effect of psychotropic substances on the reaction of self-stimulation," Byull. Eksp. Biol. Med., 83: No. 4, 429.

Borisova, M. N., Gurevich, K. M., Ol'shannikova, A. E., and Ravich-Shcherba, I. V. (1976), "Certain problems of the psychophysiology of individual differences," Vopr. Psikhol., No. 5, 19.

Bovard, E. W. (1961), "A concept of hypothalamic functioning," Perspect. Biol. Med., 5: No. 1, 52.

Bovard, E. W. (1962), "The balance between negative and positive brain system activity," Perspect. Biol. Med., 6: No. 1, 116.

Bozhovich, L. I. (1970), "Social, personal and practical trends as determinants of children's behavior," in: The 20th International Psychology Congress [in Russian], Moscow, p. 13.

Bragina, N. N., and Dobrokhotova, T. A. (1977), "The problem of functional asymmetry of the brain," Vopr. Filosof., No. 2, 135.

Brown, B. (1971), "Awareness of EEG—subjective activity relationships detected within a closed feedback system," Psychophysiology, 7: No. 3, 451.

Bruner, J. S., and Postman, L. (1947), "Emotional selectivity in perception and reaction," J. Pers., 16: 69.

Brushlinsky, A. V. (1966), "The process of seeking the unknown in the course of solving mental tasks," in: New Studies in the Pedagogical Sciences [in Russian], Moscow, p. 129.

Brushlinsky, A. V. (1967), "On the psychology of the creative process," in: Man and Creativity [in Russian], Nauka, Moscow, p. 13.

Buchtel, H. A., Campari, F., DeRisio, C., and Rota, R. (1976/77), "Hemispheric differences in discriminative reaction time to facial expressions: preliminary observations," Boll. Soc. Ital. Biol. Sper., 52: No. 18, 1447.

Bunnell, B. N., Sodetz, F. J., and Shalloway, D. I. (1970), "Amygdaloid lesions and social behavior in the golden hamster," Physiol. Behav., 5: No. 2, 153.

Burton, M. J., Rolls, E. T., and Mora, F. (1976), "Effects of hunger on the responses of neurons in the lateral hypothalamus to the sight and taste of food," Exp. Neurol., 51: No. 3, 668.

Cardner, H., Ling, P., Flamma, L., and Silverman, J. (1975), "Comprehension and appreciation of humorous material following brain damage," Brain, 98: No. 3, 399.

Casey, K. L., and Keene, J. J. (1973), "Unit analysis of the effects of motivating stimuli in the awake animal: pain and self-stimulation," in: Brain Unit Activity during Behavior, C. C. Thomas, Springfield, p. 115.

Chasov, V. A. (1959), "Psychological analysis of suggestion and its practical application," Candidate's Dissertation in Psychology, Leningrad State University, Leningrad.

Cherkes, V. A. (1967), "Instinctive and conditioned reactions in cats with excised amygdala nuclei," Zh. Vyssh. Nervn. Deyat., 17: No. 1, 70.

Cherkes, V. A. (1978), The Frontal Brain and Elements of Behavior [in Russian], Naukova Dumka, Kiev.

Chkhartishvili, Sh. N. (1967), "The problem of will in psychology," Vopr. Psikhol., No. 4, 72.

Chkhartishvili, Sh. N. (1971), "The social situation and motive forces of the development of the human personality," in: Proceedings of the 4th All-Union Congress of Psychologists [in Russian], Tbilisi, p. 71.

Church, R. M. (1959), "Emotional reactions of rats to the pain of others," J. Comp. Physiol. Psychol., 52: 132.

Connor, J., and Watson, P. (1977), "A device for presenting attack opportunity as a reinforcer for operant behavior," Behav. Res. Methods Instrum., 9: No. 4, 349.

Cytawa, J. (1979), "The nature of reinforcement in ingestive instrumental conditioning," in: Abstracts of Symposium on Instrumental Conditioning, Jablonna.

Cytawa, J., and Trojniar, W. (1976), "The state of pleasure and its role in instrumental conditioning," Acta Nerv. Super., 18: No. 1/2, 92.

Danin, D. S. (1976), "Why art?" Vopr. Filosof., No. 10, 111.

Dashkevich, O. V. (1970), "Emotions and their regulation in sport," Author's Abstract of Candidate's Dissertation in Medical Sciences, Moscow.

Dawkins, R. (1977), The Selfish Gene, Oxford University Press, New York.

Deets, A., Harlow, H., Singh, S., and Blomquist, A. (1970), "Effects of bilateral lesions of the frontal granular cortex on the social behavior of rhesus monkeys," J. Comp. Physiol. Psychol., 72: No. 3, 452.

Deglin, V. L. (1973), "A clinical experimental study of unilateral electroconvulsive incidents," Zh. Nevropatol. Psikhiat., 73: No. 11, 1609.

Deglin, V. L., and Nikolaenko, N. N. (1975), "The role of the dominant hemisphere in regulating emotional states," Fiziol. Cheloveka, 1: No. 3, 418.

DeJong, R., Italbashi, H., and Olson, J. (1969), "Memory loss due to hippocampal lesions," Arch. Neurol., 20: No. 4, 339.

Delgado, J. (1969), Physical Control of the Mind, Harper and Row, New York.

Delgado, J. (1971), The Brain and Consciousness [Russian translation], Mir, Moscow.

Denisova, Z. V. (1978), Mechanisms of Emotional Behavior of the Child [in Russian], Nauka, Leningrad.

Denisova, Z. V., Brendsted, A. N., and Tarakanov, P. V. (1978), "Interhemisphere asymmetry of theta activity in children with emotional problems," Zh. Vyssh. Nervn. Deyat., 28: No. 1, 169.

Desiderato, O., and Newman, A. (1971), "Conditioned suppression produced in rats by tones paired with escapable or inescapable shock," J. Comp. Physiol. Psychol., 77: No. 3, 427.

Deutsch, J. A., and Howarth, C. I. (1963), "Some tests of a theory of intracranial self-stimulation," Psychol. Rev., 70: No. 5, 444.

Diligensky, G. G. (1976), "The problem of the theory of human needs," Vopr. Filosof., No. 9, p. 30; (1977), No. 2, 111.

Dimond, S. J., Farrington, L., and Johnson, P. (1976), "Differing emotional response from right and left hemispheres," Nature, 261: No. 5562, 690.

Divac, I., and Kosmal, A. (1978), "Subcortical projections to the prefrontal cortex in the rat as revealed by the horseradish peroxidase technique," Neuroscience, 3: 785.

Dlag, J. (1977), "Aggression and submission in monkey societies," Anim. Behav., 25: No. 2, 465.

Dneprov, V. (1968), The Subjective and the Moral [Russian translation], Inostr. Lit., No. 10, 193.

Dobrokhotova, T. A. (1968), "Pathology of the emotional sphere with tumor disease in the frontal lobes of the brain," Zh. Nevropatol. Psikhiatr., 68: No. 3, 418.

Dobrokhotova, T. A., and Bragina, N. N. (1975), "Spatial-temporal factors in the organization of neuropsychic activity," Vopr. Filosof., No. 5, 133.

Dobrokhotova, T. A., and Bragina, N. N. (1977), Functional Asymmetry and Psychopathology in Focal Damage to the Brain [in Russian], Meditsina, Moscow.

Dodonov, B. I. (1978), Emotion as a Value [in Russian], Politizdat, Moscow.

Dostoevsky, F. M. (1958), Collected Works, Vol. 9 [in Russian], Goslitizdat, Moscow.

Douglas, R. (1972), "Pavlovian conditioning and the brain," in: Inhibition and Learning, Academic Press, New York, p. 529.

Douglas, R., and Pribram, K. (1966), "Learning and limbic lesions," Neuropsychologia, 4: No. 3, 197.

Dozlovskaya, M. M., and Waldman, A. V. (1972), "Vegetative correlates of emotional reactions," in: Experimental Neurophysiology of Emotions [in Russian], Nauka, Leningrad, pp. 173-219.

Drobnitsky, O. G. (1972), "Social and biological factors of human development," Vopr. Filosof., No. 9, 109.

Dubinin, N. P. (1972), "The social and biological in the contemporary human problem," Vopr. Filosof., No. 10, 50.

Dubrovsky, D. I. (1976), "The information approach to the problem 'consciousness and brain'," Vopr. Filosof., No. 11, 41.

Dubrovsky, D. I. (1978a), "Consciousness and brain," Priroda, No. 8, 91.

Dubrovsky, D. I. (1978b), "Consciousness and information: toward an analysis of the problem of the ideal," Filosof. Nauki, No. 6, 46.

Dzhalagoniya, Sh. L. (1972), "Producing neurotic states in monkeys with intact brains and with damaged frontal lobes," Zh. Vyssh. Nervn. Deyat., 22: No. 4, 708.

Dzheliev, I. T., Lagutina, N. I., and Fufacheva, A. A. (1963), "Central mechanisms of regulating blood circulation and respiration in monkeys," Fiziol. Zh. SSSR, 49:

Eisenberger, R. (1972), "Exploration of rewards that do not reduce tissue needs," Psychol. Bull., 77: No. 5, 319.

Epstein, S., and Bahm, R. (1971), "Verbal hypothesis formulation during classical conditioning of the GSR," J. Exp. Psychol., 87: No. 2, 187.

Ershov, P. M. (1972), Theatrical Direction as Practical Psychology [in Russian], Iskusstvo, Moscow.

Ershov, P. M., and Simonov, P. V. (1965), "What is to be done with feeling?" Teatr, No. 11, 56.

Fedoseev, P. N. (1973), "Culture and morals," Vopr. Filosof., No. 4, 23.

Feierbakh, L. (1955), Collected Philosophical Works, Vol. 1 [in Russian], Moscow.

Feigenberg, I. M. (1963), "Probability predictions in brain activity," Vopr. Filosof., No. 2, 59.

Feigenberg, I. M. (1965), "Interaction of analyzers and its clinical significance," Author's Abstract of Doctoral Dissertation, Moscow.

Filippycheva, N. A., and Faller, T. O. (1978), "Functional significance of the medial sections of the frontal lobes of the human brain," in: Location and Organization of Cerebral Function [in Russian], Moscow.

Flynn, J. P. (1967), "The neural basis of aggression in cats," in: Neurophysiology and Emotion, Rockefeller University Press, New York, p. 40.

Fonberg, E. (1965), "The role of amygdala nuclei in the behavior of animals," in: Reflexes of the Brain [in Russian], Nauka, Moscow.

Fonberg, E. (1967), "The motivational role of the hypothalamus in animal behaviour," Acta Biol. Exp., 27: No. 3, 303.

Ford, J. G., Bremner, F. J., and Richie, W. R. (1970), "The effect of hours of food deprivation on hippocampal theta rhythm," Neuropsychologia, 8: No. 1, 65.

Fress, P. (1975), in: Experimental Psychology, 5th edn. [in Russian], Progress, Moscow, p. 111.

Friedman, M., Brown, A., and Roseman, R. (1969), "Voice analysis test for detection of behavior patterns. Responses of normal men and coronary patients," J. Am. Med. Assoc., 208: No. 5, 828.

Frolov, M. V., and Sviridov, E. P. (1974), "Amplitude of the T-peak of the EKG as a correlate of emotional stress," Zh. Vyssh. Nervn. Deyat., 24: No. 5, 1052.

Fromm, E. (1960), Man for Himself, Holt, Rinehart and Winston, New York.

Frost, R. O., Burish, T. G., and Holmes, D. S. (1978), "Stress and EEG alpha," Psychophysiology, 15: No. 5, 394.

Ganelina, I. E. (1975), Ischemic Heart Disease and Individual Traits of the Organism [in Russian], Nauka, Leningrad.

Gantchev, G., Danev, S., and Koitcheva, V. (1967), "La frequence cardiaque en cours d'un travail de differente responsibilite et sa correlation avec la quantite de l'information recue et elaboree," Activ. Nerv. Super., 9: No. 1, 25.

Gantman, Yu. N. (1971), "Satisfaction through activity in connection with personality traits," Candidate's Dissertation in Psychological Science, Moscow State University, Moscow.

Gershuni, G. V., Bogdanov, B. V., Vikarchuk, O. Yu., Mal'tsev, V. P., and Chernigovskaya, T. V. (1976), "Human recognition of various types of sound signals made by apes," Fiziol. Cheloveka, 2: No. 3, 407-408.

Garai, L. (1966), "The historically materialistic approach to the problem of specific human needs," Vopr. Psikhol., No. 3, 61.

Garai, L. (1968), "Historical materialism and the problem of personality," Vopr. Filosof., No. 9, 19.

Gellhorn, E. (1948), Regulatory Function of the Autonomic Nervous System [Russian translation], Inostr. Lit., Moscow.

Gellhorn, E. (1960), "The tuning of the autonomic nervous system through the alteration of the internal environment (asphyxia)," Acta Neuroveget., 20: No. 4, 514.

Gershuni, G. V. (1971), "Certain traits of brain activity," in: Mechanisms of Regulation of Physiological Functions [in Russian], Nauka, Leningrad, p. 43.

Gershuni, G. V., Bogdanov, B. V., and Vakarchuk, O. Yu. (1977), "A study of the recognition by man of a long-distance orienting sound signal of monkeys," Fiziol. Cheloveka, 3: No. 6, 1090.

Gershuni, G. V., Bogdanov, B. V., and Vakarchuk, O. Yu. (1976), "Recognition by man of various sound signals produced by monkeys," Fiziol. Cheloveka, 2: No. 3, 407.

Gilyarov, M. S. (1976), "Feedback and direction of the evolutionary process," Vestn. Akad. Nauk SSSR, No. 8, 68.

Glaubman, H., Orbach, I., Aviran, O., et al. (1978), "REM deprivation and divergent thinking," Psychophysiology, 15: No. 1, 74.

Gloor, P. (1960), "Amygdala," in: Handbook of Physiology, Vol. 2, Am. Physiol. Soc., Washington, D.C., p. 1395.

Golding, W. (1973), Tales of William Golding [Russian translation], Inostr. Lit., No. 10, p. 204.

Gorfunkel', P. L. (1971), "Review: P. V. Simonov. Theory of reflection and the psychophysiology of emotions," Vopr. Filosof., No. 10, 154.

Gorsky, Yu. M. (1978), Informational Aspects of Control and Simulation [in Russian], Nauka, Moscow.

Greenberg, R., and Pearlman, C. (1974), "Cutting the REM nerve: An approach to the adaptive role of REM sleep," Perspect. Biol. Med., 17: No. 4, 513.

Greene, J. T. (1969), "Altruistic behavior in the albino rat," Psychon. Sci., 14: No. 1, 47.

Grigor'yan, G. A. (1978), "Current concepts of the mechanisms of self-stimulation," Usp. Fiziol. Nauk, 9: No. 3, 73.

Grindel', O. M., Bragina, N. N., Dobronravova, I. S., and Dobrokhotova, T. A. (1974), "Generalized rhythmic theta activity in the human EEG when the mediobasal structures of the brain are damaged," in: Fundamental Problems of the Electrophysiology of the Brain [in Russian], Nauka, Moscow, p. 261.

Gryzlova, I. N. (1976), "The relations of features of perceptive activity in emotiogenic situations of various kinds and certain personality characteristics," in: A Neurophysiological Approach to Analysis of Intraspecific Behavior [in Russian], Nauka, Moscow, p. 143.

Hailman, H. (1967), "The ontogeny of instinct," Behavior, Suppl. 15.

Hare, R. (1973), "Orienting and defensive responses to visual stimuli," Psychophysiology, 10: No. 5, 453.

Hebb, D. O. (1946), "On the nature of fear," Psychol. Rev., 53: 259.

Hegel, G. (1968), Esthetics, Vol. 1 [Russian translation], Iskusstvo.

Hegel, G. (1970), "Works of various years," Vopr. Filosof., No. 5, 121.

Henke, P. G. (1977), "Dissociation of the frustration effect and the partial reinforcement extinction effect after limbic lesions in rat," J. Comp. Physiol. Psychol., 91: No. 5, 1032.

Henke, P., and Maxwell, D. (1973), "Lesions in the amygdala and the frustration effect," Physiol. Behav., 10: No. 4, 647.

Hess, W. R. (1968), Psychologie in biologischen Sicht, Georg Thieme Verlag, Stuttgart.

Hinde, R. A. (1975), Animal Behavior [Russian translation], Mir, Moscow.

Hirsh, R. (1974), "The hippocampus and contextual retrieval of information from memory: A theory," Behav. Biol., 12: No. 4, 421.

Hodge, F. A. (1935), "The emotions in a new role," Psychol. Rev., 42: 555.

Hunt, S. M. (1979), "Hypnosis as obedience behaviour," Br. J. Sociol. Clin. Psychol., 18: No. 1, 21.

Huston, J. P. (1971), "Relationship between motivating and rewarding stimulation of the lateral hypothalamus," Physiol. Behav., 6: No. 6, 711.

Huston, J. P. (1972), "Inhibition of hypothalamically motivated eating by rewarding stimulation through the same electrode," Physiol. Behav., 8: No. 8, 1121.

Ilyutchenok, R. (1979), "The emotiogenic brain structures in conditioning mechanisms: conditioned evoked potentials and motor responses," in: Abstracts of Symposium on Instrumental Conditioning, Jablonna.

Ioffe, M. E., and Samoilov, M. I. (1972), "Feedback in complex defensive reflexes," Zh. Vyssh. Nervn. Deyat., 22: No. 3, 466.

Isaacson, R. L. (1978), "The limbic system contributions to goal-directed behavior," in: Abstracts of US—USSR Symposium, Irvine.

Isaacson, R. L., and Pribram, K. H. (1975), The Hippocampus, Vol 2: Neurophysiology and Behavior (1975), Plenum Press, New York.

Ivanitsky, A. M. (1976), Brain Mechanisms of Signal Evaluation [in Russian], Meditsina, Moscow.

Izard, C. E. (1977), Human Emotions, Plenum Press, New York.

Jarrard, L. E., and Becker, J. T. (1977), "The effects of selective hippocampal lesions on DRL behavior in rats," Behav. Biol., 21: No. 3, 393.

Johnston, V. S., and Chesney, G. L. (1976), "Electrophysiological correlates of meaning," Science, 186: No. 4167, 944.

Jonas, A. D., and Jonas, D. F. (1975), "The influence of early training on the varieties of stress responses, an ethological approach," J. Psychosom. Res., 19: No. 5/6, 325.

Jonas, A. D., and Jonas, D. F. (1975), "The influence of early training on the varieties of stress responses, an ethological approach," J. Psychosom. Res., 19: No. 5/6, 325.

Kapitsa, P.L. (1977), "The scientific and social approach to resolving global problems," Vopr. Filosof., No. 1, 46.

Karli, P., Vergnes, M., Eclancher, F., Schmitt, P., and Chaurand, J. P. (1972), "Role of the amygdala in the control of 'mouse-killing' behavior in the rat," in: Neurobiology of the Amygdala, B. E. Eleftheriou (ed.), Plenum Press, New York, p. 553.

Khananashvili, M. M. (1978), Information Neuroses [in Russian], Meditsina, Leningrad.

Kharkevich, A. A. (1960), "The value of information," Probl. Kibern., No. 4, 53.

Khayutin, V. M. (1967), "Development of concepts on the function of cardioaortic and synocarotid zones (automatic protection, self-regulation, adaptive control)," Fiziol. Zh. SSSR, 53: No. 12, 1469.

Kimble, D., and Kimble, R. (1970), "The effect of hippocampal lesions on extinction and 'hypothesis' behavior in rats," Physiol. Behav., 5: No. 7, 735.

Kling, A. (1972), "Effect of amygdalectomy on social-affective behavior in nonhuman primates," in: Neurobiology of the Amygdala, B. E. Eleftheriou (ed.), Plenum Press, New York, p. 511.

Koeb, B. (1974), "Social behavior of rats with chronic prefrontal lesions," J. Comp. Physiol. Psychol., 87: No. 3, 466.

Konapasky, R., and Telegdy, G. (1977), "Conformity in the rat: A leader selection of door color versus a learned door-color discrimination," Percept. Motor Skills, 44: No. 1, 31.

Konorski, J. (1967), Integrative Activity of the Brain, Chicago Univ. Press, Chicago.

Konorski, J., Santibanez, H., and Beck, J. (1968), "Electrical hippocampal activity and heart rate in classical and instrumental conditioning," Acta Biol. Exp., 28: No. 3, 169.

Koolhaas, J. M. (1978), "Hypothalamically induced intraspecific aggressive behaviour in the rat," Exp. Brain Res., 32: No. 3, 365.

Korczynski, R., and Fonberg, E. (1976), "Instrumental reactions and food and water intake in medial amygdala rats," Acta Neurobiol. Exp., 36: 667.

Korinevskaya, I. V. (1978), "Development of a conditioned defensive reflex against a background of rhythmic electrical stimulation of the septum," Neurofiziologiya, 10: No. 3, 239.

Korneva, T. V. (1978), "Certain factors that determine precision in auditory evaluation of emotional states," in: Speech, Emotion, and Personality [in Russian], Leningrad, p. 18.

Kositsky, G. I. (ed.) (1977), Preventive Cardiology [in Russian], Meditsina, Moscow.

Kostandov, E. A. (1977), Perception and Emotion [in Russian], Meditsina, Moscow.

Kostandov, E. A. (1978), "Consciousness and elicited electrical activity of the cerebral cortex," Zh. Vyssh. Nervn. Deyat., 28: No. 6, 1151.

Kostandov, E. A., and Arzumanov, Yu. L. (1980), "Hemispheric asymmetry of the R_{300} wave on unconscious emotional words," Zh. Vyssh. Nervn. Deyat., 30: No. 2, 327.

Kovalev, A. N., Smirnov, L. M., and Rabinovich (1976), "The connection between the inner structure of the EEG and emotiveness," in: New Studies in Psychology, No. 1(14) [in Russian], Pedagogika, Moscow, p. 88.

Kozintsev, G. (1965), "Nine years with *Hamlet*," Iskusst. Kino, No. 9, 59.

Krimova, M. M. (1968), "Effect of intellectual-emotional stress on heart activity," Zh. Vyssh. Nervn. Deyat., 18: No. 2, 266.

Kudryavtsev, V. N. (1974), "Sociopsychological aspects of antisocial behavior," Vopr. Filosof., No. 1, 98.

Kudryavtsev, V. N. (1978), Law and Behavior [in Russian], Yurid. Lit., Moscow.

Kuroda, I., Fujiwara, O., Okamura, N., and Utsuki, N. (1976), "Method for determining pilot stress through analysis of voice communication," Aviat. Space Environ. Med., 47: No. 5, 528.

Lacey, J., Kagan, I., Lacey, B., and Moss, H. (1963), "The visceral level: Situational determiners and behavioural correlates of autonomic response patterns," in: Expression of the Emotions in Man, International Universities Press, New York, p. 161.

Landfield, P., McGough, J., and Tusa, R. (1972), "Theta rhythm: A temporal correlate of memory storage processes in the rat," Science, 175: No. 4017, 87.

Lebedinsky, M. S., and Myasishchev (1966), Introduction to Medical Psychology [in Russian], Meditsina, Leningrad.

Leont'ev, A. N. (1970), "Emotions," in: Philosophical Encyclopedia, Vol. 5 [in Russian], Moscow, p. 553.

Leont'ev, A. N. (1971), Needs, Motives, and Emotions [in Russian], Izd. MGU, Moscow.

Leont'ev, A. N., and Sudakov, K. V. (1978), "Emotions," in: The Great Soviet Encyclopedia, Vol. 30 [in Russian], Moscow, p. 169.

Levi, V. (1973), I and We [in Russian], Molodaya Gvardiya, Moscow.

Lilov, A. (1977), On the Nature of Art [in Russian], Iskusstvo, Moscow.

Lindsley, D. B. (1951), "Emotion," in: Handbook of Experimental Psychology, S. S. Stevens (ed.), Wiley, New York.

Livanov, M. N. (1972), Spatial Organization of Brain Processes [in Russian], Nauka, Moscow.

Lobachevsky, N. I. (1976), "The origins of geometry," Nauka Zhizn', No. 5, 39.

Lomov, B. F. (1971), "The role of practice in the development of a theory of general psychology," Vopr. Psikhol., No. 1, 26.

Lomov, B. F. (1976), "Relations of the social and the biological as a methodological problem in psychology," Vopr. Filosof., No. 4, 83.

Lomov, B. F. (1977), "The problem of the social and biological in psychology," in: The Biological and the Social in Human Development [in Russian], Nauka, Moscow, pp. 34-65.

Lomov, B. F., and Ivanitsky, A. M. (1977), "The interrelation of psychology and physiology in the study of perception," Fiziol. Cheloveka, 3: No. 6, 951.

Lomov, B. F., and Shvyrkov, V. B. (1978), "Foreword," in: Theory of Functional Systems in Physiology and Psychology [in Russian], Nauka, Moscow, p. 4.

Lorenz, K. (1967), On Aggression, Bantam Books, New York.

Luk'yanov, A. N., and Frolov, M. V. (1969), Signals of the State of the Human Operator [in Russian], Nauka, Moscow.

Luria, A. R. (1962), Higher Cortical Functions in Man [in Russian], Izd. MGU, Moscow.

Luria, A. R. (1966), "Frontal lobes and regulation of behavior," in: Frontal Lobes and Regulation of Psychic Processes [in Russian], Izd. MGU, Moscow, p. 7.

Luria, A. R. (1977), "The place of psychology in some social and biological sciences,: Vopr. Filosof., No. 9, 68.

Luria, A. R. (1978), "Functional organization of the brain," in: Fundamentals of Psychology in Natural Science [in Russian], Pedagogika, Moscow, p. 109.

Luria, A. R., and Simernitskaya, E. G. (1975), "Functional interaction of the hemispheres of the brain in the organization of verbal-mimetic functions," Fiziol. Cheloveka, 1: No. 3, 411.

MacLean, P. D. (1970), "The limbic brain in relation to the psychoses," in: Physiological Correlates of Emotion, Academic Press, New York, p. 129.

Maeda Hisao (1976), "The influence of amygdalectomy on aggressive reaction in cats," Fukuoka Acta Med., 67: No. 10, 374.

Magun, V. S. (1978), "Interactions between significance of various needs of the personality and their satisfaction," Vopr. Psikhol., No. 6, 86.

Makarenko, Yu. A. (1972), "Structure and function of the central mechanisms of reinforcement," in: Mechanisms and Principles of Goal-Directed Behavior [in Russian], Nauka, Moscow, p. 212.

Markusha, A. (1979), "Frankly speaking," Nauka Zhizn', No. 3, 63.

Maslow, A. H. (1943), "A theory of human motivation," Psychol. Rev., 50: 370.

Masserman, J. W. Wechkin, S., and Terris, W. (1964), "'Altruistic' behavior in rhesus monkeys," Am. J. Psychiatry, 121: 584.

Masson, M. (1976), "Comment l'enfant s'attache a sa mere," Sci. Avenir, No. 351, 480.
McClelland, D. C., and Atkinson, J. W. (1948), "The projective expression of needs," J. Psychol., 25: 205.
Means, L., Walker, D., and Isaacson, R. (1970), "Facilitated single-alteration go, no-go acquisition following hippocampectomy in the rat," J. Comp. Physiol. Psychol., 72: No. 1, 278.
Mekhedova, A. Ya. (1968), "Evaluation of probability of reinforcement and the alimentary conditioned reflex," Zh. Vyssh. Nervn. Deyat., 18: No. 4, 590-597.
Mekhedova, A. Ya. (1969), "Evaluation of probability of reinforcement and vegetative reactions in dogs," in: Nervous Stress and Heart Activity [in Russian], Nauka, Moscow, p. 185.
Mekhedova, A. Ya. (1971), "The role of frontal areas of the brain in the formation of conditioned reactions adequate to size and the probability of their being reinforced," Zh. Vyssh. Nervn. Deyat., 21: No. 3, 459.
Mekhedova, A. Ya. (1974), "Evaluation of probability of reinforcement in dogs after extirpation of the prefrontal cortex," Zh. Vyssh. Nervn. Deyat., 24: No. 3, 506.
Melges, F., and Popper, R. (1976), "Expectation of rewards and emotional behavior in monkeys," J. Psychiat. Res., 13: No. 1, 11.
Mendelson, J. (1970), "Self-induced drinking in rats: The qualitative identity of drive and reward systems in the lateral hypothalamus," Physiol. Behav., 5: No. 8, 925.
Menitsky, D. N., and Khananashvili, M. M. (1969), "Changes in components of emotional reactions in dogs with probable reinforcement of conditioned stimuli and extinction of conditioned reflexes," Zh. Vyssh. Nervn. Deyat., 19: No. 5, 876.
Metlov, V. I. (1979), "Critical analysis of the evolutionary approach to K. Popper's theory of cognition," Vopr. Filosof., No. 2, 75.
Mikhailov, P. (1977), "Aviation: Old and new 'risk factors'," Za Rubezhom, No. 51, 19.
Mikhailova, N. G. (1975), "Effect of various activating influences on reactions of self-stimulation," Zh. Vyssh. Nervn. Deyat., 25: No. 2, 356.
Mikhailova, N. G., and Sarkisova, K. Yu. (1977), "Effect of summation of stimulations in interaction of self-stimulation zones," Zh. Vyssh. Nervn. Deyat., 27: No. 5, 1021.

Mikhailova, N. G., Staikova, R., and Cheresharov, L. (1979), "The influence of catecholamines on motivational and reinforcement effects from self-stimulation areas," Zh. Vyssh. Nervn. Deyat., 29: No. 4, 815.

Milgram, S. (1974), Obedience to Authority, Harper and Row, New York.

Milner, P. M. (1966), Physiological Psychology, Holt, Rinehart and Winston, New York.

Moore, M., Kagan, J., and Haith, M. (1978), "'Memory' and motives," Dev. Psychol., 14: No. 5, 563.

Mora, F., Rolls, E. T., and Burton, M. J. (1976), "Modulation during learning of the responses of neurons in the lateral hypothalamus to the sight of food," Exp. Neurol., 53: No. 2, 508.

Morgan, M. (1969), "Motivation," Cambridge Res., 5: No. 3, 11,

Morrell, F., Barlow, J., and Brazier, M. (1960), "Analysis of conditioned repetitive response by means of the average response computer," in: Recent Advances in Biological Psychiatry, Grune and Stratton, New York, p. 123.

Mosidze, V. M., and Akbardiya, K. K. (1973), Functional Symmetry and Asymmetry of the Brain Hemispheres [in Russian], Metsniereba, Tbilisi.

Mowrer, O. H. (1960), Learning Theory and Behavior, Wiley, New York.

Mukhina, Yu. K. (1973), "Neuronal structure and synaptoarchitectonics of nuclei of the amygdala complex of predators," Author's Abstract of Candidate's Dissertation in Biology, Brain Institute, Academy of Sciences of the USSR, Moscow.

Naenko, N. I. (1976), Psychic Stress [in Russian], Izd. MGU, Moscow.

Nauta, W. J. (1964), "Some efferent connections of the prefrontal cortex in the monkey," in: The Frontal Granular Cortex and Behavior, J. M. Warren and K. Akert (eds.), McGraw-Hill, New York, p. 397.

Nebylitsyn, V. D. (1968), "The problem of general and specific properties of the nervous system," Vopr. Psikhol., No. 4, 29.

Nebylitsyn, V. D. (1971), "Real problems of differential psychophysiology," Vopr. Psikhol., No. 6, 13.

Newton, G. (1975), "Motivation," in: Experimental Psychology, 5th edn. [Russian translation], Progress, Moscow, p. 15.

Nikitina, L., and Nikitin, B. (1979), "Dialectics of training," Smena, No. 12, 6.

Nosenko, E. L. (1978), "Changes in the characteristics of speech under emotional stress," Vopr. Psikhol., No. 6, 76.

Novikov, S. N. (1979),"Experimental analysis of ethological-physiological mechanisms of the formation of hierarchy in laboratory mice," Author's Abstract of Candidate's Dissertation in Biology, Leningrad State University, Leningrad.

Nuikin, A. (1971), "The moral. The spiritual. The ideational," Novyi Mir, No. 1, 194.

Nunu, C. M., and Osselton, J. W. (1974), "The influence of the EEG alpha rhythm on the perception of visual stimuli," Psychophysiology, 11: No. 3, 294.

Obukhovsky, K. (1972), The Psychology of Human Inclinations [in Russian], Progress, Moscow.

Ohno, S. (1973), Evolution by Gene Duplication [Russian translation], Mir., Moscow.

Older, H. J., and Jenney, L. L. (1975), "Psychological stress measurement through voice output analysis," in: Aerospace Med. Assoc. Annu. Sci. Meeting, San Francisco, p. 179.

Olds, J. (1976), "Behavioral studies of hypothalamic functions: Drives and reinforcements," in: Biological Foundations of Psychiatry, Raven Press, New York, p. 321.

Olds, J. (1977a), Drives and Reinforcements: Behavior Studies of Hypothalamic Functions, Raven Press, New York.

Old, J. (1977b), "Neuronal 'rewards' and self-stimulation of the brain," in: Functional Significance of Electrical Processes in the Brain [Russian translation], Nauka, Moscow.

Olivier, B. (1977), Behavioral Functions of the Medial Hypothalamus in the Rat, Rijksuniv., Groningen.

Oniani, T. N. (1975), "The possibility of developing conditioned reflexes on a base of emotional reactions elicited by electrical stimulation of the limbic structures," Zh. Vyssh. Nervn. Deyat., 25: No. 2, 230.

Oniani, T. N., Uingiadze, A. A., and Abziakidze, E. F. (1970), "Hypothalamohippocampal interactions," Neirofiziologiya, 2: No. 5, 497.

Oniani, T. N., Mgaloblishvili, M. M., and Chidzhavadze, E. O. (1978), "Similarities between functional organization of the hypothalamus and the amygdala complex," in: Location and Organization of Cerebral Functions [in Russian], Moscow, p. 118.

Osipov, V. P. (1924), "The physiological origin of emotions," in: Symposium in Honor of the 75th Anniversary of I. P. Pavlov [in Russian], Leningrad, p. 109.

Parygin, B. D. (1971), Fundamentals of Sociopsychological Theory [in Russian], Mysl', Moscow.

Pavlov, I. P. (1951), Complete Works, Vol. 3, Books 1 and 2 [in Russian], Moscow, Leningrad, p. 109.

Pavlov, I. P. (1954), Pavlov's Wednesday Clinics, Vol. 1 [in Russian], Izd. Akad. Nauk SSSR, Moscow, Leningrad.

Pavlov, I. P. (1973a), Twenty Years of Experience in the Study of Higher Nervous Activity (Behavior) of Animals. The Conditioned Reflex [in Russian], Nauka, Moscow.

Pavlov, I. P. (1973b), "Natural science and the brain," in: A Twenty-Year Experiment in Objective Study of Higher Nervous Activity (Behavior) in Animals [in Russian], Nauka, Moscow, pp. 79-88.

Pavlygina, R. A. (1956), "Producing a dominant focus in the hypothalamic areas and studying its properties," Proceedings of the Institute of Higher Nervous Activity, Academy of Sciences of the USSR, Physiology Series, Vol. 2 [in Russian], Izd. Akad. Nauk SSSR, Moscow, p. 124.

Pavlygina, R. A. (1958), "Disturbances and reestablishment of higher nervous activity in producing a focus of stimulation in the hypothalamic area of a rabbit brain," Proceedings of the Institute of Higher Nervous Activity, Academy of Sciences of the USSR, Vol. 3 [in Russian], Izd. Akad. Nauk SSSR, Moscow, p. 19.

Pavlygina, R. A. (1973), "Dominants and the conditioned reflex at the generalization stage," Zh. Vyssh. Nervn. Deyat., 23: No. 4, 687.

Pavlygina, R. A., Mikhailova, N. G., and Simonov, P. V. (1975), "Self-stimulation with a constant current in rats," Zh. Vyssh. Nervn. Deyat., 25: No. 1, 29.

Pavlygina, R. A., Trush, V. D., Mikhailova, N. G., and Simonov, P. V. (1977), "Interrelation of electrical activity of brain structures in the process of motivated behavior," in: The Functional Significance of Electrical Processes in the Brain [in Russian], Nauka, Moscow.

Pigarev, M. L. (1978), Limbic Switching Mechanisms (Hippocampus and Amygdala) [in Russian], Nauka, Moscow.

Plotnikov, N. (1971), "After the play," Izvestiya, No. 207, p. 5.

Polyakov, E. L., Talan, M. I., and Chernigovsky, V. N. (1978), "Organization of the effects of the hypothalamus on vegetative functions," in: Location and Organization of Cerebral Functions [in Russian], Moscow, p. 132.

Popper, K., and Eccles, J. (1977), The Self and Its Brain, Springer International, New York.

Poshivalov, V. P. (1977), "Group behavior of mice in a communication apparatus," Zh. Vyssh. Nervn. Deyat., 27: No. 5, 1011.

Preobrazhenskaya, L. A. (1969), "A study of the correlation between hippocampal theta rhythm and frequency of heartbeat at initial stages of the development of a defensive conditioned reflex," in: Nervous Stress and Heart Activity [in Russian], Nauka, Moscow, p. 151.

Preobrazhenskaya, L. A. (1973), "Certain characteristics of the conditioned reflex of flight reinforced by painful stimulation of a partner," Zh. Vyssh. Nervn. Deyat., 23: No. 1, 51.

Preobrazhenskaya, L. A. (1974), "Changes in instrumental alimentary reflexes in transition from constant to probable reinforcement," Zh. Vyssh. Nervn. Deyat., 24: No. 5, 965.

Preobrazhenskaya, L. A. (1978), "Emotional stress in conditioned reflex switching of instrumental reflexes of various types," Zh. Vyssh. Nervn. Deyat., 28: No. 3, 505.

Pribram, K. (1961), "On the theory of physiological psychology," Vopr. Psikhol., No. 2, 133.

Pribram, K. (1967), "New biology and neurology of emotions. A structural approach," Am. Psychol., 22: No. 10, 830.

Pribram, K. (1975), "The primate frontal cortex: Progress report," Acta Neurobiol. Exp., 35: No. 5/6, 609.

Pribram, K., Douglas, R., and Pribram, B. (1969), "The nature of nonlimbic learning," J. Comp. Physiol. Psychol., 69: No. 4, Pt. 1, 765.

Protopopov, V. P. (1935), Conditions of the Formation of Motor Habits and Their Physiological Characteristics [in Russian], Gos. Med. Izd. Ukr. SSR, Kiev, Kharkov.

Protopopov, V. P. (1950), Studies of Higher Nervous Activity under Natural Conditions [in Russian], Gos. Med. Izd. Ukr. SSR, Kiev.

Punch, J. C., and King, M. G. (1976), "Effects of signaled and unsignaled stressor on ECG T-wave amplitude," Physiol Behav., 17: No. 2, 227.

Putlyaeva, L. V. (1979), "The function of emotions in the thinking process," Vopr. Psikhol., No. 1, 28.

Quastler, H. (1964), The Emergence of Biological Organization, Yale University Press, New Haven.

Rappoport, S. Kh. (1968), Art and Emotions [in Russian], Muzyka, Moscow.

Reeves, D., Martin, C., and Ghiselli, W. (1977), "Influence of amygdaloid lesions on self-punitive behavior in rats," Physiol. Behav., 18: No. 6, 1089.

Reikovsky, Ya. (1979), Experimental Psychology of Emotions [in Russian], Progress, Moscow.
Rice, G., and Gainer, P. (1962), "'Altruism' in the albino rat," J. Comp. Physiol. Psychol., 55: No. 1, 123.
Richardson, J. S. (1973), "The amygdala: Historical and functional analysis," Acta Neurobiol. Exp., 33: No. 3, 623.
Rickert, E., Bennet, T., Lane, P., and French, J. (1978), "Hippocampectomy and the attenuation of blocking," Behav. Biol., 22: No. 2, 147.
Roitbak, A. I. (1978), "The problem of the unconscious from the point of view of the neuroglial hypothesis on the formation of temporal connections," in: The Unconscious, Vol. 1 [in Russian], Metsniereba, Tbilisi, p. 606.
Rolls, E., and Cooper, S. (1973), "Activation of neurons in the prefrontal cortex by brain stimulation reward in the rat," Brain Res., 60: No. 2, 351.
Rolls, B., and Rolls, E. (1973), "Effects of lesions in the basolateral amygdala on fluid intake in the rat," J. Comp. Physiol. Psychol. 83: No. 2, 240.
Rolls, E., and Rolls, B. (1973), "Altered food preferences after lesions in the basolateral region of the amygdala in the rat," J. Comp. Physiol. Psychol., 83: No. 2, 248.
Rolls, E., Roper-Hall, A., and Sanghera, M. (1977), "Activity of neurons in the substantia innominata and lateral hypothalamus during the initiation of feeding in the monkey," J. Physiol. (London), 272: No. 1, 24.
Roscoe, A. H. (1978), "Stress and workload in pilots," Aviat. Space Environ. Med., 49: No. 4, 630.
Rotenberg, V. S. (1975), "Two types of anxiety and their effect on sleep," in: The 6th All-Union Congress of Neuropathology and Psychiatry, Vol. 1 [in Russian], Moscow, p. 261.
Rotenberg, V. S. (1978), "Dream activity and the problem of the unconscious," in: The Unconscious, Vol. 2 [in Russian], Metsniereba, Tbilisi, p. 99.
Rowell, T. E. (1974), "The concept of social dominance," Behav. Biol., 11: No. 1, 131.
Rubinstein, S. L. (1957), Existence and Consciousness [in Russian], Moscow.
Rubinstein, S. L. (1976), Problems of General Psychology [in Russian], Pedagogika, Moscow.
Rusalov, V. M. (1978), "Neurodynamic bases of individual human behavior," Doctoral Dissertation, Institute of Psychology, Academy of Sciences of the USSR, Moscow.

Rusalova, M. N. (1979), Experimental Studies of Human Emotional Reactions [in Russian], Nauka, Moscow.
Rusinov, V. S. (1967), Dominants [in Russian], Meditsina, Moscow.
Russell, W. A. (ed.) (1970), Milestones in Motivation, Appleton-Century-Crofts, New York.
Sackeim, H. A., and Gur, R. C. (1978), "Lateral symmetry in intensity of emotional expression," Neuropsychologia, 16: No. 4, 433.
Safer, M., and Leventhal, H. (1977), "Ear differences in evaluating emotional tones of voice and verbal content; human perception and performance," J. Exp. Psychol., 3: No. 1, 75.
Saint-Exupery, A. (1957), Land of Man [Russian translation], Moscow.
Saradzhishvili, P. M., Chkhenneli, S. A., and Okudzhava, V. M. (1977), "The role of the amygdala complex in the activity of the central mechanisms of emotional reactions," Fiziol. Cheloveka, 3: No. 2, 195.
Schneirla, T. C. (1959), "An evolutionary and developmental theory of biphasic process underlying approach and withdrawal," in: Current Theory and Research in Motivation, Nebraska Univ. Press, Nebraska.
Schoenfeld, W. N. (1978), "'Reinforcement' in behavior theory," Pavlovian J. Biol. Sci., 13: No. 3, 135.
Schwartz, G. E. (1975), "Biofeedback, self-regulation, and the patterning of psychological processes," Am. Sci., 63: No. 3, 317.
Schwartz, G. E., Davidson, R. J., and Maer, F. (1975), "Right hemisphere lateralization for emotion in the human brain: Interactions with cognition," Science, 190: 286.
Schwartz, G. E., Fair, P., Salt, P., et al. (1976), "Facial expression and imagery in depression: An electromyographic study," Psychosom. Med., 38: No. 5, 337.
Scott, J. P., Stewart, J. M., and de Ghett, V. J. (1973), "Separation in infant dogs," in: Separation and Depression, American Association for the Advancement of Science, Washington, D.C., p. 3.
Sechenov, I. M. (1952), Collected Works, Vol. 1 [in Russian], Izd. Akad. Nauk SSSR, Moscow.
Sechenov, I. M. (1961), Reflexes of the Brain [in Russian], Izd. Akad. Nauk SSSR, Moscow.
Segal, M., and Olds, J. (1972), "Behavior of units in hippocampal circuit of the rat during learning," J. Neurophysiol., 35: No. 5, 680.

Serzhantov, V. F., and Serzhantova, T. I. (1976), "Integrative process in modern biology and the problem of human cognition in natural science," Fiziol. Cheloveka, 2: No. 1, 3.

Shalyapin, F. I. (1957), in: Shalyapin, Vol. 1 [in Russian], Iskusstvo, Moscow.

Shingarov, G. Kh. (1970), "Methodological problems of the unity of the physiology of higher nervous activity and modern neurophysiology and psychology," Vestn. Akad. Med. Nauk SSSR, No. 1, 3.

Shingarov, G. Kh. (1970), "Interesting studies of the problem of emotion," Zh. Vyssh. Nervn. Deyat., 20: No. 6, 1320.

Shingarov, G. Kh. (1970), Emotions and Feelings as a Form of Reflecting Reality [in Russian], Nauka, Moscow.

Shipley, J. E., and Kolb, B. (1977), "Neural correlates of species-typical behavior in the Syrian golden hamster," J. Comp. Physiol. Psychol., 91: No. 5, 1056.

Shreider, Yu. A. (1976), "Striving toward a new synthesis," Vopr. Filosof., No. 10, 114.

Shuleikina, K. V. (1971), Systemic Organization of Alimentary Behavior [in Russian], Nauka, Moscow.

Shumilina, A. I. (1950), "Effect of removing the frontal areas of the cortex of the brain on conditioned reflex activity of a dog in a state of experimental neurosis," Byull. Eksp. Biol. Med., No. 1, 35.

Shustin, N. A., and Sershantov, V. F. (1974), "A discussion of the methodology of the physiological study of man," Fiziol. Zh. SSSR, 60: No. 8, 1304.

Shvyrkov, V. B. (1978), "Theory of functional systems in psychophysiology," in: Theory of Functional Systems in Physiology and Psychology [in Russian], Nauka, Moscow, pp. 11-46.

Simonov, P. V. (1962), The Method of K. S. Stanislavsky and the Physiology of Emotions [in Russian], Izd. Akad. Nauk SSSR, Moscow.

Simonov, P. V. (1964), "The relation of the motor and vegetative components of the conditioned defensive reflex in man," in: Central and Peripheral Mechanisms in Motor Activity of Animals and Man [in Russian], Nauka, Moscow.

Simonov, P. V. (1966a), What Is Emotion? [in Russian], Nauka, Moscow.

Simonov, P. V. (1966b), "The information theory of emotions and 'psychic mutagenesis'," in: Second Symposium on the Problem, "Man and Machine" [in Russian], Moscow, p. 28.

Simonov, P. V. (1968), The Disease of Ignorance. An Introduction to the Psychophysiology of Neuroses [in Russian], Nauka, Moscow.

Simonov, P. V. (1970a), The Theory of Reflection and the Psychophysiology of Emotions [in Russian], Nauka, Moscow.

Simonov, P. V. (1970b), "The problem of increasing trends toward synthesis in science," in: Methodological Problems of the Physiology of Higher Nervous Activity [in Russian], Nauka, Moscow, p. 19.

Simonov, P. V. (1972), "Emotions and cardiovascular pathology: An ethological approach," in: The 23rd Bulletin on Problems of Higher Nervous Activity, Vol. 1 [in Russian], Gorki, p. 82.

Simonov, P. V. (1975), Higher Nervous Activity in Man. Motivational-Emotional Aspects [in Russian], Nauka, Moscow.

Simonov, P. V. (1976), "Conditioned reactions of emotional resonance in rats," in: A Neurophysiological Approach to the Analysis of Intraspecific Behavior [in Russian], Nauka, Moscow.

Simonov, P. V., Anisimov, S. A., and Raibman, N. S. (1978), "Game approaches in the development of physiological data using studies of human emotional reactions as an example," Zh. Vyssh. Nervn. Deyat., 28: No. 4, 675.

Simonov, P. V., and Frolov, M. V. (1970), "Electroencephalographic symptoms of emotional stress," in: Problems of Physiology and Pathology of Higher Nervous Activity, No. 4 [in Russian], Meditsina, Moscow, p. 149.

Skinner, B. F. (1971), Beyond Freedom and Dignity, Bantam-Vintage Books, New York.

Slonim, A. D. (1976), Environment and Behavior [in Russian], Nauka, Leningrad.

Smirnov, V. M. (1976), Stereotaxic Neurology [in Russian], Meditsina, Leningrad.

Smirnov, V. M. (1977), "Review of P. V. Simonov's book, 'Higher Nervous Activity in Man'," Zh. Vyssh. Nervn. Deyat., 27: No. 2, 433.

Sokolov, E. N. (1960), "Neural model of stimulus and the orienting reflex," Vopr. Psikhol., No. 4, 61.

Sperry, R. W. (1966), in: Brain and Conscious Experience, J. C. Eccles (ed.), Springer-Verlag, New York, p. 298.

Spinoza, B. (1932), Ethics [Russian translation], Moscow.

Spirkin, A. G. (1972), "Intuition," in: The Great Soviet Encyclopedia, Vol. 10 [in Russian], Moscow, p. 343.

Stanislavsky, K. S. (1954), Collected Works, Vols. 1 and 2 [in Russian], Iskusstvo, Moscow.

Stanislavsky, K. S. (1957), Actor's Work on the Role [in Russian], Iskusstvo, Moscow.

Starr, M., and Mineka, S. (1977), "Determinants of fear over the course of avoidance learning," Learn. Motiv., 8: No. 3, 332.

Stevens, R. (1973), "Probability discrimination learning in hippocampectomized rats," Physiol. Behav., 10: No. 6, 1023.

Stoletov, V. (1976), "Formation of personality," Pravda, No. 245, 3.

Strasser, S. (1970), "Feeling as a basis of knowing and recognizing the other as an ego," in: Feelings and Emotions, M. B. Arnold (ed.), Academic Press, New York, p. 291.

Strongman, K. (1973), The Psychology of Emotion, Wiley, New York.

Suberi, M., and McKeever, W. (1977), "Differential right hemispheric memory storage of emotional and nonemotional faces," Neuropsychologia, 15: No. 6.

Sudakov, K. V. (1971), Biological Motivation [in Russian], Meditsina, Moscow.

Sudakov, K. V., and Zhuravlev, B. V. (1979), "Burstlike rhythm of neurons as a reflection of processes of anticipation of food reinforcement by hungry animals," Zh., Vyssh. Nervn. Deyat., 29: No. 3, 643.

Sukhomlinsky, V. A. (1971), "The work of the soul," Koms. Pravda, No. 53, p. 4.

Sukhomlinsky, V. A. (1979), "The birth of a citizen," Mol. Gvardiya, Moscow.

Sulc, J. (1975), "Toward the Problem of emotional changes in human voice," in: Abstracts of 2nd Intern. Congress, C. I. A. N. S., Pt. 1, Prague, p. 203.

Suvorova, V. V. (1975), Psychophysiology of Stress [in Russian], Pedagogika, Moscow.

Taubkin, V. L. (1977), "Recognition of the emotional state of a human operator by using parameters of the speech signal," Candidate's Dissertation in Biology, Institute of Higher Nervous Activity and Neurophysiology, Academy of Sciences of the USSR, Moscow.

Theorell, T., Blunk, D., and Wolf, S. (1974), "Emotions and cardiac contractivity as reflected in ballistocardiographic recordings," Pavlovian J. Biol. Sci., 9: No. 2, 65.

Tikhomirov, O. K. (1969), Structure of Human Thinking Activity [in Russian], Izd. MGU, Moscow.

Tikhomirov, O. K., and Vinogradov, Yu. E. (1969), "Emotions in the function of heuristics," in: Psychological Studies, No. 1 [in Russian], Izd. MGU, Moscow, p. 3.

Timiryazev, K. A. (1939), Works, Vol. 6 [in Russian], Sel'khozgiz, Moscow.

Tolstoy, L. N. (1955a), Anna Karenina [in Russian], Goslitizdat, Moscow.

Tolstoy, L. N. (1955b), On Literature [in Russian], Goslitizdat, Moscow.

Trojniar, W., and Cytawa, J. (1976), "Transfer from extero- to interoceptive reinforcement in the course of instrumental conditioning in rats," Acta Neurobiol. Exp., 36: No. 4, 455.

Trush, V. D., and Korinevsky, A. V. (1978), The Computer in Neurophysiological Studies [in Russian], Nauka, Moscow.

Tucker, D. M., Roth, R. S., Arneson, B., and Buckingam, V. (1977), "Right hemisphere activation during stress," Neuropsychologia, 15: No. 4/5, 697.

Ukhtomsky, A. A. (1950), Collected Works, Vol. 1 [in Russian], Izd. LGU, Leningrad.

Ukhtomsky, A. A. (1966), Dominants [in Russian], Nauka, Moscow, Leningrad.

Ukhtomsky, A. A. (1973), "Letters," Novyi Mir, No. 1, 251.

Ungher, J., Appel, E., and Sirianu, S. (1966), "Delayed responses in cat with bilateral caudate nucleus lesions," Rev. Roum. Neurol., 3: No. 4, 349.

Ursin, H. (1965), "Effects of amygdaloid lesions on avoidance behavior and visual discrimination in cats," Exp. Neurol., 11: 298.

Uryvaev, Yu. V. (1978), "Systemic analysis of the function of the frontal cortex," Candidate's Dissertation in Medical Sciences, P. K. Anokhin Scientific-Research Institute of Normal Physiology, Moscow.

Vainshtein, I. I., and Simonov, P. V. (1979), Emotiogenic Structures of the Brain and Heart [in Russian], Nauka, Moscow.

Valueva, M. N. (1967), Arbitrary Regulation of Vegetative Functions of an Organism [in Russian], Nauka, Moscow.

Valueva, M. N. (1969), "Thresholds of detecting sound signals coupled with painful stimulation of the observer or his partner," Zh. Vyssh. Nervn. Deyat., 19: No. 4, 714-715.

Valueva, M. N. (1976), "The conditioned reflex as a method of studying complex forms of motivation in man," in: The Neurophysiological Approach to the Analysis of Intraspecific Behavior [in Russian], Nauka, Moscow, p. 134.

Vernadsky, V. I. (1977), Reflections of a Naturalist, Vol. 2 [in Russian], Nauka, Moscow.

Vilyunas, V. K. (1976), The Psychology of Emotional Phenomena [in Russian], Izd. MGU, Moscow.

Vinnitsky, I. M., and Il'yuchenok, R. Yu. (1973), "Development of defensive conditioned reflexes in amygdalectomized rats," Zh. Vyssh. Nervn. Deyat., 23: No. 4, 766.

Vinogradova, O. S. (1975), The Hippocampus and Memory [in Russian], Nauka, Moscow.

Volterra, V. (1976), A Mathematical Theory of the Struggle for Existence [in Russian], Moscow.
Voronin, L. L. (1976), "Cellular mechanisms of conditioned reflex activity," Zh. Vyssh. Nervn. Deyat., 26: No. 4, 705.
Vygotsky, L. S. (1956), Collected Psychological Works [in Russian], Izd. Akad. Pedagog. Nauk RSFSR, Moscow.
Vygotsky, L. S. (1965), The Psychology of Art, Iskusstvo, Moscow.
Vygotsky, L. S. (1970), "Spinoza and his teaching on emotions in the light of modern psychoneurology," Vopr. Filosof., No. 6, 127.
Waldman, A. V. (1972), "Principal problems in the study of emotional behavior in experiments with animals," in: Experimental Neurophysiology of Emotions [in Russian], Nauka, Leningrad, p. 6.
Waldman, A. V. (1978), "Theory of the functional system and modern psychopharmacology," in: Theory of Functional Systems in Physiology and Psychology [in Russian], Nauka, Moscow, p. 111.
Waldman, A. V., Zvartau, E. E., and Kozlovskaya, M. M. (1976), Psychopharmacology of Emotions [in Russian], Meditsina, Moscow.
Waldman, A. V., and Ignatov, Yu. D. (1976), Central Mechanisms of Pain [in Russian], Nauka, Leningrad.
Walter, W. G. (1953), The Living Brain, Norton, New York.
Walter, W. G. (1954), "Theoretical properties of diffuse projection systems in relation to behaviour and consciousness," in: Brain Mechanisms and Consciousness, Oxford Univ. Press, Oxford, p. 345.
Wasman, M., and Flynn, J. (1962), "Directed attack elicited from hypothalamus," Arch. Neurol., 6: No. 3, 220.
Wetzel, W., Ott, T., and Matthies, H. (1977), "Post-training hippocampal rhythmic slow activity ('theta') elicited by septal stimulation improves memory consolidation in rats," Behav. Biol., 21: 32.
White, N. (1973), "Self-stimulation and suppression of feeding observed at the same site in the amygdala," Physiol. Behav., 10: No. 2, 215.
White, N., and Weingarten, H. (1976), "Effects of amygdaloid lesions on exploration by rats," Physiol. Behav., 17: No. 1, 73.
Whittaker, E., Gilchrist, J., and Fischer, J. (1952), "Perceptual defence or response suppression?" J. Abnorm. Social Psychol., 47:732.
Wilkinson, R., ElBeheri, S., and Gieseking, C. (1972), "Performance and arousal as a function of incentive, in-

formation load, and task novelty," Psychophysiology, 9: No. 6, 589.
Williams, C. E., and Stevens, K. N. (1969), "On determining the emotional state of pilots during flight: An exploratory study," Aerospace Med., 40: No. 12, 1369.
Williams, C. E., and Stevens, K. N. (1972), "Emotions and speech: Some acoustical correlates," J. Acoust. Soc. Am., 52: No. 4(2), 1238.
Wolkenstein, V. M. (1931), The Practice of Modern Esthetics [in Russian], Moscow, Leningrad.
Wyrwicka, W. (1975), "The sensory nature of reward in instrumental behavior," Pavlovian J. Biol. Sci., 10: No. 1, 23.
Yakobson, P. M. (1977), "Expression in the art of an actor," Vopr. Psikhol., No. 1, 86.
Yankelevich, B. M. (1965), "The algorithm of actions of an operator in accident situations," Vopr. Psikhol., No. 6, 119.
Yaroshevsky, M. G. (1967), "The psychology of science," Vopr. Filosof., No. 5, 79.
Yaroshevsky, M. G. (1973), "Category regulation in scientific activity," Vopr. Filosof., No. 11, 74.
Yaroshevsky, M. G. (1975), "Ukhtomsky and the problem of motivating behavior," Vopr. Psikhol., No. 3, 3.
Yerkes, R. M., and Dodson, J. D. (1908), "The relation of strength of stimulus to rapidity of habit formation," J. Comp. Neurol. Psychol., 18: 459.
Zagrodska, J., and Fonberg, E. (1977), "Amygdalar area involved in predatory behavior in cats," Acta Neurobiol. Exp., 37: No. 2, 131.
Zagrodska, J., and Fonberg, E. (1978), "Predatory versus alimentary behavior after amygdala lesions in cats," Physiol. Behav., 20: No. 5, 523.
Zenkov, L. R. (1978), "Some aspects of the semiotic structure and functional organization of "right-hemisphere thinking," in: Unconsciousness, Vol. 1 [in Russian], Metsniereba, Tbilia, p. 740.
Zenkov, L. R., and Panov, G. D. (1976), "Visual elicited potentials of the right and left hemispheres of the brain with presentation of alternates of a picture with different degrees of resolution," Fiziol. Cheloveka, 2: No. 5, 818.
Zvartau, E. E., and Patkina, N. A. (1974), "Motivational components and self-stimulation in behavioral reactions elicited by electrical stimulation of the hypothalamus in cats," Zh. Vyssh. Nervn. Deyat., 24: No. 3, 529.

INDEX